I0418280

When Life Gives You Homeschool Lesson Plans

WHEN LIFE GIVES YOU HOMESCHOOL LESSON PLANS

The Humorous and Practical Guide
to Stress-Free Homeschooling

EBONY JACKSON, MSc. Ed.

GOLDEN COMPASS
BOOKS

Copyright © 2023 by Ebony Jackson

All rights reserved.

No portion of this publication may be reproduced, distributed, or transmitted in any form or by any means, including photocopying, recording, or other electronic or mechanical methods, without the prior written permission of the author or publisher, except in the case of brief quotations embodied in critical reviews and certain other noncommercial uses permitted by copyright law.

The information provided in this book is for general informational purposes only. The author and publisher have made every effort to ensure the accuracy and reliability of the information provided herein. However, the information is provided "as is" without warranty of any kind. This book does not constitute legal, financial, medical, or educational advice. Readers are advised to consult a qualified professional before making any decisions based on the content of this book. Additionally, homeschooling laws vary by location, and it is the responsibility of the reader to consult local laws and regulations to ensure compliance with all legal requirements in their area.

ISBN: 979-8-9891881-0-9 (Paperback)

Library of Congress Control Number: 2024906577

Printed in the United States of America

Published by Golden Compass Books

Sign up for Ebony Jackson's Homeschool Newsletter at: www.homeschoolknockouts.com/newsletter

Dedication

To my Mommy, Betty Jean, whose unwavering belief in me has always propelled me forward in chasing my dreams. Thank you for being my greatest supporter and for believing in the power of my words.

* * *

To Daddy, "Top", I cherish our Sunday conversations, nestled between the morning political news shows and the kickoff of our favorite NFL game matchups. I miss you every day and feel your presence from above, watching over me.

* * *

To my sister, Aretha Jackson, whose brilliant ideas sparked creativity at every turn. This book is not just a product of my imagination but a testament to the countless hours of support, advice, and encouragement you have always provided. What would I do without my big sis?

* * *

To my fellow Homeschool Knockouts, this book is a tribute to each of you—the diplomatic peacekeepers who turn sibling rivalries into cooperative reading sessions on the living room floor. It's for all the impromptu history lessons in the car, the field trips that began with a flat tire, and the science experiments that didn't go quite as planned. It's for every last-minute writing exercise that unexpectedly taught us the beauty of words and the joy of communication. For every unsung victory, every sock puppet play, and every day we choose this crazy homeschool journey over something 'easier'—this book is as much yours as it is mine. Thank you for turning every day into an adventure and every challenge into a story worth telling.

Learning is not compulsory... neither is survival.

— W. Edwards Demin

Contents

Introduction

It's 9:00 a.m. and your home has morphed into a three-ring circus. Your 7-year-old is on a mission to convert the living room into a full-fledged math lab, measuring everything in sight (who needs math worksheets anyway?). The dog's losing its mind at the Amazon delivery guy, and your youngest has discovered the joys of finger painting—only on the walls, naturally.

You're explaining fractions for what feels like the fifth time this week, only to see your 4th grader's eyes glaze over. Meanwhile, your middle schooler's simple question about space has somehow led you down an hour-long rabbit hole on simulation theory.

Amid all this chaos, your preschooler has constructed a fortress from every blanket and cushion in the house. And your high schooler? Well, he's somewhere in the house—if only you could remember where you last saw him.

In the middle of the noise, mess, and never-ending questions, one thing is clear: homeschooling is an adventure like no other. And that's where I step in.

I'm Ebony, your guide through this beautiful chaos, and I've got a few tricks up my sleeve because when life gives you homeschool lesson plans, you're not just surviving, your thriving in your homeschooling journey.

Why Listen to Me?

You might be wondering, "What makes this Ebony character qualified to guide me through the homeschooling wilderness?" Well, let me tell you:

1. **I've Lived It:** This isn't just theoretical mumbo-jumbo. I've lived the homeschool life for over 15 years, complete with science experiments gone wrong and history lessons that somehow ended with us all speaking in terrible British accents.

2. **I'm a Teacher of All Trades:** From teaching ESL students in Japan to instructing adult learners, and crafting curricula for Big Education™, I've collected more teaching tricks than a magician's hat. And I'm pulling them all out for you.

3. **I'm Nosy (In a Good Way):** Thanks to my YouTube channel, Homeschool Knockouts, and years of chatting and ear-hustling with other homeschool parents, this book is like a potluck of brilliant ideas. I brought the southern potato salad of experience, and everyone else brought their secret sauce.

4. **I See the Big Picture:** We're tackling everything from curriculum choices to keeping your sanity intact. Yes, those are two separate challenges. Usually.

5. **I Love a Good Resource:** If checklists, planners, and templates are your thing, you're in the right place.

6. **I'm Not Just Making This Stuff Up:** That Master of Science degree in Education (tucked away in a drawer somewhere) isn't just for show. I've turned countless educational theories into practical, real-life strategies—without all the academic fluff.

What Makes This Book Different?

This isn't just another collection of tips and tricks. It's your comprehensive guide to transforming from a frazzled home educator to a confident homeschool maven. Here's a taste of what you'll learn:

- How to design a curriculum that doesn't make your kids run screaming for the hills

- Tricks for teaching multiple kids without growing extra arms

- Tips for balancing homeschooling with work, life, and the occasional desire to hide in the closet with chocolate

- Methods for adapting your teaching for kids who march to the beat of their own drum (or full marching band)

- How to homeschool without selling a kidney to pay for it

- Self-care strategies, because you can't pour from an empty coffee cup (or wine glass, we don't judge)

Now, you might be thinking, "Sounds great, but is this book really for me?" Well, let's see...

Who's This Book For?

- Homeschool rookies wondering if 'lesson plan' is code for something magical

- Anyone who's ever looked at homeschool curriculum and thought, "But what if...?"

- Veteran homeschoolers looking to shake things up (in a good way, not a "kids-with-fizzy-soda" way)

- Parents of special-needs kids who are special in more ways than one

- Families juggling more kids than a circus act

- Working parents trying to balance conference calls and fractions

As we move through the chapters ahead, you'll find practical strategies for every aspect of homeschooling. From setting up your space and creating schedules to preparing for your first day and managing your budget, we've got you covered. And when burnout comes knocking (because it will), you'll have an arsenal of self-care techniques at your fingertips.

But it's not all serious business. You'll also find plenty of real-life stories that will have you laughing, nodding along, and feeling a lot less alone on this adventure. Because if there's one thing I've learned in my years of homeschooling, it's that a good sense of humor is just as important as a good lesson plan.

Ultimately, my mission is simple: to equip you with the tools and confidence to homeschool with less stress and more joy, creating a family legacy of curiosity, growth, and happiness. Together, we'll transform homeschooling into an experience that's not just manageable, but truly memorable for both you and your children.

So, are you ready to turn this three-ring circus into the greatest educational adventure on Earth? Grab that coffee mug, take a deep breath, and let's get started. The journey ahead is going to be amazing, and I'm thrilled to be your guide.

Happy homeschooling!

PART I - THE HOMESCHOOLING FOUNDATION

Ready to embark on your homeschooling adventure? Let's lay down a solid foundation first. In this section, we'll guide you through the ins and outs of deciding to homeschool, complete with some fascinating historical tidbits to impress your friends at dinner parties. You'll find a handy quick-start guide to get you up and running in no time, and we've broken down the legal mumbo jumbo into plain English, so you can kick off your journey with confidence. These opening chapters are your essential toolkit for a well-rounded, empowered homeschooling experience. But, if you're itching to dive straight into the nitty-gritty, skip ahead to Part II, where the practical side of homeschooling takes center stage.

1

Homeschooling?

You Have the Best Seat in the House!

Two roads diverged in a wood, and I—

I took the one less traveled by,

And that has made all the difference.

— Robert Frost, from the poem "The Road Not Taken"

WELCOME TO HOMESCHOOLING 101 where the only rule is: there are no rules! Deciding to homeschool might be the most brilliant idea you've ever had, or it could be the wildest adventure you've ever signed up for (or both); the jury's still deliberating. So, say goodbye to rigid classroom norms and hello to a world where learning is as boundless as your imagination. I'm here to guide you through this wonderfully unpredictable, caffeine-fueled journey of educating your children at home.

Think back to those early days when you taught your child how to ride a bike without training wheels, coached them through tying their shoes for the hundredth time, helped them memorize their home address like it was a secret code, or how to count using the spoons in the kitchen drawer.

*It's all about understanding that you've been in the educator's seat
ever since you taught your baby to say "Mama." You have always
been their teacher. Just without curriculum and with fewer field trips
to the aquarium.*

Whether you're a birth parent, an adoptive parent, or a grandparent, those
moments marked the beginning of your homeschooling journey. Now, it's just
about adding some official flair (and a bit of paperwork) to your natural teaching
instincts.

First things first, let's tackle the giant elephant in the room—convincing your
kids (and let's not forget yourself) that homeschooling is not just a viable option,
but a thrilling adventure. You're battling formidable foes: pervasive social expectations, the entrenched narratives of traditional schooling, and—the toughest of
them all—the seductive lure of 'me time' days.

But here's the deal: Homeschooling is like crafting your own educational
journey, complete with detours, shortcuts, and scenic routes that traditional
schools just can't offer. It's about turning "What did you learn at school today?"
into "What do we want to discover today?" It's about making learning as natural
as breathing and as exciting as opening a treasure chest.

To navigate this epic journey successfully, it's crucial to maintain a positive
mindset. I'll take it a step further and say that one must channel the wisdom and
patience of a Jedi, much like Master Yoda himself. Why channel a Jedi? Consider
those challenging days—maybe it's the seventh day of explaining a math concept
your child still can't grasp, or when you've read the same historical passage four
times, and it still doesn't make sense. In such moments, when you're searching
for that Jedi-like calm and focus, mantras can be invaluable. These are simple,
repeatable phrases that remind us of our goals and help maintain our composure.
Gather as many mantras as you find helpful, as they can be lightsabers in the thick
of educational battles. Here are eight to start with:

1. **Learning Happens Everywhere.** At the grocery store, it's a math or
   economics lesson. During bedtime stories, it's a literature discussion. On
   nature walks, it's a biology field trip. The world is your classroom.

2. **Flexibility is Our Superpower.** Stuck on a subject? Change gears.
   Found a sudden interest in dinosaurs? Let's pivot and explore. Home-

schooling allows you to bend, twist, and turn the curriculum to fit your child's curiosity and pace.

3. **We're in This Together.** Because sometimes, you need the reminder that this is a team effort. You're not just the teacher; you're a learner too. And there's beauty in discovering new things alongside your children.

4. **Effort Over Outcome.** This mantra is a lifesaver when progress seems to be crawling. It redirects attention from the frustration of not seeing immediate results to appreciating the value of persistent effort. Remember, persistence is a key part of the learning journey.

5. **Mistakes Are Just Pit Stops on the Road to Understanding.** Remind your child that every mistake is an opportunity to learn something new. This mantra can help keep spirits high, even when the answers seem elusive. It can also transform a culture of fear around mistakes into one of growth and curiosity.

6. **Patience Breeds Comprehension.** Sometimes, concepts just need time to simmer. Encourage a break or a change of activity, and then revisit the tricky material. This mantra helps reinforce the idea that sometimes, giving the brain a rest can lead to breakthroughs.

7. **Understanding Comes, Not All at Once, but in Pieces.** This mantra reminds us that learning, much like a puzzle, happens piece by piece. It's a great one to recite when your child (or you!) becomes frustrated with the seemingly slow progress of learning challenging subjects.

8. **Persistence Trumps Talent.** For difficult subjects, it's vital to remember that consistent effort often leads to more success than raw talent. It's easy to assume that a child who excels is just "naturally good at math" or that a struggling reader "wasn't born with a love for books." However, reinforcing to both you and your child that diligent reading and regular review of concepts are more effective than relying solely on innate ability can truly make a difference in learning outcomes.

Now, not only are these mantras useful for encouraging a more positive learning experience, but they also foster a resilient mindset that is essential in and out of academic environments. Incorporating these mantras into daily routines fosters strong character traits along the way. By repeating these phrases during demanding learning sessions or challenging everyday moments, you can help transform a potentially stressful experience into a more manageable and even enjoyable one. So, the next time the going gets tough, channel your inner Jedi and remember: the force of patience and persistence is strong!

This is the way.

---------- **Summary** ----------

As you stand on the brink of this homeschooling journey, remember that it's a path less traveled. And it's yours to shape, decorate, and savor. Embrace the freedom to tailor each day to your family's unique rhythm and interests. You'll create an educational experience that's as enriching as it is unforgettable. So, take a deep breath, relish the adventure, and always cherish the fact that you have the best seat in the house—front and center—teaching and growing with your children every step of the way.

2

Getting Started

A Guide for the Bewildered and Hesitant

I said school starts tomorrow. I didn't say I was going to be there.
— Kim Harrison

Y OU'VE COMMITTED TO HOMESCHOOLING—NOW what? Get ready for a front-row seat to your child's "Aha!" moments and the occasional "Why is there glitter in the math book?" scenarios. No more morning rush or school drop-off lines – now your biggest challenge is making sure everyone actually gets out of bed. You might find yourself saying things like, "No, building a pillow fort is not today's art project," and "Yes, I guess we can call that a science experiment."

This chapter kickstarts your journey, offering practical guidance and inspiration to help you confidently tackle the initial steps. We'll break down the essentials into manageable chunks, setting the stage for more detailed insights in the chapters to come. For now, let's dive into the main points:

- Establish your **homeschool vision**.

- Set realistic, achievable **goals**.

- Navigate the bureaucratic jungle of **state laws**.

- Pick the best **start date** for your homeschool year.

- Determine what **subjects to teach.**

- Create a **budget** that won't make you panic.

- Organize a functional **learning space**.

- Craft a **routine** that won't drive you to drink (more coffee).

Now that you have a snapshot of what to expect, let's delve deeper. We aim to equip you with essential tools to stay grounded and avoid feeling overwhelmed. Consider this checklist your trusty sidekick, clarifying things when they seem murky. For a printable version of this checklist, visit my website at: www.home schoolknockouts.com/resourcelibrary

HOMESCHOOL PLANNING CHECKLIST

- **Find Your Homeschool 'Why.'** What drives your decision to home-school? Is it the personalized education, the flexibility and freedom, closer family bonds, concerns about conventional schooling, health reasons, or deeply held values and beliefs? It might seem like a straight-forward question, but the answer can be as complex and layered as your favorite triple-decker sandwich, with each reason adding its unique flavor to your decision.

- **Create Your Homeschool Vision.** Before you start transforming your living room into a learning space, it's crucial to know what you're aiming for. Consider these two visions:

— *Short-Term Vision.* Think about what you want to achieve in the coming year. Maybe it's seeing your child read their first book or getting through a math curriculum without either of you crying. Visualize your daily life in these scenarios. You might be surprised how envisioning little Cartman reading by himself can motivate you to tackle those phonics lessons with gusto.

— *Long-Term Vision.* Now, let's think big. Where do you see this homeschool journey taking your child? College? A trade? Entrepreneurship? The Military? This is your chance to dream big—but also to ground those dreams in reality.

- **Set Achievable Goals.** Setting goals is less about crafting perfect student achievement badges and more about not going insane. An example? "By the end of the year, Jamie will be able to multiply without using her fingers." This is much better than "Jamie will master algebra," which, while enticing, is slightly less achievable.

- **Know Your State Laws.** Every state has its circus or set of laws for homeschooling. Some states require you to register as a private school, while others just want an occasional nod that you're not letting the kids use social media as their primary education. Make sure you're compliant to avoid the "I accidentally broke the law" panic. Websites like the Home School Legal Defense Association (www.hslda.org) can help you avoid these legal faux pas. For a more detailed discussion on this topic, refer to Chapter 3, "Homeschooling Laws."

- **Decide When to Start Homeschooling.** Is there ever a perfect time to start homeschooling? Short answer: no. Long answer: still no, but you have options. Some folks start in September to keep in sync with traditional schools, which helps when signing up for local classes or sports. Others jump in mid-year after a particularly tearful parent-teacher conference. Choose what feels right for your family, and don't look back. See Chapter 6, "Homeschool Routines" and Chapter 11, "The First Day of School" for more information.

- **What to Teach—Curriculum Choices.** Choosing a curriculum can feel like being lost in the wilderness. There are countless philosophies here—from classical to Montessori to unschooling. Think about what matches your child's style. Does Emma love workbooks, or does she prefer building castles out of spaghetti? Tailor your approach accordingly, and remember, it's okay to mix and match. We'll tackle this in more detail later in Chapter 7, "The Curriculum Jungle" and Part IV - Philosophies, Approaches, & Methods."

- **Set a Budget.** Budgets are boring but necessary. You might think, "We're saving money by not buying school uniforms," but then you see the prices of some science kits (yes, $200 for a glorified baking soda volcano). Track your spending, hunt for deals, and remember that libraries and the internet are your best friends. See Chapter 9, "Homeschooling on a Budget," for more information.

- **Get Organized—Space and Resources.** You don't need a Pinterest-perfect homeschool room to be effective. Just dedicating a specific area can help maintain peace and order. Even a corner of the kitchen table can be transformed into a learning zone with some creative storage solutions. See Chapter 5, "Getting Organized" for the scoop.

- **Create a Routine That Works.** Routines are less about rigid schedules and more about creating a flow that works for everyone. Start simple. Math doesn't always have to be at 9:00 a.m. sharp. Maybe your kids do best after they've had time to wake up fully—so reading over breakfast might be your golden hour. Be flexible, adjust as needed, and yes, coffee breaks (for you) count as educational planning time. For more details, see Chapter 6, "Homeschool Routines," for examples of planners, routines, and checklists.

- **Start Teaching.** Begin with simple lessons and activities to ease into the homeschooling routine. You can use a mix of hands-on and online resources to engage your child and supplement your curriculum. Factor in breaks and keep them motivated throughout the day. See Chapter 13, "The Art of Teaching."

- **Manage Your Expectations.** Not every day will be an educational triumph. Some days, your homeschool will resemble a chaotic carnival rather than a center of learning. And that's okay. Just know that tomorrow is a fresh start. See Chapter 13, "The Art of Teaching," for more tips.

- **Assess Your Child's Progress.** Use ongoing assessments and evaluations to stay updated on how your child is doing. It's like a caring check-in to make sure they're moving forward in their learning adventure. Remember that your child's needs might change over time, so be ready to adjust your approach and curriculum accordingly. For more details, see Chapter 16, "Assessing Progress."

- **Build Your Homeschool Community.** One of the most critical steps in your homeschooling journey is building a network of fellow homeschooling families. This community will be your lifeline, your support system, and your saving grace. Connect with other homeschoolers through local co-ops, online forums, homeschool days at the museum, parks, and other places. These are the people who will commiserate with you over failed lesson plans, cheer on your successes, and swap strategies for teaching fractions. See Chapter 14, "The Socialization Myth."

- **Prepare for Challenges and Setbacks.** Homeschooling isn't always rainbows and sunshine, so it's important to be prepared for challenges and setbacks. Stay organized and be flexible when unexpected situations arise. Don't be afraid to ask for help or advice from other homeschooling families or professionals. For more information, see Part VI "Challenges & Triumphs" for more details.

- **Celebrate Your Homeschool Successes.** Homeschooling is a unique and rewarding experience, so don't forget to celebrate your successes along the way! Keep a portfolio of your child's selected work and progress throughout the year. Recognize achievements big and small, whether it's finishing a long classic novel or completing a long division problem without tears. And most importantly, celebrate the bond and memories you're creating with your child. Check out Chapter 11, 'The Art of Teaching,' for additional details.

- **Embrace the Mantras.** When the chaos rises, have a few go-to phrases to keep your zen. Try repeating, "This moment is just a moment," or "Every day brings new chances," to ground yourself during those more tumultuous teaching episodes. Or, refer to the mantra list from Chapter 1. These simple affirmations can help keep your spirits high and your patience intact.

---------- **Summary** ----------

As we wrap up this chapter, keep in mind that homeschooling is an adventure that's as rewarding as it is challenging. It's normal to feel a mix of excitement and nervousness as you step into this role with full force. You've been your child's first teacher from the very start, and now you're just putting a more formal stamp on all those daily lessons. You'll find that with each day comes a chance to grow, not just for your children, but for you as well. The beauty of homeschooling lies in its flexibility—adapt and change as you discover what works best for your family's unique rhythm. Celebrate the victories, learn from the setbacks, and continue this journey with a sense of purpose and a dash of humor. Here's to finding joy in the chaos and making education a meaningful part of your family's daily life.

3

Homeschooling Laws

Law & Order: Homeschooling Unit

Laws are like sausages, it is better not to see them being made.
— Otto von Bismarck

A LRIGHT, LET'S HIT PAUSE for a second. Before you fully commit to this homeschooling journey, it's essential to take a step back and get a clear understanding of your state's homeschooling laws. Consider it akin to checking the HOA rules before renovating your house. A bit of research at this stage can save you from running into avoidable obstacles and headaches later on.

Homeschooling, legal in all 50 states of the United States, comes with its own intricate maze of regulations. This chapter is your guide through the dense thicket of legalities, designed to let you focus on what truly matters—providing an unparalleled education for your children, whether they're embarking on their educational journey or navigating the later stages. Websites like the Home School Legal Defense Association (hslda.org) are stellar choices for helping you locate and decipher your state's legal requirements. But rest assured, within these pages, you'll find your clear path and you'll cut through the underbrush of legal confusion. So, arm yourself with a highlighter or pen, and let's get going.

STATE NOTIFICATIONS —PLAYING DETECTIVE WITH THE DEPARTMENT OF EDUCATION

Before you begin homeschooling, it is crucial to research and decipher your state's requirements for notifying your local school district or your state about your intent to homeschool. Depending on your state, you may need to inform your local school district of your decision to homeschool. Some states are more relaxed, treating it like a casual RSVP to a garden party. Other states require a more detailed notification with specified deadlines. Basically, they want a letter that's just one step below the Declaration of Independence. In short, they want a letter just shy of the Declaration of Independence. And like any good detective series, deadlines are everything. Miss one, and your homeschool plans could unravel like a cliffhanger season finale. So, pay attention!

Properly notifying your local school district or state ensures that you adhere to the law and lays the groundwork for a successful homeschooling experience. Every great adventure starts with a solid foundation, and homeschooling is no exception. Before you get carried away with curriculum planning and field trip scheduling, take some time to familiarize yourself with your state's homeschool laws. You know what they say: an ounce of prevention is worth a pound of cure.

REGULATIONS UNVEILED—THE MANY SHADES OF HOMESCHOOL LAWS

Understanding your state's specific requirements is essential. Each state in the United States of America has its own unique set of regulations governing home-schooling, ranging from relaxed to downright persnickety (I've been waiting to use that word). For example, in Texas, homeschoolers are considered private schools and are only required to teach reading, spelling, grammar, mathematics, and good citizenship. On the other hand, New York has more stringent regulations, requiring homeschoolers to submit a notice of intent, an Individualized Home Instruction Plan (IHIP), quarterly reports, and annual assessments. In one state, you might need to submit a detailed educational plan, while in another, a simple notification of intent to homeschool could suffice.

Start by visiting your state's Department of Education website to get the lay of the legal land. Prepare yourself for a scavenger hunt of sorts, as homeschool regulations are often tucked away in the deepest recesses of the website. Once you have found the pertinent information, compile a checklist containing all the necessary requirements and deadlines, such as the compulsory age for starting school. This will help ensure that you are fully compliant with the law.

RECORD KEEPING—WHEN DID I BECOME AN ARCHIVIST?

Believe it or not, record keeping—or navigating the kingdom of endless paper trails— is a crucial aspect of homeschooling that you'll need to embrace if you want to stay on the right side of the law. As much as we'd like to focus solely on the fun aspects of homeschooling, paperwork, and documentation are necessary evils that accompany this educational adventure. Depending on your state's regulations, you may need to keep track of attendance, lesson plans, test scores, and more. Stay organized from the get-go to avoid last-minute record-keeping scrambles.

Here are **four key aspects** of homeschool documentation to keep in mind:

1. **Attendance Records:** Most states require homeschoolers to maintain attendance records to prove that your child is meeting the minimum number of instructional hours or days required by law. Say hello to your new best friend—the attendance log! You can download it for free at: www.homeschoolknockouts.com.

2. **Curriculum and Lesson Plans:** Depending on your state, you may need to submit curriculum information or even detailed lesson plans. Have these documents handy and well-organized, as they might be subject to review by the state.

3. **Assessments and Evaluations:** While standardized testing may not be your cup of tea, some states require homeschoolers to participate in these assessments. Keep records of any test scores or evaluations, as they can serve as valuable documentation of your child's academic progress.

4. **Portfolios:** A portfolio is a collection of your child's work, showcasing their growth and achievements throughout the year. While not required by all states, a well-maintained portfolio can be a powerful tool during evaluations and potential transitions back into the public school system.

THE CURRICULUM CONUNDRUM—WHAT THE HECK DO I TEACH?

Charting the course between state demands and personalized learning is a tricky tightrope you've got to walk, especially for high school. Will your state require you to follow the public school's curriculum so closely that you'll basically become a schoolteacher at home (minus the students vaping in the bathroom)? Or will you have the freedom to choose your own adventure, crafting a syllabus that feels like an exciting literary jaunt?

And if your child dreams of playing NCAA college sports, you'll need to ensure your curriculum meets specific academic standards to maintain eligibility. It may sound overwhelming, but with careful planning, you can strike the right balance. Remember, you're in charge of your homeschool, but it's essential to follow the rules to keep everything on track. For guidance on selecting and implementing curriculum, see Chapter 7, "The Curriculum Jungle."

CHARTER, PRIVATE, OR UMBRELLA?—CHOOSING YOUR PATH TO THAT DIPLOMA

One of the many perks of homeschooling is the freedom to choose the educational path that best suits your family's needs. Depending on your personal preferences and state regulations, you may choose to align your homeschool with a charter school, a private school satellite program (PSP)/umbrella school, or maintain complete independence (private school). Each option offers unique benefits, and the choice often depends on the family's educational philosophy, desired level of support, and personal preferences. Understanding the different types of homeschooling options can be helpful for families considering this educational path. Here are definitions for each type mentioned:

•**Homeschool Charter:** A homeschool charter is a publicly-funded school that operates independently of the traditional public school system. These schools can provide curriculum, resources, funds, and guidance. Some homeschool charters might even provide part-time on-campus classes, extracurricular activities, and access to resources like libraries and computer labs.

•**Private School Satellite Program (PSP):** An independently run educational institution not funded by the government. PSPs are also known as umbrella schools, and they offer some level of support and legal protection for a home-schooling family. Many have homeschool programs, giving families curriculum support and access to activities, while allowing children to be educated at home. These schools may be secular or religious.

•**Private School Affidavit (PSA):** In states like California, filing a PSA legalizes your homeschool as a private school, subjecting you to state laws. In essence, you are telling the state that you, not an outside entity like a PSP, are a private school. This option offers full control over curriculum and scheduling, but requires you to manage records, testing, and administration.

TESTING TANGO

State testing requirements for the homeschool community can vary significantly depending on the jurisdiction. In some states, they visit like a once-a-year comet, demanding only an annual test. Others, however, prefer to make frequent appearances, like nosy neighbors, asking for periodic evaluations or even entire portfolios. Still, others have the laissez-faire attitude of a hipster coffee shop, "Just do your thing, man." Refer to the Home School Legal Defense Association's website (hslda.org) or your state's department of education for guidance.

WHERE ELSE IS HOMESCHOOLING LEGAL?

1. **Australia:** The Land Down Under has seen a steady increase in home-schooling over the years. Australian parents can choose from a variety of curriculum options, and homeschoolers often form networks to share resources and socialize. Most regions require homeschooling families to register with their state or territory's education department and to follow specific guidelines.

2. **Brazil:** Homeschooling was legalized in Brazil in 2018, allowing parents to educate their children at home as long as they follow the Brazilian National Curriculum. Homeschooling families must register with their local education authority and submit to annual assessments.

3. **Canada:** Homeschooling is legal in all Canadian provinces and territories, with each jurisdiction implementing its own regulations and requirements. Some provinces, such as Alberta and British Columbia,

offer financial support and resources for homeschooling families.

4. **France:** Homeschooling is legal, but parents must notify local authorities and submit to regular inspections to ensure that a suitable education is being provided.

5. **Japan:** Homeschooling is less common in Japan, where the education system is highly structured and rigorous. However, a small number of families have chosen to homeschool, often due to concerns about bullying or the desire to provide a more customized education.

6. **Kenya:** Homeschooling is growing in popularity and is legal, with parents required to register with the Ministry of Education and sometimes present a case for homeschooling.

7. **New Zealand:** Homeschooling is legal in New Zealand, and parents must obtain a Certificate of Exemption from the Ministry of Education. To receive this certificate, parents must demonstrate their ability to provide a suitable education, including an outline of their teaching methods and resources.

8. **Russia:** Homeschooling is legal in Russia, and parents have the option to educate their children at home under the supervision of a certified tutor.

9. **South Africa:** Homeschooling is legal in South Africa, but parents must register their children with the Department of Basic Education. While the South African government requires homeschoolers to follow the national curriculum, the enforcement of this requirement is inconsistent.

10. **United Kingdom:** Homeschooling is legal in all parts of the United Kingdom—England, Wales, Scotland, and Northern Ireland. While the UK government does not require a specific curriculum for homeschooling families, local authorities may conduct periodic assessments to ensure that children are receiving an adequate education.

11. **United States:** Homeschooling is legal in all 50 states, but regulations and requirements differ significantly between jurisdictions. De-

spite varying regulations, the U.S. remains one of the most home-school-friendly countries, with a well-established network of support groups and resources.

WHERE HOMESCHOOLING IS HEAVILY RESTRICTED OR ILLEGAL

1. **China:** The government requires all children to attend public or private schools. Homeschooling is generally not recognized as a legal option, although some families still practice it in secret.

2. **Germany:** Homeschooling is generally illegal, with rare exceptions. The law mandates that all children attend a recognized school.

3. **Greece:** Homeschooling is not considered a legal alternative to public or private schools, and all children must attend school from ages six to 15.

4. **Spain:** While the Spanish constitution guarantees the right to education, it does not allow for homeschooling as an alternative to compulsory attendance in a school.

5. **Sweden:** Homeschooling is heavily restricted, with permissions granted under exceptional circumstances, and it is subject to strict oversight.

6. **Turkey:** Compulsory education laws require attendance at recognized schools, making homeschooling not permissible.

The homeschooling statistics around the world information is based on insights from Christopher Klicka's articles in Practical Homeschooling Magazine, as printed in issue no. 35, 2001, and no. 55, 2003.

---------- **Summary** ----------

Homeschooling has established itself across the globe, reflecting the unique characteristics and viewpoints of different cultures. Its flexibility has enabled it to thrive in a variety of environments, showing that it's more than an American phenomenon; it's a worldwide educational movement that crosses international and cultural lines. Homeschooling can be an incredibly rewarding experience for both you and your child, but it's essential to stay informed about homeschool laws to ensure smooth sailing on your educational voyage.

As a homeschooling parent, you are taking on a tremendous responsibility--one that, when approached with diligence and seriousness, can yield lasting benefits for your child and your family. By familiarizing yourself with state regulations, keeping diligent records, knowing any testing requirements, and choosing the ideal path to a diploma, you'll be well-equipped to guide your child through their homeschooling years and beyond. And, who knows? Maybe your homeschooling adventure will be picked up for a second season.

* * *

For more specific information on homeschooling laws in the United States, you can visit the websites of prominent homeschooling organizations such as the Home School Legal Defense Association (hslda.org) and the National Home Education Research Institute (nheri.org), which provide information on legal issues, research, and support for homeschooling families.

4

History of Homeschooling
From Socrates to Sweatpants

The mind is not a vessel to be filled, but a fire to be kindled.
                                                    – Plutarch

ONCE UPON A TIME, in a world not so different from our own, parents thought homeschooling was for that one family who lived at the end of the cul-de-sac in a house made of recycled materials and compost with a rusty RV in the cracked driveway. But then, something extraordinary happened, and homeschooling burst forth from its granola-filled cocoon, becoming an option for the average family.

Before the dawn of standardized tests and yellow school buses, homeschooling was the norm, not the exception. It was the original form of education, the old-school way (quite literally!) of imparting knowledge before it was mainstream. In fact, homeschooling boasts a rich tapestry of history spanning thousands of years, replete with its own share of drama, innovation, and the occasional comedic twist.

Homeschooling is defined as an educational approach wherein children are taught at home, either by their parents or a designated tutor, rather than attending a conventional public or private institution. This method allows for a custom-tailored curriculum, adaptive scheduling, and an environment specially crafted to a child's individual needs and learning pace. But before we discuss homeschooling today, let's go back in time.

HOMESCHOOLING THROUGH THE AGES

Ancient Times: Our story begins in the ancient world, where the likes of Socrates, Plato, and Aristotle were educated at home. Envision the dinnertime dialogue in such a household: a child's innocent inquiry, "What are we eating for dinner, Mother?" could be met with a ponderous pause and then, "Consider, offspring, the nature of sustenance—is it not but a fleeting pleasure amidst the pursuit of wisdom?" It's a scene where every question is a doorway to existential exploration, and every answer is a lesson in thinking deeply. Meanwhile, the kiddo's just sitting there eyeballing the mutton with garlic sauce thinking, "Can we just eat already? Who's looking for a philosophical treatise when your stomach is growling?"

Middle Ages: Homeschooling wasn't just old school—it was the school for young nobles who might as well have been auditioning for a medieval reality show: 'Ye Olde Game of Thrones.' Mornings were for sharpening wits with the trivium—grammar, logic, and rhetoric. This was kind of like prepping for verbal jousts, with scholarly tutors leading the charge armed with classical texts and scriptures. Come afternoon; it was time to swap books for falcons, needlepoint, and fancy footwork in courtly dance because what's nobility without the skills to impress at the grand feast? Tutors, often clergy with brains and brawn, were the original life coaches, schooling these blue bloods in everything from ethical estate management to the fine art of not tripping over one's robe.

Colonial America: In colonial New England, homeschooling was all the rage, and not just for the Puritans with their serious Bible study vibes. Everyone was in on the action—Quakers, rebels, indigenous folk, and even that one family with the weird accent from who knows where. Formal schools were as rare as a fun Saturday night in the stocks, so parents doubled as teachers, ensuring their kids could read, write, and not get lost in the woods. Children picked up skills like little sponges—boys becoming a jack-of-all-trades and girls mastering the 'keep the home fires burning' arts. They learned how to plant crops with the precision of a Swiss watchmaker because who wants to find a turnip where the carrots should be? Carpentry was a hit, too, helping kids build anything from a chicken coop to a soapbox for the town crier. And let's not forget the all-important art of bartering—because when you need a new horse or a fancy lace bonnet, you'd better have some serious haggling chops. It was practical education with a side of wilderness survival, preparing kids for everything from raising a barn to outsmarting a bear—useful stuff if they ever planned to be the star of 'Colonial Survivor'.

Historical references and insights on homeschooling were drawn from the Institute for Education PolicyJohns Hopkins University, which provides a comprehensive overview of homeschooling's evolution. Additional academic insights were accessed via SpringerLink, an online platform offering access to a wide range of scientific, technical, and educational resources, including journals, books, and reference works.

---------- **Summary** ----------

The history of homeschooling is a fascinating journey that spans centuries and continents. From its ancient roots to its contemporary resurgence, homeschooling has proven to be a resilient and adaptable educational method that continues to inspire and educate millions of students worldwide. As we look to the future, one thing is certain: homeschooling will continue to grow and adapt, shaping the minds and hearts of the next generation of thinkers, dreamers, and doers.

PART II - PRACTICAL HOMESCHOOLING

Let's transition from the foundations of Part I to actual practice. These chapters are a treasure trove of tips and tricks for managing the daily realities of homeschooling. From getting organized to creating enriching learning environments, and from curriculum selection to crafting effective lesson plans, Part II provides the nuts and bolts of running a successful homeschool. Whether you need to declutter like a pro, weave a routine that doesn't unravel by midday, or navigate the curriculum jungle without losing your way, this section has you covered. I'll guide you through planning lessons without breaking a sweat, stretching your budget to perform educational alchemy, and making that first day of school feel like a grand opening instead of a grand closing. Jump in and make your homeschooling journey smooth, efficient, and enjoyable.

5

Getting Organized

Fred Sanford Meets Marie Kondo

For every minute spent organizing, an hour is earned.
— Benjamin Franklin

A S A MODERN-DAY HOMESCHOOLER, you must be an alchemist of sorts, transforming the everyday spaces of your home into vibrant hubs of learning. Whether your home resembles the eclectic clutter of Fred Sanford's junkyard from TV's *Sanford and Son*, mirrors the pristine calm of a Marie Kondo-inspired sanctuary, or boasts a style that's entirely your own, there's a perfect way to organize and energize your space for this educational journey.

This chapter serves as your organizational toolkit, showcasing practical tips, real-life examples, and proven strategies to help you create your ideal homeschool haven. It also takes into account three distinct budget levels to suit various financial needs. You'll find strategies for optimizing lighting, creating ambient sounds, and organizing learning materials. Whether accommodating special needs, setting up a central hub, or managing costs, this chapter offers realistic solutions that respect your financial boundaries. These strategies also build a vibrant launchpad where your kids can learn, thrive, and generally run amok.

Start with the basics and then expand as you go. Below, you'll find a range of options to transform your space into a true learning sanctuary. But before you somersault in headfirst, consider these four essential tips to get you started on the right foot:

THE #1 Essential(s): Whiskey and a Secret Room
(Just kidding ... sort of.)
All joking aside. Here are the four essential tips:

1. **Dedicated Workspace:** Opt for a spot that's quiet, brightly lit, and free from distractions.

2. **Work Surface:** Provide a sturdy surface like a desk, table, or lap desk for their activities.

3. **Comfy Seating:** Make sure your child has a supportive chair or seating arrangement.

4. **Essential Supplies:** Keep pencils, pens, paper, crayons, scissors, and notebooks nearby.

Now that we've covered the basics, you're ready to expand, enhance, or declutter your space. Let's now build on the four foundational essentials we've outlined.

DEDICATED WORKSPACE—FOCUS FOUND!

Consistency is the name of the game when it comes to homeschooling. Carving out a dedicated learning environment in your abode provides a familiar backdrop where your kiddos can focus and feel at ease. Perhaps it's a forgotten corner of the living room, a seldom-used guest room (lucky you!), or even a closet. Choose your spot, and then deck it out with all the essentials: a desk, a comfy chair, bookshelves, storage solutions, and enough lighting to keep the shadows at bay.

Setting aside a dedicated learning space within your home will provide a consistent environment where your children can focus and feel comfortable. You don't need a massive, sprawling space or a Pinterest-worthy room to achieve this goal. Anything can be a desk: a kitchen table, a piano bench, a ping-pong table, a folding table, and even a TV tray table. Get creative! Just avoid using your bed or a massage table (I have seen this happen), as these might have the unintended side effect of lulling you and your progeny into a deep slumber. All you need is a quiet, clean, and organized area where your kids can concentrate on their work. Here's how you can implement this with three different budgets/concerns in mind:

Frugal Budget

Trick Out Their Learning Pad: A low budget doesn't mean compromising on a quality learning environment. Focus on multi-functional furniture like a foldable desk and stackable chairs that save space and money (think Ikea). Utilize existing items around the house, such as a dining room table or a comfortable armchair, for the learning setup. Decorative elements can be handmade or sourced from thrift stores, such as DIY wall art or second-hand educational posters. Equip the space with affordable learning aids from the dollar stores, thrift/charity shops, homemade experiment kits, and library books.

Example: Sarah's family loves music but is mindful of their budget. They've created a cozy music corner in their living room by clearing out a nook where Sarah can practice on her keyboard. By repurposing a foldable desk and a couple of second-hand chairs, they managed to save space and money while still providing Sarah with a dedicated area for her music sessions. They found a used keyboard and a couple of second-hand guitars at a local thrift store. The walls are decorated with homemade posters of Sarah's favorite musicians, crafted from magazine cutouts and old concert flyers, creating an inspiring yet cost-effective mini-concert hall. This setup not only saves space with furniture choices but also enhances Sarah's learning environment without a significant financial outlay.

Premium Budget

Trick Out Their Learning Pad: When the budget allows, tailor the homeschooling environment to align closely with your child's interests and educational needs. Consider investing in advanced educational tools such as high-tech telescopes, high-quality microscopes, large wall-sized whiteboards, boxed sets of classic books or biographies, or large laminated wall maps (to name a few).

Example: Bobby is a visual and kinesthetic learner with a deep interest in astronomy. His parents have set up an "outer space" corner in his room featuring a high-tech telescope connected to a laptop for star mapping, a motorized model of the solar system, and a shelf dedicated to a curated selection of astronomy books. They've also invested in a high-definition solar system wall mural that makes Bobby feel like he's studying among the stars.

Special Needs and Other Options

Trick Out Their Learning Pad: For children with special needs, incorporate specialized tools and technology designed to meet their specific requirements—such as visual aids for better comprehension, sensory toys to help manage stress or furniture to help improve focus. Additionally, consider your child's learning style when setting up the room. If your child is an auditory learner, for example, stock up on headphones and access to audiobooks or other auditory resources. If you're raising a hands-on learner, cram the space with manipulatives and materials that scream, "Touch me!"

Alternatively, don't be afraid to get creative and let your homeschooling space reflect your family's passions and interests. Love medieval history? Deck your walls with tapestries and the occasional coat of arms. Is your family obsessed with all things STEM? Turn your workspace into a mini laboratory complete with 3D printers, beakers and microscopes. Encourage your children to adorn the space with their artwork, posters of their favorite subjects, or motivational quotes that don't make you roll your eyes.

Example: Alex has autism and sensory processing issues. His family designed a sensory-friendly area with minimal visual distractions and soft, calming colors on the walls. They included a variety of sensory toys and tools, like a weighted blanket to provide calming deep pressure, a bean bag chair that molds to his body for enhanced comfort and support, a stress ball for tactile input, and a small indoor swing to help Alex regulate his sensory needs throughout the day.

SEATING—NOBODY LEARNS WELL WITH A NUMB BUM!

When it comes to seating, choose chairs that are comfortable but not too comfortable. We're talking Goldilocks-level comfort: not too hard, not too soft, but just right. Let's examine these examples:

Frugal Budget

Example: Simple, budget-friendly chairs from thrift stores with DIY cushioned seats and backrests work for Pam. She added homemade lumbar support using rolled-up towels secured with rubber bands, providing the necessary support for long study sessions.

Premium Budget

Example: Michael's parents have selected high-end task chairs that feature adjustable lumbar support and breathable mesh fabric. These chairs are designed to provide optimal comfort and maintain posture, which is essential for long hours of study, ensuring he stays focused without strain.

Special Needs and Other Options

Example: John, grappling with sensory processing challenges, benefits from accommodations tailored to soothe and support. His learning space is thoughtfully equipped with two chairs: a cushioned rocking chair positioned in a quiet corner for breaks, offering gentle, rhythmic motion to enhance his sense of security, and his desk chair, outfitted with fidget chair bands. These bands offer a discreet outlet for his excess energy, helping him maintain focus and stay calm while engaged in tasks.

AMBIENCE—SETTING THE MOOD

Now, let's talk lighting and beyond. The ideal homeschooling environment has enough natural light to keep the room bright and airy but not so much that you start to wonder if you're in a greenhouse. Add some cozy lamps for those rainy days or late-night study sessions—because even calculus looks better in a warm glow. Aim for a delicate balance of sunshine and shade that whispers, "Learn, my child, but don't forget to frolic."

Don't stop at lighting, though. Bring in some greenery! A few potted plants here and there can make your space feel alive, and they might even become your new best friends when you need a break from the daily grind. And, while we're on the topic of life, how about a fish tank? The gentle gurgle and the sight of fish darting around can be both soothing and mildly entertaining—until they start staring at you like they understand chemistry better than you do.

For that perfect background noise, white noise machines can drown out the inevitable chaos from the rest of the house. Or, if you're feeling fancy, go for the sounds of a babbling brook or gentle rain. There are phone apps that you can download for a portable white noise option.

Finally, let's talk about movement. Yes, movement! Invest in a few wobble stools or exercise balls. They'll help your kids channel their energy without bouncing off the walls—literally. With this setup, your homeschool space won't just be a place of learning; it'll be a haven of comfort, curiosity, and maybe a little bit of controlled chaos. Here's how you can make this happen:

Frugal Budget

Example: Instead of expensive LED strips, Sean uses string lights bought from a dollar store, hung along the walls and across the ceiling to create a cozy, inviting atmosphere. When it's time to focus, Sean switches on a cheap desk lamp with a warm light for the right amount of light. For greenery, he has a few low-maintenance succulents on the windowsill, adding a touch of nature with minimal care. An old smartphone connected to a budget-friendly speaker plays white noise or nature sounds from free apps to mask household noises. Motivational quotes printed on card stock from his printer and taped to the walls add inspiration.

Premium Budget

Example: In Cy's homeschooling room, LED lights are cleverly positioned to create a gaming-like mood. These color-changing LED strips, carefully placed along the walls, ceiling, and furniture, are controlled by a remote, allowing Cy to customize the lighting to suit his mood, whether he's focused on studying or taking a well-deserved break. Sports quotes on art canvases add inspiration above his vertical rack of weights, which he uses to sculpt his athletic body for football. This setup allows Cy to customize his environment for both study, relaxation, and athletic training.

Special Needs and Other Options

Example: In Emily's homeschooling room, special considerations have been made to create a sensory-friendly environment beyond lighting accommodations. Alongside soft, adjustable lighting fixtures, the room features elements known to promote calmness and focus. Lush, green ferns are strategically placed throughout the space, providing visual interest and a connection to nature, which can have a grounding effect for individuals with sensory sensitivities.

A small fish tank adds another calming element, with the gentle movement of the fish and the sound of flowing water creating a tranquil atmosphere. Additionally, a white noise machine softly hums in the background, masking distracting noises from outside her window and promoting a sense of relaxation. These sensory-friendly additions, from plants to aquatic features and white noise, work in harmony to support Emily's comfort and concentration during homeschooling activities.

LISTEN UP! LET'S TALK ABOUT SOUND

In crafting an ideal learning environment at home, sound management is key. Consider the refined melodies of Mozart to potentially boost cognitive function, or the steady hum of a white noise machine to keep the daily noise of barking dogs, buzzing dishwashers, and your neighbor's choice music at bay. On the other hand, there's merit in welcoming the natural ebb and flow of household sounds, treating sporadic interruptions as teachable moments in adaptability, calmness, and composure—even when unexpected sounds intrude, like the sudden whoosh of a toilet during a virtual class or zoom call. Here's how to implement this:

Frugal Budget

Example: To help her children stay focused during their homeschooling sessions, Laura uses an old radio/CD player to play soft instrumental music in the background. She alternates between musical CDs and a classical radio station, which is a handy backup if the CDs get scratched or lost. This simple setup helps to create a calm atmosphere and effectively minimizes distractions from external noises.

Premium Budget

Example: For children with sensory processing issues, managing auditory input becomes crucial. Tom's parents have created a sensory-friendly zone that includes soundproofing panels to minimize echo and background noise. Additionally, they provide Tom with adaptive headphones that play specially curated soundscapes, which are designed to reduce anxiety and improve focus during learning activities. These soundscapes include natural sounds like soft rain or gentle ocean waves, which are particularly comforting for children who might be overwhelmed by more conventional noise.

Special Needs or Other Options

Example: In Sam's homeschooling space, his parents have set up a dedicated quiet area, complete with noise-canceling headphones and a white noise machine. This helps Sam and his siblings to focus during their independent study time, even when there's a lot of activity happening in the rest of the house.

ORGANIZE YOUR SPACE: KEEP IT TOGETHER—LITERALLY AND FIGURATIVELY!

Here's the scoop: to excel at homeschooling, having an organized space is essential. A cluttered environment can be distracting, making it hard for children to focus. No worries if your living room currently resembles a paper factory explosion—these tips will help you turn things around. Creating a tidy, dedicated learning area not only clears the clutter but also sets the tone for a productive homeschool day. Involve your children in the process by encouraging them to take responsibility for their space. A simple daily clean-up routine at the end of each day can make a big difference and teach valuable organizational habits. Here are a few organizational ideas you can implement:

- **Daily Bins**: Each day of the week gets its own bin. Load it up with the day's books, supplies, and assignments. It's like a daily to-do box—when the bin's empty, school's out! Don't forget to give those math manipulatives their own labeled bin, too. This way, those colorful counting cubes and pattern blocks stay corralled instead of ending up in the kitchen sink or mysteriously under the couch.

- **Workboxes**: Workboxes are similar to daily bins and are an organizational system where individual tasks and activities are placed in separate, easily accessible containers or boxes to promote independence and structure in your child's daily learning. They're perfect for keeping those subject-specific manipulatives, like geometric shapes for math or letter tiles for spelling, organized and within easy reach. It's like a little treasure chest of learning! Check out Sue Patrick's videos on Workboxes.

- **Reading Corner**: Create a cozy nook with a comfy chair, good lighting, and a mini-library set up on a bookshelf or in a basket. It's perfect for quiet reading time or just chilling with a book. You could even tuck in a small basket of word-building manipulatives, like letter magnets or sight word cards, for hands-on literacy practice in between chapters.

- **Create Learning Zones**: Set up areas for each subject like you're planning a mini theme park. Math Land over here, Science World over there, and Art Alley right in the corner. Each zone can have a little sign that your kids help make. Consider designating a "manipulative station" in Math Land or Science World with clear containers for all those tools of the trade—base ten blocks, animal counters, measuring spoons, you name it!

- **Tech Station**: Set up a charging station where all devices live when they're not in use. No more "I can't do math, my tablet's dead!" Plus, keeping tech in one spot helps with screen time rules.

- **Command Center**: Establish a central, organized area in the home, typically the kitchen, to keep everyone coordinated. This area usually features a large calendar, whiteboard, and/or cork board to help the family stay on schedule and efficiently manage daily tasks and activities. Each kid can have a color-coded section for their assignments and reminders.

- **Delegate like a Boss**: Put the kids on cleanup duty and make it fun! Maybe toss in a little challenge—fastest tidy-upper gets first dibs on snack time? Turn organizing into a team sport. Set a daily five-minute "tidy-up time" where everyone pitches in. Maybe play their favorite song as a timer, and they have to race to beat the song! Don't forget to include gathering those runaway manipulatives as part of the challenge—whoever finds the most wins extra kudos.

Frugal Budget

Example: The Martin family devised a color-coded system to keep their home-schooling paraphernalia from staging a coup. Blue for math, red for reading, and green for science—everything's matched up and easy to find. Each subject was assigned a color, and all materials for that subject were kept in matching bins and folders purchased from the dollar store. They keep it simple but effective. Dollar store bins and baskets help sort supplies, and a DIY pegboard on the wall holds all their tools and materials. A second-hand bookshelf keeps all their books organized, and they use an old coffee table as a multifunctional workspace. They even repurposed an old shoe rack into a tech station where all the devices can charge overnight.

Premium Budget

Example: The Bustamante's have gone all out with a custom-built homeschool room. Each child has their own desk with built-in storage, ergonomic chairs, and personalized shelves. The room features a smart board, interactive learning tools, and a cozy reading nook with a built-in bookcase. They even have a mini-fridge stocked with healthy snacks to keep everyone energized.

Special Needs or Other Options

Example: With four children in different grades, the Carter's use a mobile cart system where each child has a designated cart labeled with their name. Each cart is organized with hanging files for completed assignments, in-progress work, and new assignments, alongside bins for each subject's materials, adapted to their grade level.

ORGANIZE YOUR DAY: SCHEDULE SMARTER—PLAY HARDER!

Getting organized in homeschooling is like crafting your own secret recipe—when you get it just right, everything falls into place. The secret ingredients? A well-chosen calendar, a thoughtful schedule, and a consistent routine. These elements aren't just mundane tasks; they're the magical ingredients that transform chaos into calm and make your homeschool journey a delightful adventure.

Consider what your ideal homeschool day looks like. Are you an early riser who prefers to tackle challenging subjects before noon, or do you favor a flexible, student-led schedule that matches your child's natural learning pace? Perhaps you like a rhythmic approach, schooling for six weeks followed by a week off.

The possibilities are numerous and can help you organize and optimize your day effectively.

Here's a brief overview to get you thinking about the various calendars, routines, and schedules we'll explore further in Chapter 6, "Homeschool Routines."

Homeschool Calendars

Calendars are essential for tracking your homeschool year, planning lessons, and scheduling breaks. They help you visualize the big picture and ensure you're covering all necessary subjects and activities. Some families prefer a traditional academic calendar that follows the local school district's schedule, while others opt for a year-round calendar with shorter, more frequent breaks. There's also the option of a custom calendar that fits your unique lifestyle, allowing for vacations, family events, and spontaneous learning opportunities.

Homeschool Routines

Routines provide a framework for your daily activities, helping to create a sense of predictability and stability. A well-established routine can reduce decision fatigue and make transitions between tasks smoother. Routines can be as structured or as flexible as needed. For example, a morning routine might include breakfast, a brief physical activity, and then diving into academics, while an afternoon routine could involve hands-on projects, outdoor exploration, or creative pursuits. The key is to find a rhythm that works for your family and stick to it consistently.

Homeschool Schedules

Schedules are the detailed, time-specific plans that outline your day-to-day activities. Unlike routines, which offer a general structure, schedules are more precise and help ensure that each task is given adequate time. You might have a block schedule, where larger chunks of time are dedicated to fewer subjects, allowing for deeper immersion. Alternatively, a loop schedule can be employed, where subjects are rotated in a sequence, ensuring that everything is covered without the pressure of fitting it all into a single day. Daily, weekly, or even monthly schedules can be designed to keep your homeschool organized and on track.

By integrating calendars, routines, and schedules into your homeschool planning, you create a cohesive system that supports both learning and family life.

These tools not only help manage time effectively but also allow for flexibility and adaptability, ensuring a balanced and enriching homeschooling experience. In the next chapter, we will delve deeper into the specifics of these organizational tools, providing detailed strategies and examples to help you tailor them to your unique needs.

---------- **Summary** ----------

As we wrap up this chapter, let's take a step back and appreciate the tapestry we've woven—a space for learning that's as dynamic and vibrant as life itself. Setting up the ultimate homeschool haven is more than just snagging a spot with good light and cozy seats. It's all about creating a vibe where you and your learners feel pumped and tuned into our big, wild world. It's also about building a place that lets your kids flex their brain muscles and soar, no matter what curveballs come zipping their way.

Yeah, there'll be those days when your living room looks like a tornado hit it, the Wi-Fi decides to bail, or your kiddos turn your master lesson plan into a fleet of paper planes—and it's not even 7:58 AM on a Monday. But isn't rolling with the punches, adapting, and learning how to dance in the rain pretty much life 101? With the right organization, you'll be able to face those hiccups head-on, turning them into moments of creativity rather than stress, and keeping your homeschool days running smoothly.

6

Homeschool Routines

How to Weave One Without Unraveling

Your daily routine determines your success.

— John C. Maxwell

I MAGINE THIS: IT'S THE first day of your homeschool adventure. Your pristine, color-coded schedule is flawless—math from 8:00 a.m. to 9:00 a.m., science from 9:00 a.m. to 10:00 a.m., and so on, with every subject neatly slotted into its designated hour. You've got highlighters, lesson plans, and manipulatives all lined up, complete with healthy snacks and perhaps a little educational podcast playing in the background. You're convinced that you've cracked the code to homeschooling—thinking this structured approach is the key to a successful homeschool day.

But by 10:00 a.m. reality comes crashing in. The toddler is staging a protest over a missing blue cup that would make a seasoned activist proud. The dog decides that this is the perfect time to practice his barking skills, right in the middle of your read-aloud session. The older kids are either locked into an epic debate over whether a hot dog is a sandwich or mysteriously disappearing every time you try to start a new lesson. Your preschooler has turned a simple craft project into an abstract art installation—on the living room wall. And the laundry you thought you'd quickly fold during their art time? Forget it. Meanwhile, the lesson plans are somewhere under a pile of crayons and scattered worksheets. Suddenly, that strict schedule feels more like a straitjacket than a helpful guide and you're left seriously questioning your life choices and wondering how on earth anyone manages to make this work.

Sound familiar? Don't worry, you're not alone. The truth is, no matter how perfect that schedule looks on paper, life has a way of laughing at our best-laid plans. But here's the good news: that's where the magic happens. Flexibility isn't just a backup plan—it's the secret sauce to homeschooling success.

Welcome to the chapter on crafting a homeschool routine. In this section, we'll tackle the essentials of creating a structured yet flexible homeschool environment that suits your family's unique needs. We'll talk about the several different types of homeschool calendars, explore the differences between routines and schedules, break down various types of daily/weekly schedules, and provide practical examples to help you find the right fit. You'll also discover how to balance structure with flexibility and incorporate essential breaks and downtime.

Now that you have an overview of what we'll cover, we'll start with the foundation of any successful homeschool routine: understanding your family's unique dynamics. Start by observing your family's natural patterns and rhythms. This insight will help you choose a homeschool calendar and daily routine that align perfectly with your family's lifestyle.

KNOW THY FAMILY—UNDERSTAND YOUR FAMILY'S RHYTHM

Every family has its own natural rhythms. Some families are up at the crack of dawn, ready to seize the day. Others might not hit their stride until after a leisurely breakfast and a bit of quiet time. Start by observing when your kids are most alert and productive. Are they little morning larks who jump out of bed ready to learn? Or, are they night owls who do their best thinking after dinner? Let's consider several examples:

Example #1: Take the Johnson family. Their youngest, Noah, is an early riser, bursting with energy and questions at 7:00 a.m. Meanwhile, their teenager, Emma, emerges from her room around 10:00 a.m., grumpy and groggy, but transforms into a learning powerhouse by late afternoon. So, they split their day to match these rhythms. Morning is for Noah's academics and creative projects, while Emma tackles her most challenging subjects in the afternoon. It's not a traditional setup, but it works for them.

Example #2: The Thompson family, a single-parent household, starts their day with breakfast together at 8:00 a.m., allowing for a slow start that accommodates everyone's morning moods. They engage in light activities like reading or drawing until everyone is fully awake.

Here are two ways to assess your family's lifestyle and rhythms to choose the best homeschool calendar, routine, and schedule:

Assess Your Family's Rhythm

1. Daily Activity Log

Keep a detailed log of your family's daily activities for at least one to two weeks. Record when each family member wakes up, eats meals, engages in activities, and goes to bed. Note periods of high and low energy, as well as moments of focus and distraction.

Steps:

- **Track Wake and Sleep Times:** Observe and record when everyone naturally wakes up and goes to bed. This will help identify whether your family functions better in the morning, afternoon, or evening.

- **Monitor Energy Levels:** Note when family members are most energetic and productive versus when they need rest or downtime.

- **Identify Patterns:** Look for consistent patterns or routines that naturally occur, such as mealtimes, nap times for younger children, or moments when the household is typically quiet or active.

2. Lifestyle Commitment and Analysis

Evaluate your family's lifestyle and external commitments to understand how they will impact your homeschool. Consider work schedules, extracurricular activities, special-needs therapies, and any other regular obligations.

Steps:

- **Assess Work Schedules:** Determine the work hours of each parent and how they influence the family's daily routine. Consider how flexible or rigid these schedules are.

- **Review Extracurricular Activities:** List all extracurricular activities, such as sports, music lessons, or community events, and note their schedules and/or financial commitments. Identify any potential conflicts or opportunities for incorporating these activities into the homeschool routine.

- **Plan Around Commitments:** Create a schedule that accommodates these commitments, ensuring that there is enough flexibility to adapt to changes or unexpected events. This might mean having a more structured routine on certain days and a more flexible approach on others.

By using these methods, you can gain a comprehensive understanding of your family's lifestyle and dynamics, helping to create a homeschool calendar, routine, and schedule that fits their unique needs and promotes a harmonious learning environment.

HOMESCHOOL CALENDARS, SCHEDULES, & ROUTINES

Once you have the lay of the land with your family dynamics, it's time to start planning your homeschool calendar, routine, and schedule. It's important to grasp the differences amongst these terms because they can be confusing. While they might seem similar, they serve different purposes in your homeschooling journey. Let's break them down.

Types of Homeschool Calendars

A homeschool calendar refers to the overall structure and timeframe within which your homeschooling occurs. Think of it as the "big-picture" view of your homeschooling year. Homeschool calendars define the start and end dates of your school year, the breaks you take, and how you spread your school days across the months.

Traditional Calendar: Mirrors the typical school year with a long summer break. The traditional calendar, running from August/September through May/June, is the familiar calendar many of us experienced in the public school system. Rooted in the agrarian needs of early farmers, this approach has stood the test of time. It offers several perks: you get to vacation when neighborhood kids and cousins do, enjoy all the summer activities, and feel that nostalgic burst of excitement and energy every fall. This calendar mirrors the typical public-school calendar, with set school days, weekends, national holidays off, and a long summer break. Each day typically runs from around 8:00 a.m. to 3:00 p.m., just like a conventional school day.

> **Example:** The Smith family follows a traditional calendar, starting their lessons at 8:30 a.m. and wrapping up by 3:00 p.m. They take a one-hour lunch break at noon and have short breaks between subjects. They enjoy a summer break from June to August and follow the local school district's holiday calendar.

Calendar-Year Calendar: Starts the school year in January, aligning academics with the calendar year for a fresh start after the New Year. Some families choose to kick off their school year in January, taking December off to enjoy the holidays. This gives everyone a chance to recharge and return ready for new subjects after the New Year's festivities. The calendar year divides the year into balanced segments with shorter, more frequent breaks, which can help prevent burnout. This method also allows families to travel during less busy times, making vacations more enjoyable and affordable. By spreading out breaks throughout the year, it keeps the learning experience fresh and exciting for both parents and children.

> **Example:** The Johnson family uses calendar-year schooling for six weeks followed by a one-week break. They also take a three-week break in December and another in June. Their shorter breaks help keep the kids engaged and reduce the pressure of a long school year.

Sabbath Calendar: Implements six weeks of schooling followed by one week off, repeating this cycle throughout the year. The Sabbath calendar incorporates a recurring one-week break every seventh week, inspired by the concept of taking a sabbath rest. This method provides regular downtime and opportunities for rest and enrichment activities.

> **Example:** The Davis family follows a Sabbath calendar, homeschooling for six weeks and then taking the seventh week off. This rhythm helps them stay refreshed and provides time for special projects, field trips, or family vacations.

Year-Round Calendar: Spreads learning throughout the year with shorter, more frequent breaks. The year-round calendar (similar to the calendar schedule) spreads schooling throughout the entire year, typically with shorter breaks throughout rather than one long summer vacation. The start date can be at any time of the year. This can help maintain continuity in learning and reduce the need for extensive review after long breaks.

> **Example:** The Martinez family uses a year-round calendar, homeschooling for three weeks and taking one week off throughout the year. They take shorter breaks but have more of them, keeping their learning consistent and allowing for flexibility in planning vacations and family time.

Customized Calendar: Includes unique breaks and schooling periods based on your personal preferences and lifestyle. This approach offers the ultimate flexibility, allowing you to design a homeschooling calendar that best fits your family's rhythm and commitments.

> **Example:** The Rodriguez family uses a customized calendar to support their world schooling lifestyle. They travel to different countries throughout the year, aligning their schooling periods

with their travel schedule. During their travels, they take breaks to immerse themselves in local cultures, learn new languages, and visit historical sites. They might spend two months in Spain, schooling in the mornings and exploring in the afternoons, followed by a month-long break to travel through France and Italy. This customized approach ensures that their children's education is enriched by real-world experiences and cultural immersion, making learning both exciting and relevant.

SCHEDULES AND ROUTINES

Understand Schedules and Routines

Let's start by clearing up a common confusion: the difference between a schedule and a routine. A schedule is a detailed plan that outlines specific times and the order for each activity, similar to what you'd find in a traditional school. This includes the subjects taught, the duration of each lesson, and the sequence of activities. In contrast, a routine is a general sequence of activities, sometimes with specific intentions, but without strict time constraints. It provides structure while allowing for more flexibility.

Schedules can be great for families who thrive on predictability and structure. They help ensure that everything gets done and can be particularly useful for parents balancing work and homeschooling.

Routines, on the other hand, are ideal for families who need more flexibility. They reduce the pressure of sticking to exact times, which can be a lifesaver on days when everything seems to go off the rails. By focusing on the order of activities rather than strict timing and being strategic with your order, routines can accommodate the unexpected twists and turns of daily life while still providing structure.

Let's compare the two with a visual example:

Sample Time-Based Schedule

TIME	SUBJECT/ACTIVITY
9:00 AM	Math
9:45 AM	Science
10:30 AM	History
11:15 AM	Writing/Handwriting
12:00 PM	Lunch
1:00 PM	Social Studies
1:45 PM	Reading

Sample Routine

SUBJECT/ACTIVITY	INTENTION
Math After Breakfast	This could be at 8:30 AM one day and 9:00 AM the next, depending on how the morning goes.
Read-Alouds Between Science and Handwriting	This provides a natural transition and break between different types of learning.
Challenging or Undesirable Subjects Right Before Lunch	This ensures that the most demanding work is tackled when energy levels are higher, and lunch serves as a reward and break afterward.
Science and History Group Lessons on Tuesday and Thursday Mornings/Afternoons	Instead of a fixed time, you can start these lessons after everyone is settled and ready to focus, whether that's 9:00 AM or 10:00 AM.

We'll explore schedules and routines in more detail later. Now that you've grasped the distinction between them, let's move on to the three main types of schedules.

Homeschool Schedules

Now that we understand homeschool calendars and the difference between a routine and a schedule, let's examine the three main types of schedules:

Traditional Schedule: A Blast from the Past

What It Is

The homeschool traditional schedule is like taking a page straight out of a 1950s classroom playbook. Imagine a school year that starts in late August or early September and ends in May or June, with a long summer break to recharge those educational batteries. Your days are neatly packaged from 8:00 a.m. to 3:00 p.m., Monday through Friday, just like in the public school system. It's an option for those who crave structure and enjoy aligning their lives with the conventional academic calendar. While it has its benefits of routine and predictability, it's essential to balance it with a bit of flexibility to avoid burnout and keep the learning journey enjoyable.

How It's Implemented

Picture this: your homeschool day kicks off at 8:00 a.m. sharp. You dive into math, then shuffle through science, english, and history, all punctuated with perfectly timed breaks and a lunch hour that mirrors a public school's cafeteria schedule. By 3:00 p.m., the final bell rings (well, metaphorically), and the academic day wraps up.

Benefits

1. **Familiarity:** This schedule is a comfort zone for those of us who grew up with it. It's like a warm, educational blanket.

2. **Alignment with Public Schools:** You can vacation when your neighbors do, participate in local summer camps, and not feel out of sync with the rest of the world.

3. **Routine and Predictability:** Kids (and parents) know what to expect every day, which can reduce the chaos and keep everyone on track.

4. **Nostalgia Factor:** There's something magical about that back-to-school energy in the fall and the blissful countdown to summer vacation.

5. **Working Parents:** Can be particularly useful for parents balancing work and homeschooling, as it mirrors traditional work hours and provides a clear structure.

Disadvantages

1. **Rigidity:** Life is unpredictable, and this schedule can feel a bit too stiff when unexpected events or opportunities arise.

2. **Burnout Potential:** Nine months straight of daily grind with a long break at the end can lead to burnout for both kids and parents.

3. **Summer Slide:** The long summer break can sometimes lead to the infamous "summer slide," where kids forget what they learned.

Block Schedule: Dive Deep and Conquer

What It Is

The homeschool block schedule is like the superhero of schedules, swooping in to save the day with focus and flexibility. Instead of hopping from subject to subject every hour, you dedicate larger blocks of time to fewer subjects each day. This method allows for more in-depth exploration and less time wasted on transitions.

How It's Implemented

Imagine your homeschooling day as a series of immersive experiences. Instead of juggling multiple subjects in one day, you dive deeply into just one or two. For instance, Monday might be all about history and science, with a solid two-hour block dedicated to each. Tuesday shifts the focus to one and a half hour blocks of English and math, and so on. This way, kids get to fully immerse themselves in a subject without the constant stop-and-start of a traditional schedule.

Benefits

- **In-Depth Learning:** Allows students to dive deep into subjects, fostering better understanding and retention.

- **Fewer Transitions:** Less time wasted moving between subjects, which means more productive learning time.

- **Flexibility:** Easier to accommodate longer projects, experiments, viewing documentaries, and field trips without disrupting the flow.

- **Reduced Burnout:** With fewer subjects per day, both students and parents can focus better and avoid feeling overwhelmed.

Disadvantages

- **Possible Gaps:** There's a risk of forgetting material if too many days pass between sessions on the same subject.

- **Adjustment Period:** It might take time for both parents and kids to get used to the longer focus periods.

- **Planning Intensive:** Requires careful planning to ensure all subjects are covered adequately over time.

On the following page is a sample breakdown of two block schedules (also referred to as block routines):

Weekly Block Schedule (Routine)

Block	Monday	Tuesday	Wednesday	Thursday	Friday
Morning Mastery (8:30 AM - 10:30 AM)	Mathematics, Language Arts	History	Mathematics, Language Arts	History	Mathematics, Language Arts
Mid-Morning Discovery (10:30 AM - 12:30PM)	Science, Writing	Art	Science, Writing	Art	Science, Writing
Lunch & Leisure (12:30 PM - 1:30 PM)	Lunch	Lunch	Lunch	Lunch	Lunch
Afternoon Exploration (1:30 PM - 3:30 PM)	Electives (Coding, Drawing, etc.)	Electives (Physical Education, Music)	Electives (Coding, Drawing, etc.)	Electives (Physical Education, Music)	Electives (Coding, Drawing, etc.)

Times listed are only a suggestion to give you a frame of reference.

Daily Block Schedule (Routine)

Block	Time Slot	Activities
Morning Focus	8:30 AM - 10:30 AM	**Monday-Friday:** Core subjects like math and language arts (reading, writing, grammar, handwriting)
Mid-Day Exploration	10:30 AM - 12:30 PM	**Monday and Wednesday:** History, Geography, PE; **Tuesday and Thursday:** Science, Art/Poetry, PE; **Friday:** PE only
Lunch & Relaxation	12:30 PM - 1:30 PM	Lunch and free time for relaxation
Solo/Catch Up/Creative Time	1:30 PM - 3:30 PM	Electives, individual learning, finishing work, music, crafts
Wind Down	3:30 PM - 5:00 PM	Read alouds, snack, free time, outdoor play, optional educational movie/show/program.

Times listed are only a suggestion to give you a frame of reference.

Loop Schedule

What It Is

A loop schedule is a simple yet effective way to organize a list of subjects or activities into a rotating cycle, regardless of the day of the week. This approach ensures you cover those easily neglected subjects/interests without the stress of fitting everything into a rigid daily timetable.

How It's Implemented

1. **Make an "All Subjects" List**
   Start by jotting down every subject or activity you're planning to teach—yes, everything. This is your master list. You want to get it all down so nothing slips through the cracks. Think of it as your brain dump to keep things from, well, getting dumped.

2. **Create a "Daily Loop" List**
   Now, take a good look at that master list and pick out the subjects that absolutely need to happen every day (or almost every day). We're talking the non-negotiables like math, reading, and whatever else keeps your homeschool ship afloat. These are your "most days" essentials.

3. **Craft a "Weekly Loop" List**
   Here's where the loop magic happens. List out the subjects or activities you want to hit at least once a week—like history, art, or music. Feeling fancy? Make multiple loops like "Language Arts Loop," "Electives Loop," or the ever-popular "Morning Basket Loop." This is your chance to mix in the fun stuff that might not fit into your daily grind. Go wild!

4. **Start at the Top**
   Once you've got your loops ready, start at the top of your weekly list and tackle the first item. Didn't finish it? No problem—just pick up where you left off next time. No need to stress; you're in the loop now.

5. Keep on Looping

As you finish each subject or activity, cross it off with a flourish. When you reach the bottom of the list, loop back up to the top and start again. It's like the world's most satisfying to-do list that never judges you for taking your time.

Take a look at the three loop schedule examples below and on the following page that I've created to give you a sense of how to craft your own. They all get the job done—some are no-fuss, while others bring a little extra flair. If you'd like a free blank copy of these or any of the other loop schedules I've designed, just pop over to my website and snag yours at: www.homeschoolknockouts.com/resourcelibrary.

Sample Loop Schedule #1

Sample Loop Schedule #2

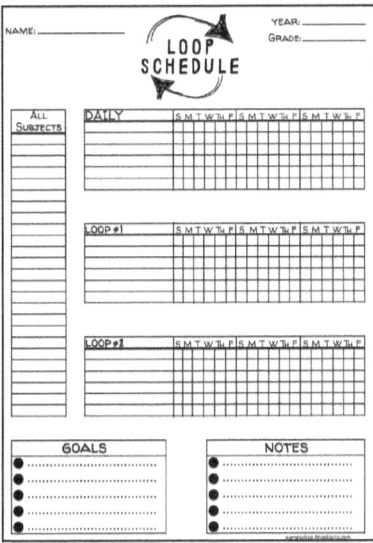

Sample Loop Schedule #3

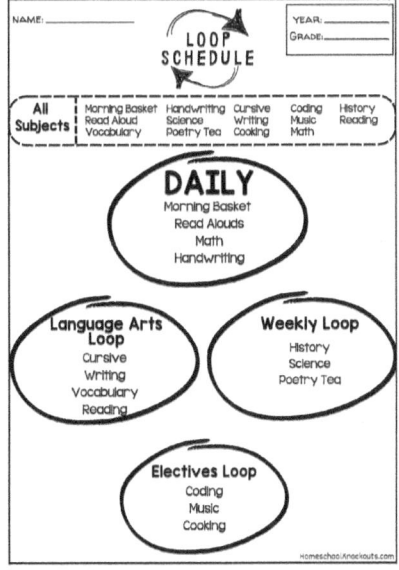

Benefits

- **Flexibility**: Adapts to daily life. If something unexpected happens, just pick up where you left off. No rigid timetable stress.

- **Comprehensive Coverage**: Ensures all subjects get attention. Prevents neglecting any subject for a balanced education

- **Reduces Burnout**: Spreads out the workload. Makes learning more manageable and less overwhelming for everyone.

Disadvantages

- **Lack of Routine**: The flexible nature can disrupt daily routines. Some kids need consistency and might struggle without it.

- **Potential for Procrastination**: No set deadlines can lead to delaying less-favored subjects. Requires discipline to cover all subjects.

- **Tracking Challenges**: Hard to keep track of progress. Can lead to confusion and missing subjects or activities.

STRUCTURE YOUR DAY AND WEEK

Creating a flexible, but structured, routine can help keep both you and your child on track. Here are some simple ways to structure your homeschool day and week:

- **Morning Routine:** Start with a consistent morning routine to set the tone for the day. This could include breakfast, morning chores, and a short family meeting to discuss the day's plans.

- **Breaks:** Incorporate regular breaks to prevent burnout. A 10–15-minute break after each 45 minutes to one hour of focused work can make a huge difference.

- **Afternoon Activities:** Use the afternoon for hands-on activities, projects, and extracurriculars. This is a great time for art, music, physical education, and field trips.

- **Weekly Themes:** Assign specific themes or subjects to different days of the week. For example, Mondays could be for science experiments, Tuesdays for history projects, Wednesdays for writing projects, and so on.

CORE COMPONENTS OF A HOMESCHOOL DAY

To create a balanced and engaging homeschool day, it's essential to integrate various core components that cater to different learning styles and interests. Here's how you can blend academic time, hands-on learning, and creative activities to make your homeschool experience enriching and enjoyable.

Academic Time

Academics are the bread and butter of homeschooling. But instead of thinking of it as a rigid education setup, imagine it as a personalized learning adventure. You can make math fun with manipulatives, explore science through hands-on experiments, bring history to life with storytelling, and turn reading into an interactive story time. Writing can be an exciting process with creative prompts and projects.

Example: Start the day with a math scavenger hunt around the house. Afterward, you can have a science session in the kitchen and turn baking into a chemistry lesson. Reading time could involve cozying up with a good book and then discussing the story over a cup of hot chocolate or lemonade.

Hands-on Learning

Incorporate practical, hands-on learning activities. This approach not only makes learning fun but also helps kids grasp concepts better through real-world applications.

Example: Picture a history lesson where you build a model of an ancient city with clay and craft materials. Or a geography lesson that involves creating a giant map on the living room floor and exploring different cultures through food, music, and crafts.

Creative Time

Don't forget to carve out time for creativity. Art, music, and imaginative play are crucial for a well-rounded education. They help kids develop critical thinking skills and express themselves.

Example: Set up an art station where your kids can paint, draw, or craft whenever they feel inspired. Schedule a weekly music session where you learn new songs together or explore different musical instruments. Imaginative play could involve setting up a pretend store or acting out a favorite story.

Think of academic time as your main course, hands-on learning as the delicious sides, and creative time as the dessert that leaves everyone smiling. Balancing these components ensures your homeschool day is nutritious and delightful.

BALANCE STRUCTURE AND FLEXIBILITY

Finding the right balance between structure and flexibility in your homeschool routine can be like Goldilocks trying to find the perfect bowl of porridge—not too hot, not too cold, but just right. Too much structure can lead to burnout and rebellion, while too much flexibility can result in chaos and unfinished work. Here are some examples on how to add structure and flexibility to your day.

Hyper-Scheduled Day

Your day is planned down to the minute. Breakfast at 7:00 a.m., math at 8:00 a.m., science at 8:45 a.m., handwriting at 9:15 a.m., reading at 9:30 a.m., history at 9:50 a.m., writing at 10:30 a.m., drawing at 11:20 a.m., PE at 11:45 a.m. with no room for spontaneity or delays. By noon, everyone is stressed, and the joy of learning has vanished. Sound familiar? That's the danger of a hyper-scheduled day.

Too-Laid-Back Day

Now, imagine the opposite: You wake up whenever, start the day whenever, and maybe get around to some schoolwork—if you feel like it. By the end of the day, you realize that nothing substantial was accomplished, and everyone feels a bit lost. That's the risk of being too laid-back.

Finding the Sweet Spot

The key is to find a middle ground that works for your family. This might mean having a general structure with set learning blocks but allowing for flexibility within those blocks. Here are a few ideas to get you thinking:

Example: A balanced day could start with a morning routine that includes breakfast and a family meeting to discuss the day's plan. Then, you have a block of academic time where you focus on core subjects, but you're flexible about the order and duration. If your child is deeply engaged in a science experiment, you can let them continue without worrying about the clock. Early afternoons could be reserved for hands-on activities, field trips, or free play, with a gentle reminder that you'll return to academics after lunch/free time.

Imagine your homeschool day like a jazz performance: there's a basic structure, but plenty of room for improvisation. As long as you're hitting the key notes, it's all good! Find your family's rhythm, and don't be afraid to change the tune as you go.

INCORPORATE BREAKS AND DOWNTIME

Even the most enthusiastic learners need breaks. Short breaks throughout the day help maintain focus, reduce stress, and improve overall productivity. Think of breaks as little pit stops that keep your homeschool engine running smoothly. Now, not all breaks are created equal. Here are a few types of breaks or downtime to consider for your homeschool day:

Tiered Breaks

Implementing the Pomodoro Technique can be a game-changer. This method involves 25 minutes of focused work followed by a 5-minute break. After four sessions, take a longer break of 15-30 minutes. This approach keeps learning fresh and prevents burnout.

Example: Start with 25 minutes of math, followed by a 5-minute break to stretch or grab a snack. Then, jump into 25 minutes of reading, another 5-minute break, followed by 25 minutes of science, another short break, and finally 25 minutes of history. After completing these four focused sessions, reward yourself with a 20-minute break to play a board game, read a book, or enjoy some outdoor time.

Physical Breaks

These involve movement and are great for burning off energy. Activities like jumping jacks, a quick game of tag, or a short walk can refresh the mind and body.

Example: After a focused learning session, let your kids run around the yard for a few minutes or have a quick indoor obstacle course.

Quiet Breaks

These are perfect for recharging quietly. Activities like reading a favorite book, drawing, working on a puzzle, or simply resting can be very restorative.

Example: After a noisy group activity, let your kids spend 5-10 minutes reading quietly or listening to calming music.

Creative Breaks

Encourage creativity during breaks. Let your kids do a quick craft, play with building blocks, or invent a short story.

Example: A 10-minute break to draw their favorite scene from a favorite book from the morning's lesson or build a Lego structure related to what they're learning can be a great reset.

Social Breaks

Let your kids interact with each other or with friends. This can be through a quick phone call, a playdate, a weekly social group on Outschool, or a group game.

Example: A mid-afternoon break for a playdate or a video chat with a friend can provide social stimulation and a fun break from academics.

View breaks as the commercial breaks during your favorite TV show. Just the right amount of time to grab a snack, stretch your legs, and get ready for the next exciting segment of your homeschool day. Too few breaks, and everyone's zoning out. Too many breaks, and you'll never get through the show. Find your family's perfect break balance, and watch productivity soar!

---------- Summary ----------

In the whirlwind of homeschooling, finding a routine that works for your family is like discovering a well-kept secret. The key is balancing structure with flexibility, creating a learning environment where everyone thrives. Understanding your family's natural rhythms, differentiating between routines and schedules, and exploring various scheduling options can transform chaos into harmony. Whether you lean towards a traditional schedule, embrace the freedom of a year-round approach, or mix it up with a loop schedule, the goal is to craft a routine that fits your unique needs. With practical tips, real-life examples, and a dash of humor, this chapter equips you to weave a homeschool routine that keeps everyone engaged, productive, and smiling. Remember, the best homeschool routine is one that adapts to the unexpected twists and turns of daily life, ensuring that learning remains a joyful adventure.

7

The Curriculum Jungle

Where's the Map When You Need One?

Sometimes you make the right decision, sometimes you make the decision right.

— Dr. Phil McGraw

ERE'S THE THING ABOUT homeschool curriculum choices: it's like ordering takeout from five different great restaurants and expecting a five-star meal at the end. In theory, it sounds fantastic. You get a little bit of this, a little bit of that, and before you know it, you've concocted the perfect education for your child. But when you're in the thick of it, facing the curriculum circus, things can get a little...well, messy. With so many options and paths to choose from, you'll quickly find yourself in a labyrinth. There are textbooks, online courses, educational approaches, learning/teaching styles, and lifestyle situations to consider.

Whew! But don't worry. This chapter is divided into three parts to make the process manageable. Part I covers the big picture, where we align curriculum with your family's goals, styles, and needs. Part II delves into the details of researching and selecting curriculum. Finally, Part III focuses on customizing the curriculum to suit your child.

So, where do we begin? Tackling the curriculum jungle might seem overwhelming, but by breaking it down into manageable steps, you can create a clear path forward. To simplify the process, I've put together a quick eight-step curriculum checklist that will guide you through each stage, from setting goals to being flexible with your choices.

1. **Set Goals:** Determine what you want to achieve academically, socially, and emotionally for your child.

2. **Learn Your Child's Learning Style:** Are they are visual, auditory, kinesthetic, or logical learners?

3. **Identify Your Homeschool Philosophy:** Reflect on your educational beliefs and approach. Are you leaning towards classical education, Montessori, unschooling, or a mix?

4. **Assess Your Teaching Style:** Consider how you best teach and what resources you feel comfortable using.

5. **Establish a Budget:** Determine how much you are willing and able to spend on educational materials and resources

6. **Research and Review:** Look into different curriculum options and read reviews from other homeschooling families. Focus on the big picture (goals, child's needs, budget) and the details (contents overview, required materials/class pricing, teacher involvement, optional materials, intended audience, worldview, and pros/cons.)

7. **Try Samples:** Many curriculum or publishing companies offer sample lessons or trial periods. Use these to see how well they fit. For example, many online curriculum providers offer a few weeks of free access or a few sample chapters, allowing you to gauge how well the curriculum fits before making a full commitment.

8. **Be Flexible:** Be open to adjusting and changing the curriculum if it doesn't meet your child's needs.

With the checklist in hand, we can now take a broader view. Let's start with Part I—The Big Picture, where we will explore how to set clear, achievable goals and more for your homeschooling journey.

PART I—THE BIG PICTURE

Before we get lost in the maze of curriculum options, let's take a moment to map out our plan and get clear on our goals. Are you aiming for academic excellence, sparking a love for learning, or addressing specific areas of improvement? Defining your overall and subject-specific goals is essential. Whether it's getting your kid to dive into novels, nail essay writing, conquer math challenges, or explore fascinating science concepts, knowing what success looks like is the first step. Don't forget the fun and important extras—art, sports, and social skills! And remember, every child learns differently.

SET GOALS

Holistic Development

Are you aiming for your child to develop a well-rounded set of skills and attributes, encompassing academic, social, emotional, and physical aspects?

Example: You want your child to not only achieve high grades but also build strong social skills, emotional resilience, and physical health through activities like team sports and mindfulness practices.

Creative and Critical Thinking

Do you want to encourage your child to think creatively and critically, nurturing their ability to solve problems and innovate?

Example: You focus on project-based learning, where your child engages in activities that require creative problem-solving, such as building models, coding projects, or participating in debates and discussions.

Social and Emotional Learning

Is your goal to enhance your child's social and emotional intelligence, ensuring they develop empathy, self-awareness, and effective communication skills?

Example: You incorporate activities like group projects, peer mentoring, and reflective journaling to help your child understand and manage emotions, build healthy relationships, and make responsible decisions.

Lifelong Learning

Are you fostering a mindset that values continuous learning and curiosity beyond the classroom?

Example: You encourage your child to explore interests through extracurricular activities, library visits, and online courses, instilling a love for discovering new things and adapting to an ever-changing world.

Physical and Mental Well-Being

Are you placing an emphasis on your child's physical health and mental well-being as a foundation for academic success?

- **Example:** You ensure your child balances their academic workload with regular physical activities, healthy eating, sufficient sleep, and stress management techniques like meditation or yoga.

Ethical and Moral Development

Is your focus on instilling strong ethical values and moral integrity in your child's education?

Example: You engage your child in discussions about ethics and morality, encourage volunteer work, and provide opportunities for them to reflect on their actions and their impact on others.

Subject-Specific Goals

Determine specific milestones for each subject. Here are some examples:

- **Reading Proficiency:** Aim for your child to read a novel on their own, improve reading comprehension, or enjoy a variety of genres by the end of the year.

- **Writing Skills:** Set goals like writing a paragraph without frustration, gradually building up to more complex writing tasks.

- **Math Skills:** Target mastering basic arithmetic, understanding fractions and decimals, or tackling algebraic concepts, depending on the grade level. Consider goals that prepare them for real-world consumer math.

- **Science Understanding:** Expose them to a variety of science topics, ensuring they gain a solid grasp of fundamental principles and the ability to conduct simple experiments.

Realistic and Achievable Goals

Ensure your goals are realistic and achievable within your timeframe. A useful method for crafting effective goals is the S.M.A.R.T. framework. S.M.A.R.T. stands for Specific, Measurable, Achievable, Relevant, and Time-bound. Here's a breakdown:

- **Specific:** Clearly define what you want to achieve.

- **Measurable:** Determine how you will measure progress and know when the goal is achieved.

- **Achievable:** Set goals that are realistic and attainable.

- **Relevant:** Make goals relevant to what you want to accomplish. Your "why are we doing this?"

- **Time-bound:** Set a deadline for achieving the goal

Using this framework can help you create structured and attainable goals. Here are two examples to get you going:

If your child struggles with reading:

- **Specific:** Improve reading comprehension and fluency.

- **Measurable:** Read for 20 minutes daily, three times a week, and complete a reading comprehension worksheet once a week.

- **Achievable:** Choose books that are one level below the current reading level to build confidence and fluency.

- **Relevant:** Reading is crucial for overall academic success.

- **Time-Bound:** Achieve this goal over the next three months, with a review at the end of each month to adjust as needed.

If your child is strong in writing:

- **Specific:** Improve creative writing skills by writing more short stories.

- **Measurable:** Write one short story every two weeks, each with at least 1,000 words.

- **Achievable:** Spend 30 minutes each day working on the stories and get feedback from mom, an online teacher, or an older sibling.

- **Relevant:** Enhance creative writing skills to help with future writing projects and boost overall writing confidence.

- **Time-bound:** Achieve this goal over the next three months.

Don't forget to include goals for other skills and interests, such as:
- **Art and Creativity:** Encourage artistic expression by setting goals for completing specific projects or learning new techniques.

- **Physical Education:** Set goals for regular physical activity, improving fitness levels, or participating in sports.

- **Social Skills:** Include goals for developing social skills, teamwork, and communication, if applicable.

UNDERSTAND YOUR CHILD'S NEEDS

A successful homeschooling experience begins with understanding your child's unique needs, interests, and learning styles. By considering their strengths, weaknesses, and the subjects that captivate them, you can tailor the curriculum to maximize their potential for academic success and personal development. Let's break this down.

Learn Your Child's Learning Style

To build an effective homeschool curriculum, you need to understand your child's learning style. Are they visual, auditory, kinesthetic, or a combination? Observing their natural preferences and adapting your teaching style can ensure a fruitful homeschooling experience. Here are some tips for choosing the best curriculum based on your child's learning style (refer to Chapter 12, "Teacher, Know Thyself (and Your Student)," for more information on learning styles):

- **Visual Learners:** Benefit from a curriculum with lots of diagrams, charts, and pictures. Look for textbooks and workbooks with plenty of visual aids.

- **Auditory Learners:** Benefit from audio resources, such as podcasts, audiobooks, lectures, dictation, and narration. They may also enjoy group discussions and debates.

- **Kinesthetic Learners:** Learn best through hands-on activities and projects. Look for a curriculum that offers opportunities for physical activities, experiments, and manipulatives.

- **Logical Learners:** Enjoy a curriculum that is organized logically and sequentially with clear procedures or steps. They might also enjoy puzzles and problem-solving activities.

Choose an Educational Philosophy

Choosing the right homeschool curriculum can be guided by understanding different homeschool philosophies. For example, if your child loves being outside, the Charlotte Mason Method might be a good fit. If your child is a bookworm, the Classical Method might be a better choice. For a complete list of philosophies, see Part IV "Philosophies, Approaches, and Methods"). Here are some key philosophies and how they can help you select a curriculum that fits your child's needs:

Charlotte Mason (Chapter 18)

- **Philosophy:** Emphasizes short lessons, rich literature, nature study, and nurturing a love for learning through "living books" rather than dry textbooks.

- **Curriculum Choice:** Seek materials that include a wide range of literature, nature journals, and art appreciation. Prioritize real-world experiences and hands-on learning.

Classical Education (Chapter 19)

- **Philosophy:** Focuses on the trivium, a three-part process of training the mind, including grammar (fundamental facts and rules), logic (critical thinking and understanding), and rhetoric (expressing ideas effectively).

- **Curriculum Choice:** Emphasize reading classic literature, studying history and Latin, and engaging in logical discussions and debates.

Eclectic Homeschooling (Chapter 20)

- **Philosophy:** Combines elements from various educational philosophies to create a customized approach. It is flexible and adapts to the child's needs.

- **Curriculum Choice:** Mix and match different resources and programs that suit your child's learning style and interests. Perhaps Charlotte Mason method for reading and science and the classical approach for history and writing. Adapt and change the curriculum as needed.

Montessori (Chapter 21)

- **Philosophy:** Focuses on self-directed activity, hands-on learning, and collaborative play. Encourages independence and respects a child's natural development.

- **Curriculum Choice:** Choose resources that provide a prepared environment with manipulative materials and activities that allow children to learn at their own pace.

Unit Studies (Chapter 23)

- **Philosophy:** Integrates multiple subjects around a central theme, making learning more interconnected and meaningful.

- **Curriculum Choice:** Select unit study programs that allow you to explore topics deeply and across various subjects such as science, history, math, and literature.

Unschooling (Chapter 24)

- **Philosophy:** Child-led learning driven by the child's interests and passions rather than a structured curriculum. Emphasizes real-world learning experiences.

- **Curriculum Choice:** Provide a variety of resources, opportunities, and activities based on your child's interests, including books, field trips, projects, and online resources.

Waldorf Education (Chapter 25)

- **Philosophy:** Focuses on holistic education that nurtures the child's body, mind, and spirit. Emphasizes creativity, imagination, and hands-on learning.

- **Curriculum Choice:** Look for programs that integrate arts and crafts, storytelling, music, and nature activities. Avoid early use of technology and focus on experiential learning.

Take your time researching these homeschool approaches and choose one (or more) that best aligns with your family's educational goals. See Chapter 17 on "Homeschooling Approaches" for more methods and approaches.

PART II—THE DETAILS

Alright, folks, it's time to move from the lofty talk about goals, styles, needs, and philosophies to the practical side of how to actually pick a curriculum. With so many options available, the selection process can feel overwhelming. That's where a checklist comes in handy. A checklist can really help you cover all the important points and make a well-informed decision. We've got everything covered: research tips, content overview, target audience, special education considerations, pricing, teacher involvement, necessary/optional materials, and more. By going through each of these points, you can make smart choices that best meet your educational goals and needs. Below is an eight-step checklist to help you choose and compare different options like a pro.

Curriculum Research—The Ultimate Checklist

Step 1: Research and Evaluate

- **Online Reviews:** Websites such as Cathy Duffy Reviews, The Homeschool Mom, or Homeschool.com offer comprehensive reviews on various homeschooling curricula. Use them!

- **Community Insights:** Join local homeschooling groups, educational communities, or online forums like those on Facebook and elsewhere. Subscribe to your favorite homeschooling YouTube channels. Interacting with experienced homeschooling parents can offer real-world insights and recommendations that are not evident through online reviews alone.

- **Visit Publishers and Test Drive:** Check out the websites of curriculum publishers to look at sample materials, placement tests, sample lesson plans, and scope and sequence documents. These can be an excellent way to see if a particular teaching style and content engage your child effectively

- **Check for Accreditation and Standards Compliance:** If this applies to you, ensure the curriculum adheres to relevant educational standards or is accredited, which is crucial for maintaining an official record of your child's academic progress (especially if you have older children who want to play sports at a NCAA college or university).

Step 2: Content Overview

Understand what the curriculum covers. Grab the materials and flip through them from the first page to the last page. Ask these five questions:

1. What subjects and topics are included?

2. Is there a clear scope and sequence that logically progresses from one concept to the next?

3. Are there teaching notes? Does it provide a sample teaching day or a pacing week?

4. Is it a 3-day, 4-day, or 5-day a week curriculum?

5. Don't forget to consider the depth and breadth of the topics. Are they just skimming the surface, or do they take a deep dive into each subject? This will help you ensure that the curriculum is comprehensive and robust enough to meet your child's needs.

Step 3: Target Audience

Who is the target audience for this curriculum and is it appropriate for your child?

- **Suitability for Different Learning Levels:** Who is this curriculum for? Gifted, struggling, or average students? Motivated students? *Example: A curriculum that includes advanced problem-solving tasks may be ideal for gifted students, while one with more foundational skills might suit struggling learners.*

- **Age, Maturity, and Grade-Level Suitability:** Make sure the curriculum matches your child's age, maturity, and/or grade level. *Example: A nine-year-old advanced reader might be capable of reading To Kill a Mockingbird, but the content may introduce topics more suitable for an older child. Also, publishers have their grade/age recommendations, but you know your child. Place them where you think they can be successful.*

- **Special Education Considerations:** If you have children with special-education needs, it's important to find a curriculum that meets their unique requirements. More on this in Chapter 29, "The Special-Needs Child."

- **Layout & Structure:** Opt for curricula that balance text with visuals—diagrams, charts, and illustrations aid comprehension. Ensure the layout includes ample white space and uses bullet points or numbered lists to break down complex information into manageable chunks.

- **Adaptability:** Choose a curriculum that allows for alternative assessments like oral presentations or projects instead of written exams.

- **Balanced Materials:** Textbook and/or workbook pages that are too text-heavy can be overwhelming for children with ADHD. For a child with dyslexia, look for materials that include text-to-speech options, visual aids, and simplified reading passages. See Chapter 29, "The Special-Needs Child" for more details.

Step 4: Price

- **Your Budget:** Determine your budget early in the process and stick to it! In addition to textbooks and workbooks, factor in costs such as online class fees, test booklets, answer booklets, teacher manuals, subscription fees, supplemental materials, manipulatives, and any necessary technology. See Chapter 9, "Homeschooling on a Budget" for more information.

- **Curriculum Prices:** Costs range from free resources to more expensive 'all-in-one' or comprehensive packages. For most curricula, however, you can simply purchase materials piecemeal throughout the year as you progress through the content.

- **PDF files and eBooks:** These can be cost-effective option as you can use them with multiple children year after year. Also, look for opportunities to buy used materials or to share resources with other homeschooling families.

Step 5: Teacher Involvement

Level of Preparation Required (Definitions)

- **No Prep:** Ideal for parents who prefer a structured approach with minimal additional work. Pre-made worksheets, activities, and lesson scripts are ready to use, allowing for immediate use without any prior preparation.

- **Low Prep:** Suitable for those who want some level of customization while still having a solid foundation. Basic outlines and materials are provided, requiring only minor adjustments or additional materials to tailor the lessons to the specific needs of the child.

- **High Prep:** For parents who are comfortable with creating detailed lesson plans from scratch. Involves significant preparation, including the development of customized materials, undergoing training to effectively teach the content, and gathering or setting up necessary resources.

Daily Lesson Planning

- **No Prep:** Lessons are fully scripted, requiring the parent to simply follow along. This approach saves time and ensures consistency in instruction.

- **Low Prep:** While lesson plans are provided, they allow for minor adjustments to better fit the specific timing or unique needs of students, offering a balance between structure and flexibility.

- **High Prep:** Parents are responsible for developing comprehensive, tailored lesson plans each day. This includes setting specific objectives, planning engaging activities, and designing assessments to measure student understanding.

Curriculum Flexibility

- **Rigid:** The curriculum is strictly defined with little room for deviation. Suitable for educators who prefer a highly structured environment where all lessons and activities are predetermined.

- **Moderate:** Offers some flexibility, allowing teachers to adapt lessons and activities to better suit their teaching style or the needs of their students. This approach provides a balance between structure and adaptability.

- **Highly Flexible:** The curriculum can be easily modified or supplemented. Parents have the freedom to tailor the content to their preferences, incorporate different teaching styles, and address diverse student needs.

Support for Differentiated Instruction

- **Minimal:** Limited resources and strategies are available for addressing the diverse learning needs of students. This approach may be suitable for homogeneous groups where differentiation is less critical.

- **Moderate:** Provides some strategies and materials for varying instruction based on student abilities and learning styles. This level supports moderate differentiation to address different student needs.

- **Extensive:** Offers a comprehensive set of tools and resources for tailoring instruction. This includes a wide range of strategies and materials designed to accommodate individual learning styles, levels, and abilities, ensuring that all students can access and engage with the content.

Step 6: Resource Materials - Must-Have vs. Nice-to-Have (Your Call)

- **Textbooks:** Essential for providing a structured and comprehensive overview of the subject matter. They serve as the primary source of information and reference.

- **Workbooks:** Used for practice and reinforcement of concepts taught in the textbooks. They contain exercises and activities to help students apply their knowledge.

- **Teacher Manuals:** Provide detailed guidance on how to effectively deliver the curriculum. They include lesson plans, teaching strategies, and answers to workbook exercises.

- **Test Booklets:** Used to assess student understanding and progress. They contain quizzes, tests, and other forms of assessment to evaluate learning outcomes.

- **Supplemental Materials:** Includes manipulatives, visual aids, and other resources that enhance the learning experience. These materials help to illustrate concepts and engage students in hands-on learning.

- **Digital Resources:** E-books, online platforms, and other digital tools offer interactive and multimedia content. These resources can provide additional support and enrichment opportunities for students.

- **Optional Enrichment Materials:** Additional resources that can be used to further enhance the learning experience. These may include advanced reading materials, project kits, and other activities that go beyond the standard curriculum.

Additional Resources:

- **Online Help:** Many curricula offer a comprehensive online help center or online forums where parents can find answers to frequently asked questions, step-by-step guides, and troubleshooting tips. This resource is crucial for quick and convenient support.

- **Tutorials:** Video tutorials and interactive guides (created by other parents or teachers) can assist parents in understanding how to effectively use the curriculum and its associated tools.

PART III – CURRICULUM CUSTOMIZATION

I Bought Curriculum, Now What?

A major benefit of homeschooling is the flexibility to tailor your child's education to their unique interests and needs. After selecting a curriculum, it's wise to adapt it to align with what excites and motivates your child. Here are some suggestions:

Incorporate Project-Based Learning

One effective way to cater to your child's interests is through project-based learning. This method allows the child to engage in projects that reflect their passions, whether it's art, science, or literature.

Example: If your child is interested in nature, you could design a curriculum around environmental science that includes activities like planting a garden or visiting nature reserves.

Utilize Technology and Multimedia Resources

In today's digital age, technology can be a valuable tool in homeschooling. Here are some ways to incorporate technology into your lesson plans:

- **Educational Websites:** Websites like Khan Academy, National Geographic Kids, and BBC Bitesize offer free educational resources and interactive lessons.

- **Apps and Games:** There are numerous educational apps and games that make learning fun and interactive. Apps like Duolingo for language learning and Prodigy for math can be excellent supplements.

- **Virtual Field Trips:** Explore museums, national parks, and historical sites through virtual tours. This can be a great way to enhance your geography, history, and science lessons.

Adapt Learning Pace to Child's Needs

Every child learns at their own pace, and homeschooling allows you to adapt to that pace. If your child excels at math but struggles with reading, you can spend more time on literacy skills while accelerating their math studies. This personalized approach helps in maintaining their interest in both subjects without feeling overwhelmed.

Engage with Experts and Community Resources

Sometimes, the best way to foster a child's interest is to connect them with experts or community resources. This could be arranging meetings with professionals in their field of interest, attending workshops, or participating in community projects. Such interactions can provide practical knowledge and inspire deeper engagement with the subject matter.

Regularly Reassess and Evolve the Curriculum

Interests can change, and it's important to remain flexible and reassess the curriculum periodically. This doesn't mean a complete overhaul but adjusting parts of the curriculum to introduce new subjects or phasing out others that no longer captivate your child's interest. Regular feedback sessions with your child can help you gauge their interest levels and make necessary adjustments.

Finding the Right Balance

So, how do you find the right balance between customization and getting through equivalent fractions? The truth is, there's no one-size-fits-all answer. It will depend on your child's individual needs and preferences, as well as your own level of involvement and commitment.

Importance of Flexibility and Open-mindedness

One approach might be to set aside time each day or week for your child to pursue their own interests. Maybe they could work on a project related to their favorite subject or read a book that they've been dying to get their hands on. At the same time, you could also incorporate new and challenging topics into their curriculum. Maybe you could introduce them to a new language or culture or teach them about a scientific concept that they've never heard of before. Ultimately, the key is to keep an open mind and be willing to experiment. Don't be afraid to try new things and see what works best for your child. And remember, even if you don't get it exactly right, your child will still be learning and growing every day.

The Pitfalls of Customization—(Or How To Avoid Creating A Spoiled Child)

I said earlier that knowing your child's learning style is key, but teaching to it is another matter. Let's start with a harsh truth: customizing your child's curriculum to fit their interests and needs is a lot harder than it sounds. Sure, it's tempting to think that you can tailor every lesson to your child's strengths and passions, but the reality is that there are only so many hours in a day and so much material that needs to be covered. Also, you run the risk of creating a spoiled child who only wants to learn about things that interest them.

So, does your child's learning style actually matter all that much? Sure, some children might prefer visual aids or hands-on activities over reading a textbook, but at the end of the day, they need to develop skills in reading, writing, and math, regardless of their preferred learning style (unless there's a learning disability).

Now, before you spend hours pouring over different curricula and trying to match them to your child's learning style, take a deep breath and relax. Your child will be just fine with whatever curriculum you choose as long as you are engaged, make it interesting, and stay involved in their learning process. So, while it's important to incorporate your child's interests into their curriculum, it's equally important to expose them to new and challenging ideas. You never know what might spark their curiosity and lead them down a new path. Just food for thought.

---------- **Summary** ----------

Homeschooling can feel like navigating a dense curriculum jungle, but with this chapter as your trusty guide, you can find a clear path forward. Start by setting clear academic, social, and emotional goals for your child. Figure out their learning style—whether they're a visual, auditory, kinesthetic learner, or a mix—and pick an educational philosophy that resonates with you. Jump into curriculum options with a detective's eye, consider reviews, community feedback, and accreditation. Don't forget to set a budget that covers the essentials like textbooks and workbooks. Decide how hands-on you want to be, and customize the curriculum to fit your child's interests, using tech, hands-on projects, and expert tips. Keep things fresh by regularly reassessing your approach. With the right balance of structure and flexibility, you'll create a unique and engaging education that fits your family like a glove.

8

Lesson Planning for Couch Potatoes

The Playbook for Lesson Prep

The best time to plant a tree was 20 years ago. The second best time is now.

— Chinese Proverb

L ESSON PLANNING, FAR FROM being the villain in your homeschooling story, is actually your trusty sidekick, the Robin to your Batman. It's your secret weapon in maintaining order amidst the chaos of learning at home. Some may question its importance, asking, "Why bother with lesson planning?" The answer is simple: it's the foundation that supports and guides your teaching journey. A well-crafted lesson plan is the backbone of successful homeschooling, providing structure, clarity, and a roadmap for achieving educational goals.

However, many parents find lesson planning to be a chore, envisioning hours spent in concentrated effort. But it doesn't have to be that way. In this chapter, we'll explore the step-by-step process of creating impactful lesson plans in three parts: planning, execution, and helpful strategies. We'll delve into understanding your homeschooling goals, breaking down the curriculum, developing a lesson plan, balancing core subjects with electives and extracurricular activities. Additionally, we'll explore how to assess your child's progress. So, grab your chocolate, queue up your Netflix playlist, and get comfortable on the couch—let's start lesson planning!

If you're eager to get straight to the practical stuff or need a quick overview, here is a quick-start guide with essential pointers to get you going fast. The detailed playbook will follow.

HOW TO CRAFT YOUR HOMESCHOOL LESSON PLAN

A Quick-Start Guide

Step 1: Set Clear Goals

This step is a lot like the first step in curriculum planning. Take a moment to consider what you want to achieve with your lesson planning. Ask yourself:

- What are your academic goals for the year?

- Are there any specific skills or subjects you want your child to focus on?

- What interests does your child have that you can incorporate into your lessons?

- Setting clear goals will give you a roadmap and keep you focused throughout the year.

Step 2: Create a Schedule

Decide how you want to structure your homeschooling days. Here are a few questions to guide you:

- Which schedule will you follow? Traditional? Year round? Block? Loop? Sabbath?

- How many hours a day and days a week will you dedicate to home-schooling?

- How will you balance core subjects with enrichment activities?

Remember, flexibility is one of the biggest benefits of homeschooling. Your schedule should work for you, not the other way around.

Step 3: Choose Your Resources

Now it's time to pick your resources. This could include:

- Textbooks and workbooks

- Online courses and videos

- Educational games and apps

- Manipulatives

- Library books and local resources

Don't feel pressured to use a one-size-fits-all curriculum. Mix and match resources that fit your child's learning style and interests.

Step 4: Plan Your Lessons

With your goals, schedule, and learning materials in place, it's time to plan your lessons. Using a spreadsheet, calendar, or notebook to record your plans usually helps. Break down your goals into manageable chunks. Here's how:

- Outline what you want to cover each week or month. If your curriculum comes with a pacing guide, all the better!

- Prepare daily or weekly lesson plans that include activities, assignments, and any materials needed.

- Be realistic about how much you can accomplish in a day. It's better to go at a comfortable pace than to rush through topics.

Step 5: Review and Adjust

Homeschooling is a dynamic process. Regularly review your lesson plans and ask:

- What's working well? What's not?

- Is your child engaged and learning effectively?

- Do you need to adjust your goals or resources?

That's your quick-start guide! For more in-depth information, read on as we explore each stage in detail.

PART I – THE PLANNING STAGE

Understand Your Homeschooling Goals

The first step in crafting your lesson plan is figuring out what you want your kids to achieve. Ask yourself: What should my child have under their belt by the end of the year, semester, or even just this month? Think big picture first—what's the dream outcome? Maybe it's mastering multiplication tables or knocking out an epic research paper. Whatever it is, start with that vision and break it down into long-term goals and short-term goals.

Now, long-term goals are the big milestones you want your child to reach over an extended period, like a year or a semester. These might include mastering algebra, writing a 10-page historical analysis paper, or developing fluency in reading. Short-term goals, on the other hand, are the smaller, more immediate steps that pave the way to those larger achievements. For example, a short-term goal might be completing a chapter of an algebra textbook each week with a tutor, drafting an outline for the historical analysis essay, or mastering phonics skills. By setting both long-term and short-term goals, you create a clear, manageable path for your child's educational journey.

Here are three categories to help you organize your long-term and short-term goals, complete with examples:

Three Types of Goals

1. **Academic Goals:** "By the end of the semester, my child will be able to multiply and divide fractions."

2. **Personal Development/Character Goals:** "For the next four weeks, my child will develop a daily routine and stick to it, using a planner to track activities and assignments."

3. **Extracurricular Goals:** "My child will participate in a swimming club and compete in at least three swim meets by the end of the year."

Now that you've aced goal-setting, let's start planning your homeschool year with a big-picture yearly calendar!

Start with the Yearly Calendar—The Big Picture

Depending on what type of schedule you use—whether it's traditional, year-round, sabbath, etc. (refer to Chapter 6, "Homeschool Routines" for more about schedules)—start with an overview by setting up a yearly calendar in a spreadsheet, calendar, or notebook. This is where you'll plug in your holidays, vacation days, and seasonal breaks.

In addition to those days, plan for the start date and end date of your school year, and any planned days off for special events or family activities. For example, you might start the school year after Labor Day and end in early June, with breaks in the winter, spring, and around major holidays like Thanksgiving and Christmas. Additionally, consider including time for standardized testing, portfolio reviews, and extracurricular activities like field trips and co-op classes.

You can highlight key dates and events using different colors or markers to easily distinguish holidays, breaks, and special activities. This visual organization will make it easier to stay on track and adjust plans as needed.

I have several free yearly calendar templates on my website that can help you get started with lesson planning. Visit www.homeschoolknockouts.com/resourcelibrary for the freebies.

Be sure to check your state's requirements to see if they require a certain number of school days, instructional hours, or mandatory subjects. Resources like the Home School Legal Defense Association (hslda.org) can provide detailed information on state-specific regulations and help you ensure your calendar is compliant.

Breaking Down Curriculum

Once you've set your goals and have your yearly calendar partially filled out, it's time to break down your curriculum. Tackling a homeschool curriculum for lesson planning means going through all the instructional materials. Take it slow and do a little bit each day. If you try to go through all the curriculum for all your children at once, it's going to be overwhelming.

Start by casually flipping through any teacher manuals and look at everything from the first page to the last. Pay attention to any pacing charts you find—they're great for helping you figure out how much time to spend on each topic. Also, look out for any scope and sequence section, usually at the beginning of the book. This part is key because it outlines what topics and skills you'll cover and when. Don't skip over the teacher notes; they're full of useful tips and strategies.

And those sample teaching days or weeks? They give you solid examples of how to implement your lessons throughout the week. After you go through the teacher resources, go through the student materials. By taking note of all these elements, you'll be able to create a comprehensive and well-paced lesson plan that fits your homeschooling needs perfectly.

Planning Methods—Choose One, Two, or All

When you're planning homeschool lessons, you can approach it a few ways: by each child, by subject, or a combination. The best approach is entirely up to you. Try them all out and see which ones you prefer.

By Child:
- List each child and their core subjects (e.g., 1st grade subjects differ from 12th grade).

- Outline each subject's curriculum for the week on a monthly calendar.

- Identify key concepts to cover.

- Plan daily lessons and activities tailored to each child's needs.

- When finished with the first child, move on to the next child.

- **Benefits:** This method allows for personalized attention to each child's individual needs and learning pace.

By Subject:
- Start with a core subject (e.g., math) and list all children taking that subject.

- Outline the subject's curriculum for the week on a monthly calendar.

- Identify key concepts to cover and adjust for different ages/grades.

- Plan daily lessons and activities for each subject, accommodating different learning levels.

- When finished with one subject (e.g., math), move on to the next subject (e.g., English).

- **Benefits:** This method helps streamline lesson planning and ensures consistency across all children for each subject.

Combination:
- Plan math and language arts individually for each child at their level.

- Outline the curriculum and key concepts for these subjects on a monthly calendar.

- Plan science, history, Bible, and art together for all children, incorporating age-appropriate activities.

- Create a balanced schedule that includes both individual and group learning sessions.

- **Benefits:** This method balances individualized attention with group learning, making it suitable for families with children of varying ages.

How Many Weekly Lessons to Teach?

Alright, let's figure out how to plan your homeschool lessons without going bananas. Figuring out how many lessons you need per week for each subject can be a game-changer. Planning weekly feels way less overwhelming than trying to map out the entire year in one go. So, here's a nifty little calculation to help you out based on a 36-week or 180-days school year:

Step 1: Total Lesson Count
- Start by counting the total number of lessons in your curriculum. We'll use math as our example because, well, numbers. Let's say Primary Mathematics has 160 lessons.

Step 2: Weekly Breakdown
- Now, grab that total lesson count and divide it by the number of weeks in your school year. So, 160 lessons ÷ 36 weeks = roughly 4.44 lessons per week.

Step 3: Keep It Practical
- Let's be real, nobody wants to deal with .44 of a lesson. Round it to something that works for you – maybe 4 or 5 lessons a week, depending on your groove.

Do you need to stick to this plan exactly? Definitely not! Think of it more as a set of friendly guidelines. By breaking it down like this, you keep things manageable and dodge the dreaded homeschool burnout spiral. Plus, you get the flexibility to adapt as you go. You'll tweak things to fit your own schedule and life because, let's face it, stuff happens.

The number of lessons, their complexity, seasonal breaks, holidays, and even those pesky colds will all influence your pace. Some folks take two years to finish a one-year curriculum, while others zoom through it in a semester. It's all up to you—you're the boss here.

How Far Out Should You Plan Your Homeschool?

Long-range planning sounds ideal, but let's get real. Planning an entire year of lessons can feel like prepping for the apocalypse. When life throws you curve-balls—like dealing with a house issue or your spouse pursuing a master's degree—week-to-week planning is often the most practical approach.

Before tackling the weekly schedule, let's compare the benefits and drawbacks of yearly, monthly, and weekly planning.

- **Yearly Planning:** Yearly planning involves mapping out the entire academic year in advance. While it provides a comprehensive overview and long-term direction, it is rigid and can be disrupted by unforeseen events. Adjusting plans on such a large scale can be challenging and time-consuming.

- **Monthly Planning:** Monthly planning offers a balance between structure and flexibility. It allows for a detailed plan for the month while still being adaptable enough to accommodate changes. This approach provides more flexibility than yearly planning and is easier to adjust when necessary.

- **Weekly Planning:** Weekly planning is the most flexible and responsive approach. It allows for detailed planning on a short-term basis, making it easier to adapt to sudden changes and challenges. Weekly plans are manageable and can be adjusted quickly, maintaining a balance between structure and flexibility.

A week at a time keeps things manageable and sane, which is why we focus on weekly planning in this chapter.

How to Plan Your Lessons One Week at a Time

1. **Decide Subject Frequency:** Don't overload. Core subjects daily; other subjects weekly; enrichment subjects weekly or less frequently.

2. **Group Lessons for Multiple Kids:** Teach subjects like religious studies, art, history, and science together to save time and sanity.

3. **Detail Weekly Lessons:** Write brief descriptions and note supplies for each subject. Keep it simple and efficient.

Planning a week at a time is like eating an elephant one bite at a time; it makes the task manageable. This method also offers flexibility, allowing you to pivot when your kid gets obsessed with a new topic or a curriculum doesn't work out. Plus, regularly reviewing and planning keeps lessons fresh, ensuring you're always on top of your game rather than struggling to remember what you planned months ago.

You can receive several free weekly, monthly, and yearly lesson planning templates by visiting my website (I know. Another shameless plug): www.home schoolknockouts.com/resourcelibrary.

PART II – THE PRACTICAL STEPS

Craft Effective Homeschool Lesson Plans

Still with me? Awesome! Now that we've addressed the planning stage, let's get into the fun part: creating the actual lesson plan. I know it might seem like a Herculean task, but trust me, it's totally doable. Here's a straightforward process to get you started:

Review and Understand Your Curriculum

Start by thoroughly reviewing the curriculum materials for each subject. Understand the key objectives, suggested pacing, and any guidelines provided. Familiarize yourself with the overall structure to create a clear vision of your academic year.

Example: If you're using a science curriculum that covers biology, chemistry, and physics, take note of the major units within each area. Identify key concepts such as cell structure in biology, chemical reactions in chemistry, and Newton's laws in physics.

Utilize Teacher Manuals

Dive into the teacher manuals for each subject. Begin with one child and one subject, taking notes on key points, recommended schedules, and important dates. This process helps build a solid foundation for your lesson plans.

Example: For a math curriculum, the teacher manual might suggest a daily warm-up activity, a main lesson, and practice problems. Note these suggestions and plan how much time each part will take in your daily schedule.

Consolidate Subjects Across All Students

Consider planning one subject at a time for all children. This approach streamlines your process, aligns different grade levels, and facilitates joint activities and themes across ages.

Example: If you have three children studying history at different levels, plan a unit on Ancient Egypt that includes age-appropriate readings, projects, and discussions. Older children can delve into more complex topics while younger ones work on basic facts and fun activities.

Set Your School Calendar

Determine the start and end dates for your school year, as well as holidays and vacation periods. Account for local holidays, family commitments, and necessary breaks. This calendar will guide your pacing and planning.

Example: Start school the first week of September, take a break for Thanksgiving, a two-week break for Christmas, and a spring break in March. Plan to end the school year in mid-June.

Establish a Pacing Guide

A pacing guide is an essential tool for ensuring that you cover all the necessary material within the timeframe of your school year without overwhelming yourself or your children. Here's how to create an effective pacing guide:

1. **Determine the School Year Duration:** Calculate the number of weeks available in your school year, subtracting holidays, vacations, and other breaks.

2. **Identify the Total Number of Lessons:** Begin by noting the total number of lessons or units for each subject in your curriculum.

3. **Divide Lessons by Weeks:** Divide the total number of lessons by the number of available weeks to determine how many lessons you need to

cover each week. For example, if you have 180 lessons to cover in 36 weeks, you need to complete about five lessons per week.

4. **Adjust for Complexity:** Recognize that not all lessons are equal in complexity. Some topics may require more time than others. Adjust your pacing to allow more time for difficult subjects and less for easier ones.

5. **Incorporate Flexibility:** Include buffer weeks or days for review, catch-up, or unexpected events. This flexibility ensures that minor disruptions don't derail your entire schedule.

6. **Set Milestones:** Establish key milestones or checkpoints throughout the year to ensure you're on track. These can be at the end of each unit or quarter.

7. **Regular Reviews:** Periodically review and adjust your pacing guide to reflect actual progress and any changes in your schedule.

Example: For a literature curriculum with 30 chapters to be covered in 36 weeks, plan to cover one chapter per week, with extra weeks for review and special projects. Adjust if a chapter is particularly long or complex.

Curriculum Outline

Create a broad outline of your curriculum, listing main topics, units, and significant projects or assessments for each subject. This overview helps maintain focus and allows for easy adjustments throughout the year.

Example: For a history curriculum, the outline might include:
- Unit 1: Ancient Civilizations (weeks 1-6)

- Unit 2: Medieval Times (weeks 7-12)

- Unit 3: Renaissance and Reformation (weeks 13-18)

- Unit 4: Modern History (weeks 19-24)

- Unit 5: American History (weeks 25-30)

- Unit 6: Review and Final Project (weeks 31-36)

Weekly Breakdown

Develop a weekly breakdown of your curriculum outline, specifying topics and objectives. Flip through chapters to identify key points (look at headings, sub-headings, bolded topics, etc.) for your planner. Include key assignments, tests, and projects to track progress and stay organized.

> **Example:** For week 1 of your Ancient Civilizations unit, you might plan:
> - Day 1: Introduction to Ancient Civilizations
>
> - Day 2: Study of Mesopotamia
>
> - Day 3: Mesopotamian Culture and Society
>
> - Day 4: Ancient Egypt Introduction
>
> - Day 5: Egyptian Pyramids and Pharaohs

Incorporate Extracurricular Activities

List all extracurricular activities your children will participate in, such as sports, music lessons, clubs, and community service. Scheduling these ensures a holistic educational experience.

Organize Lessons in a Planner

Choose a planner that suits your needs—whether digital or print—and start entering your lessons. Popular options include Homeschool Planet, Google Calendar, and Erin Condren LifePlanner. A well-organized planner is crucial for maintaining structure.

Input Your School Calendar

Add your predetermined school year dates, holidays, and days off into your planner. This forms the backbone of your schedule, ensuring you account for all important dates.

Example: Mark the first day of school, holidays like Thanksgiving and Christmas, spring break, and the last day of school in your planner. Include any planned family vacations or special events.

Schedule Subjects

Enter each subject into your planner, detailing daily or weekly lesson plans. This step ensures that all subjects are covered systematically throughout the school year.

Example: For math, plan daily lessons from Monday to Thursday, with Fridays reserved for review or enrichment activities. Input specific topics or pages to be covered each day.

Plan Enrichment Activities

Include plans for crafts, field trips, and extra reading. These activities enrich the educational experience and provide hands-on learning opportunities.

- **Crafts:** Create a model of the solar system during the astronomy unit.

- **Field Trips:** Visit a local museum during the history unit on Ancient Greece.

- **Extra Reading:** Assign related novels or biographies to complement the history curriculum.

Regularly Review and Adjust Plans

Periodically review your plans to ensure you are on track. Be flexible and adjust as needed to accommodate changes or unforeseen challenges.

Example: At the end of each month, review your progress. If your child is struggling with a particular topic, allow additional time to review and understand the material before moving on.

Backup Your Plans

Always have a backup of your lesson plans, whether digitally or as hard copies. This precaution ensures continuity in case of technical issues or other disruptions.

Example: Save your digital planner to a cloud service like Google Drive or Dropbox. Print out key schedules and lesson plans and store them in a binder.

Implementing Your Plans

Finally, put your plans into action. Follow your schedule, be adaptable, and enjoy the homeschooling journey. Remember, flexibility is key, and it's okay to modify your plans to better suit your family's needs.

Example: Start your school year with enthusiasm, sticking to your planned schedule. If you find that certain activities or pacing aren't working, make necessary adjustments to improve the learning experience.

Structuring Your Lesson Plans

A well-structured lesson plan should include several key elements:

- **Objectives:** Clearly define what you want your child to learn by the end of the lesson.

- **Materials Needed:** List all the materials required for the lesson, from books to art supplies.

- **Instructional Methods:** How will you teach the lesson? Lecture? Hands-on activity? Discussion?

- **Activities and Assignments:** Plan activities and assignments that reinforce the lesson's objectives.

- **Assessment Methods:** Determine how you will assess your child's understanding and progress.

Let's look at some sample lesson plans to make sense of this. The following is a unit study approach of a Wizard of Oz lesson plan that I personally created because I don't have the rights to show another publisher/author's lesson plan. A curriculum will provide you all of this information. You will NOT have to create this on your own! Unless, of course, you want to design your own curriculum. I just want you to see what a lesson plan can look like.

Sample 5-Day Lesson Plan (Unit Study Approach)

Here's a suggested five-day lesson plan I created:

There's No Place Like Home(school)—A 3rd Grade Oz-some Adventure
   Objective: The child will explore literature, mathematics, tornado science, arts and crafts, and enhance reading comprehension skills.
   Materials:
   * *The Wizard of Oz* book by L. Frank Baum
   * *Tornadoes!* book by Gail Gibbons
   * *The Wizard of Oz* movie (Judy Garland version)
   * Tin foil or colored paper for Tin Man crafts
   * Paper, pencil, crayons, markers, or colored pencils for tornado drawing
   * Small fan (optional, for dramatic tornado effect)
   * Math worksheet with munchkin-themed problems (or any Oz theme)
   * Reading comprehension questions based on the book
   * Green construction paper
   Note: Feel free to mix and match the craft activities

Day 1: Monday - Setting the Stage for Adventure & Science
- **Introduce *The Wizard of Oz* (~10 minutes):** Present the book *The Wizard of Oz*. Discuss the book cover and what the book might be about. Read aloud how Dorothy was whisked away to a mystical realm by a tornado. Reenact the tornado scene using a fan (ensuring safety first!) for an enjoyable and light-hearted twist.

- **Tornado Science (~15 minutes):** Read *Tornadoes!* to learn about their formation. Watch a Brain Pop video on tornadoes. Encourage child to draw their own imaginative tornadoes, (e.g., a candy tornado or one brimming with floating unicorns).

Day 2: Tuesday - A Journey Through Literature
- **Read Aloud & Comprehension Check (~20 minutes):** Recite chosen excerpts from *The Wizard of Oz*, adopting exaggerated voices for the characters. Pause occasionally to probe child with reading comprehension questions like, "What did the Scarecrow desire from the Wizard?" and "Why do you think Dorothy's house squashed the Wicked Witch of the East?"

Day 3: Wednesday - Mathematical Munchkins and Crafty Characters
- **Munchkin Math (~15 minutes):** Direct child to complete a munchkin-themed math worksheet. Offer problems like, "If 5 munchkins each devour 2 lollipops, how many lollipops were eaten in total?" Use humor by voicing the problems in a munchkin tone.

- **Tin Man Tangrams (~15 minutes):** Help your child craft a Tin Man figure using foil or paper cut into different shapes (akin to tangram pieces). While assembling the tin men, discuss the significance of possessing a heart and the traits of a good friend.

Day 4: Thursday - Inspiring Creativity and Cinematic Appreciation
- **Watch *The Wizard of Oz* Movie - Judy Garland version (~70 minutes):** Immerse your child in the world of Oz by watching the classic *The Wizard of Oz* film together. Encourage child to pay attention to the characters, their actions, and the overall story, as it will provide the foundation for the next activity.

- **If I Governed the Land of Oz... (~10 minutes):** After the movie (if your child is up to it), encourage your child to share their thoughts on what they would do differently if they were the ruler of Oz. Engage their creativity with fun and imaginative scenarios, like assigning the Cowardly Lion as the guardian of Oz or starting an annual parade featuring all the characters of Oz. Other suggestions could include delegating household chores to flying monkeys or inaugurating a national holiday honoring puppies. The aim here is to stimulate their creative and critical thinking, as well as their leadership qualities, all within the context of the world they just experienced through the movie.

Day 5: Friday - Art and Reflection

- **Emerald City Art (~20 minutes):** Employ green construction paper to aid your child in constructing their unique "Emerald City" skyscrapers. Advocate for the inclusion of other colors to enliven their city, drawing parallels to the Technicolor magic of the Land of Oz.

- **There's No Place Like Homeschool (~5 minutes):** Conclude by reflecting on the thrilling journey through Oz and ask child about their favorite part of the lesson. Reinforce that learning can be exciting and magical, mirroring their beloved tales.

This unit study lesson plan has it all—lesson objectives, materials, a 5-day pacing guide, time estimates for each activity, and a mix of math, science, writing, reading, art, and hands-on fun. Think of unit studies as the ultimate multitaskers, blending subjects like a pro. And while you won't need to create your own lesson plans, I'm here to show you how a solid lesson plan can look in action. Remember, lesson plans are like snowflakes—no two are exactly alike!

PART III –TIPS & TRICKS

Start with Your Gut

Trust your instincts and choose a topic that speaks to you. Your passion will inspire your children.

Example: If you love mythology, create a lesson on Greek myths, exploring the stories and their influence on modern culture.

Keep Your Lesson Plan Straight

A visual daily schedule, like a whiteboard or notebook, helps keep the day's lessons on track without constantly flipping through manuals.

Example: Write out the day's subjects and activities on a whiteboard each morning, so everyone knows what to expect.

Reality Checks

Homeschool curriculum is designed for busy parents, not professional teachers. It's structured, often "open and go," minimizing guesswork and prep.

Example: Use a pre-packaged or low prep/no prep curriculum that includes lesson plans and materials, so you can focus more on teaching and less on preparation.

Drawbacks of Weekly Planning

If your weekends are crazy, planning might feel last-minute. But a 20-minute commitment weekly beats a day-long marathon annually.

Example: Set aside Sunday evening to plan the week's lessons. This short planning session can save you from daily stress and keep you organized.

Think Outside the Box

Choose a creative, unconventional topic. Your children will appreciate the break from monotony.

Example: Design a project around the history of comic books and their impact on society. Be silly and creative!

Review Your Curriculum

Ensure your lesson topic aligns with your curriculum goals and objectives, and consider state requirements (if applicable).

Example: If teaching environmental science, ensure your lessons cover required topics like ecosystems and human impact while including state-specific standards.

Select a Subject Area

Choose a subject like history, science, or literature. Then, pick specific topics within that area.

Example: For a history lesson, focus on the Renaissance period and explore its art, inventions, and key historical figures/events.

Consider Student Interests

Choose a topic that interests your children. Their engagement is crucial for effective learning.

Example: If children are interested in technology, create a lesson on the evolution of computers and their impact on daily life.

Make it Relevant

Select a topic that connects to the real world, showing children the relevance of their learning.

Example: Teach economics through the lens of current events, such as the impact of a recent economic policy change, ie. interest rate hike and its effect on buying a home.

Look for Connections

When choosing a lesson topic, look for connections between different subjects.

Example: Explore the intersection of science and art by studying the science of color and how artists use color theory in their work.

Get Inspired by Real-World Events

Keep an eye on current events and look for opportunities to bring real-world events, people, and news into your lessons.

Example: Use a current news event like a significant election to discuss the political system and voter behavior.

Ask Your Children

Ask your kiddos for their opinions and ideas. They may have unique perspectives and interests that you can incorporate into your lessons.

Example: Have a brainstorming session where your children suggest topics they are curious about such as dolphins, the Vietnam War, fashion, artificial intelligence, Michael Jackson, cybersecurity, soccer, hip-hop, 13th century life, the Bronte sisters, etc.

Keep Learning

Finally, make sure to keep learning and expanding your knowledge.

Example: Attend a workshop on the latest educational technology to learn how to integrate new tools into your classroom effectively.

By following these tips, you can think outside the box and be creative when choosing or developing a lesson topic. Remember that the goal is to create a learning environment that is engaging, fun, and memorable for your children. So, be bold, be innovative, and have fun!

Assessing Progress

Regularly tracking your child's progress is vital to ensure they are meeting their educational goals. Use formative assessments like quizzes and discussions to gauge understanding throughout the learning process. Summative assessments such as tests and projects, provide a comprehensive evaluation at the end of a unit or term. Keep records of your assessments to track improvement over time and identify areas that need more attention. For further details on assessments, see Chapter 16, "Assessing Progress."

---------- **Summary** ----------

So, there you have it. Crafting a lesson plan need not feel like you're wrestling with a flying monkey! You now have a better understanding of how to craft lesson plans that are both effective and adaptable to your homeschooling needs. From setting clear goals and choosing appropriate curricula to structuring your lessons, you can choose or create a homeschool lesson plan that is engaging, relevant, and aligned with your curriculum goals and objectives. Now, get those ruby slippers on and start planning—after all, there's no place like homeschool!

Disclaimer: Always ensure that your lesson topics align with your curriculum goals and objectives, your state's requirements (if applicable), and are appropriate for your child's grade level and abilities. For more detailed information on state-specific requirements, you can visit the hslda.org website.

9

Homeschooling on a Budget
Educational Alchemy

The best way to teach your kids about taxes is by eating 30% of their ice cream.

— Bill Murray

DISCOVER THE SKILL OF saving cents without compromising on common sense! Just as alchemists sought to transform lead into gold, educational alchemy is the creative skill of turning everyday moments and budget-friendly resources into valuable, golden learning opportunities for your children. We'll explore some financial aspects, from wisely choosing curriculum to planning exciting field trips. Additionally, I'll guide you through crafting a reliable budget, grabbing those irresistible discounts, and uncovering the best saving tips. Pro-tip for keeping your wallet happy? Start planning early! But before we do that, let's take a second to unpack what a home education budget can look like.

ANATOMY OF A HOMESCHOOL BUDGET

Creating a homeschool budget doesn't have to be a headache! Start by jotting down all your expected income, like salaries or freelance gigs. Next, list the essentials—think mortgage or rent, groceries, and utilities. Then, go into home-schooling-specific expenses like textbooks, workbooks, supplies, online classes, and field trips. Be sure to include a cushion for unexpected costs, like broken instruments, malfunctioning laptops, or new software. Also, remember to set aside some money for savings and emergencies, which is crucial to keep your finances on track. With a clear budget in place, you'll find it much easier to manage your homeschooling expenses without feeling stressed about money. For more guidance on budgeting, I highly recommend the book *Get Good with Money* by Tiffany Aliche, which is one of my favorite guides for practical and effective financial planning.

You can find several sample budget sheets on my website at www.homeschoolknockouts.com/resourcelibrary. For now, I suggest taking a quick look at two sample curriculum budgets below to get a visual sense of what I'm referring to before moving forward.

Sample Curriculum Budgets

Homeschool Budget Breakdown

With a basic understanding of what a homeschool budget could look like, it's time to delve into the specifics. By carefully evaluating the different aspects of your homeschool expenses, you'll be better equipped to prioritize spending and make informed decisions. Whether it's securing curriculum materials, ensuring ample access to extracurricular activities, or investing in technological resources, a well-organized budget breakdown will illuminate where to allocate funds for the best educational impact.

I've outlined various categories and items to consider for your budget. I've refrained from listing specific prices since costs vary widely based on location, the number of children you have, and if you prefer shiny new things or love the thrill of a good bargain! Additionally, I've provided sources where you can find these items. Keep your approach flexible, adapt the items to fit your style and budget, and you'll be on the right track. Let's explore the details of each category to provide a comprehensive guide on how to structure and manage your homeschool budget effectively.

Curriculum and Learning Materials

- **Textbooks:** Purchase from online sources like Amazon, Christianbook, Discount School Supply, and Rainbow Resource, or directly from educational publishers like Pearson and McGraw-Hill. Curriculum resell/swap groups on Facebook are another great option. Just search 'homeschool curriculum for sale' in the groups section. You'll be amazed at what's available.

- **Online Courses:** Platforms like Khan Academy, Coursera, Outschool, and Udemy provide a vast array of subjects with varying time lengths and price points, ranging from free to premium.

- **Workbooks and Practice Sheets:** Websites like Teachers Pay Teachers and Education.com offer free and affordable resources.

Supplementary Educational Resources

- **Educational Apps and Software:** Explore options available on the Google Play Store and Apple App Store. It's a good idea to browse Common Sense Media, a nonprofit that offers reviews and ratings for media and technology.

- **Library Membership:** Local libraries offer access to books, digital resources, and museum passes. Services like Overdrive offer ebooks and audiobooks, while Tumblebook offers narrated and animated children's stories. Many libraries offer free digital access to magazines and newspapers that are otherwise behind paywalls, or free access to online classes, music, and streaming movies. Not every library offers these services, but yours might. Check out the website for your local library or stop by and ask a librarian.

- **Field Trip Admissions:** Benefit from memberships or educational discounts at museums, zoos, science centers, and aquariums. *Pro tip: Explore their websites for free curriculum resources or lesson plans to enhance your visit to the exhibits.*

Art and Craft Supplies

- **Materials:** Craft stores like Michaels, Jo-Ann's, and Hobby Lobby, or online options like eBay and Etsy, have plenty of materials for the crafter, artist, designer, hobbyist, and beyond.

- **Craft Kits and Storage:** Craft stores offer kits, while IKEA and The Container Store have storage solutions.

Science and Technology Equipment

- **Scientific Tools:** Explore specialized stores like Carolina Biological Supply Company, Home Science Tools, or Steve Spangler Science.

- **Computer Upgrades and STEM Toys:** Best Buy, Newegg, Target, and educational toy stores have options to supply your tech and STEM toy needs.

Physical Education and Extracurricular Activities

- **Sports Equipment:** Sporting goods stores or sports consignment shops have affordable options.

- **Class Fees:** Community centers, recreation centers, YMCAs, or fitness gyms provide classes for a wide variety of activities.

- **Home Gym Equipment:** Visit local sports stores like Dick's Sporting Goods, Academy Sports + Outdoors, and REI. Resale shops specializing in used sports and/or gym equipment also offer fantastic bargains. You can also explore online options like Walmart, Wayfair, or Overstock.

Home Library and Reading Materials

- **Books and Subscriptions:** Local bookstores, Amazon, Barnes & Noble, and services like Audible offer various options. Library sales, yard sales and eBay are fantastic ways to build your library, especially if you're open to gently used books.

- **E-Readers:** You can find e-readers for digital books at electronics stores or on Amazon (Kindle). No Kindle device? No worries! The Kindle app is free and lets you read digital books on your phone or tablet.

Office/School Supplies and Organization

- **Printer Supplies and Organizers:** Staples, Office Depot, and similar stores offer office supplies. Of course, there is Amazon.

- **Pencils, Pens, Notebooks, Folders, Paper, and More:** You can find these essentials at major retail stores like Target and Walmart. Budget-friendly options include Dollar Tree, Dollar General, and 99-cent stores.

- **Whiteboard and Markers:** Check Amazon, Walmart, or local office supply stores.

Furniture and Learning Space

- **Desks, Chairs, Bookshelves:** IKEA, Wayfair, and second-hand stores offer affordable furniture.

- **Learning Space Décor:** You're only limited by your imagination!

Utilities and Internet

- **Laptop/Desktop Internet Bandwidth:** When choosing a plan, think about your actual usage needs to avoid overpaying. Compare plans from different providers and take advantage of bundles, discounts, or student pricing. Use data-saving tools like the "Data Saver" feature built into many web browsers like Google Chrome that reduce data usage by compressing images and scripts on web pages before they're downloaded to your device, which helps conserve data to avoid exceeding data caps.

- **Mobile Device Internet Bandwidth:** Apps like "Opera Mini" offer similar functionality as "Data Saver". The app compresses web pages before they reach your phone, reducing the data required to load them. Additionally, some mobile network providers offer data-saving tools that can reduce the quality of streaming videos and images to save data when you're on a limited plan.

- **Electric/Utilities Company:** Local service providers may offer discounts or budget plans to manage costs more efficiently. Make sure to ask about any available options!

Professional Development and Support

- **Popular Resources for Development/Support:** Homeschool Co-op membership, Homeschool convention workshops, Homeschool Legal Defense Association. These provide resources, support and/or legal advice.

Miscellaneous and Emergency Fund

- **Unplanned Opportunities and Replacements:** A savings account for unexpected needs such as last-minute field trips and broken instruments.

I know, I know. These are a lot of categories! But not all of them will apply to you. Starting with a flexible plan helps navigate unexpected or seasonal expenses.

Consider secondhand shopping or sharing resources to save money. Once you've got a handle on the basics of budgeting, let's look at five essential categories.

FIVE ESSENTIAL HOMESCHOOL BUDGET CATEGORIES

1. **Curriculum:** The academic artillery of your homeschool venture that deserves the lion's share of your resources. These are your classes, educational supplies, and materials. Everything from textbooks, workbooks, and literary works, art supplies, math manipulatives, and science experiment kits. Your choice of curriculum will form the backbone of your child's educational journey, making it a vital area of investment. And don't shy away from secondhand options or free trials to make it budget-friendly.

2. **Field Trips:** Spice up your routine with educational outings that connect learning to the real world. These trips, whether they are to museums, nature parks, or cultural landmarks, can be both educational and fun. They offer awesome ways to see how what you're learning fits into the big picture, mixing up school facts with out-in-the-world discoveries. Look out for free admission days or join forces with other homeschooling families to get group discounts.

3. **Extracurriculars:** Beyond the standard curriculum, extracurriculars like music, sports, hobbies, clubs, or coding add depth to your child's education. Not only do these activities enrich your homeschool program, but they also cater to your child's interests and foster well-rounded personal development. You don't need to overspend; find local clubs or community activities, or create your own at home.

4. **Entertainment:** Affordable fun is key to making homeschooling enjoyable. Whether it's DIY craft sessions, home baking challenges, or backyard camping adventures, frugal fun helps make homeschooling enjoyable and affordable. More than just a budgeting move, it's a mindset that rewards inventiveness and proves that the best things in life don't always come with a hefty price tag.

5. **Everything Else, Literally:** This encompasses the rest of the stuff. Don't overlook expenses like field trip souvenirs, sports fees, standard-

ized testing costs, printer ink, stationery supplies, and unexpected expenses. Even your cup of sanity-preserving coffee, tea, wine/whiskey. These sundries might seem minor but can add up quickly, so include them in your budget!

Now that these essential categories have been highlighted in your budget, it's time to morph from auditor to action planner. Let's explore how to bring real savings into these categories. A heads-up: some strategies may span multiple categories.

CURRICULUM SHOPPING ON A DIME

Ever felt the magnetic pull of a ritzy curriculum, thinking it might just be the VIP pass to homeschooling? We've all felt that tug. But here's the pro move: the first step towards financial savviness is a smart curriculum pick. Don't let the shimmering promises of famous brands or snappy packaging hoodwink you into loosening the ole coin purse. Here's a thought: a curriculum can sometimes be like a glittery outfit that dazzles in the store window but feels as practical as a waterproof towel if it doesn't fit your style. It's just cash down the tubes if it's grossly out of sync with your child's learning style or your teaching tune. So sure, the wallet's has to open, but let's do it with some finesse. After all, who's in the market for a screen door on a submarine? Put your hand down–and follow these strategies.

- **Buy Used Curriculum:** You can often find used curriculum for sale online or through local homeschool groups. Facebook has over 50 homeschool swaps, curriculum exchanges, and Buy/Sell groups. Ebay is another great resource.

- **Use Free Trial Periods:** Many online curriculum providers like ABCMouse.com, ReadingEggs.com, and IXL.com offer free trial periods, allowing you to try before you buy (at the time of this printing).

- **Teach Your Kids Together:** One of the most effective ways to save money while homeschooling is to teach your kids together. Certain subjects lend themselves easily to teaching multiple grades simultaneously: science, social studies, and literature come to mind. Not only can this approach save you money on curriculum and supplies, but it also encourages a collaborative learning environment and fosters sibling relationships. Many homeschool curricula, such as Sonlight, Ambleside Online, Moving Beyond the Page, and BookShark, offer materials that can be used across multiple grade levels (multi-level curriculum).

- **Choose a Unifying Theme:** Choosing a theme that appeals to all your children's interests and age levels is a great way to teach multiple subjects at once. For example, if your kids are interested in space, you can use this theme to teach science, math, reading, and writing. You can find a variety of free online resources, like lesson plans and worksheets, that are centered around a theme.

- **Use Open Educational Resources:** There are several reputable colleges and universities that offer free online classes or Massive Open Online Courses (MOOCs) on various subjects. Here are some well-known institutions that provide such opportunities for online learning:

  - **Massachusetts Institute of Technology (MIT) OpenCourse-Ware:** Offers a wide range of undergraduate and graduate courses across various disciplines. Website: https://ocw.mit.edu/index.htm

  - **Harvard University Online Learning:** Provides free courses, lectures, and learning materials on diverse topics. Website: https://online-learning.harvard.edu/

  - **Stanford Online:** Offers free online courses, as well as professional and continuing education programs. Website: https://online.stanford.edu/

  - **Yale University Open Yale Courses:** Provides free access to introductory courses taught by Yale professors. Website: https://oyc.yale.edu/

  - **University of California, Berkeley (UC Berkeley) Free Online Courses:** Offers a selection of free online courses in various subjects. Website: https://online.berkeley.edu/

  - **University of Oxford Podcasts:** Provides a collection of podcasts featuring lectures and seminars from Oxford University. Website: https://podcasts.ox.ac.uk/

- ○ **Carnegie Mellon University Open Learning Initiative:** Offers free online courses and interactive learning materials. Website: https://oli.cmu.edu/

- ○ **University of Michigan—Open Michigan:** Provides free educational resources and courses in various disciplines. Website: https://open.umich.edu/

- ○ **Khan Academy:** While not an institution, it provides a vast collection of free online courses and educational resources on a wide range of subjects. Website: https://www.khanacademy.org/

Note: It's important to understand that while these institutions offer free access to educational materials, *they may not grant official college credits or degrees for completing these courses.*

- **Create Your Own Curriculum:** If you're creative, resourceful, and have the time, you can create your own curriculum using free or low-cost materials. Start by defining your learning goals, curating your resources, designing your learning path, implementing a schedule, and evaluating/adapting along the way. For more information, see Chapter 7, "The Curriculum Jungle."

- **Comparison Shop:** Don't just settle for the first curriculum you find. Shop around and compare prices. You can often find the same curriculum at a lower price from a different vendor or website.

- **Attend Homeschool Conventions:** You can find great deals on curriculum and materials at homeschool conventions. The Homeschool Mom website has a comprehensive list of homeschool conventions and conferences by state. https://www.thehomeschoolmom.com/local-support/homeschool-conventions-conferences-and-events/

- **Art Class with Recycled Materials:** Teach your kids the value of recycling and creativity by using items like cardboard boxes, egg cartons, and plastic bottles for art projects. Create collages, sculptures, or imaginative crafts using these materials. This way, you'll save money on art supplies while instilling a sense of resourcefulness in your children.

- **Second-Hand Treasures:** One person's trash is another's curriculum! Garage sales, thrift stores, and online marketplaces are goldmines for budget-conscious homeschoolers. Keep an eye out for gently used textbooks, workbooks, or educational toys. With a little patience, you'll find gems at a fraction of their original price. Cha-ching!

- **Group Buys and Curriculum Sharing:** Teaming up with other homeschooling families can be a game-changer when it comes to saving money. Join forces to take advantage of group discounts, share curriculum materials, or even collaborate on projects. Remember, teamwork makes the dream work! Facebook Groups has the most comprehensive list of homeschool groups that buy/and/or share curriculum.

FIELD TRIPS—WORLD EXPLORATION WITHOUT THE FIVE-STAR PRICE TAG

Unlock the door to a world of affordable, enriching experiences right at your doorstep. Discover how to turn local and accessible destinations into unforgettable learning adventures. Rule of thumb: No matter what kind of excursion you attend, ALWAYS look on the website of the place/institution for educator options and/or deals. Alternatively, once on the premises, ask personnel if such options exist. **A closed mouth does not get fed!**

- **Free Admission Days:** Budget-conscious homeschoolers develop a sixth sense for free admission days at museums, zoos, and cultural institutions. Mark your calendar and make a day of it. These outings provide a great opportunity to break the routine, learn something new, and have a blast without spending a dime. Do remember that you're not the only one, so wear your best elbow pads to deal with the crowds. However, if you're fortunate to have "homeschool days" at your museums, zoos, science centers, etc., then you'll have the place all to yourselves. Pure paradise. Until public/private school field trips kick in. *Pro tip: Go very early in the morning (around 8:00 or 9:00) before the school buses arrive, or after 1:00 p.m. when students are heading back to the buses.*

- **Outdoor Adventures:** Nature provides a wealth of free educational opportunities, like hiking, bird watching, and stargazing. Instead of expensive field trips, explore the natural world right in your backyard or nearby park. Encourage your kids to observe insects, birds, plants, and weather patterns. Create a nature journal where they can draw or write their observations. This is an excellent way to teach your children about the environment and biodiversity on a budget.

- **Community Events:** Attend free local events, like concerts, plays, and workshops, for cultural enrichment. Find out if there are student or educator days/events and put them on your calendar. *Pro tip: Get on the mailing list of area cultural attractions/organizations like the opera, symphony, theater, botanical gardens, etc.*

- **Group Discounts:** Many attractions offer group discounts or educator discounts/perks for field trips. You can take advantage of these discounts by organizing a group of homeschooling families to visit together. Not only will you save money on admission, but you'll also have the opportunity to socialize and learn with other homeschooling families. A welcome change from spending all day with your own kids.

- **Off-Season Field Trips:** Visiting popular tourist destinations during peak season can be expensive, crowded, and overwhelming. Instead, consider taking field trips during off-seasons when there are fewer tourists and lower prices. For example, visiting a beach town in the fall or a ski resort in the spring can provide unique learning opportunities and experiences without the high costs of peak season.

- **Virtual Field Trips:** Virtual field trips can be an affordable and convenient way to supplement your homeschooling curriculum. They're also a great way to learn about subjects that might not be accessible in your local area. Many museums, zoos, and historical sites offer virtual tours and exhibits that can be accessed online. You can also take virtual tours of famous landmarks and destinations around the world, giving your kids a global perspective without leaving home.

POCKET-PLEASING PLAY: AFFORDABLE ACTIVITIES FOR ALL

Ah, the world of extracurricular activities where prices can skyrocket faster than a McDonald's Big Mac combo meal. But worry not. There are ways to offer your child diverse experiences without taking out a second mortgage.

- **The Great Outdoors:** Mother Nature is an open-air classroom just waiting for intrepid explorers. Parks, forests, and beaches offer myriad lessons in biology, geology, and more—all without a single charge. The only entrance fee is your curiosity.

- **Home-Based Clubs:** Who needs expensive extracurricular activities when you can start your own clubs at home? Host a book club, start a neighborhood sports league, set up a makeshift art studio in your backyard, or even start an "I don't want to be in a club" club. You'll be surprised at the fun and learning that can come from a little creativity and some low-cost supplies. The possibilities are endless, and the only membership fee is your imagination.

- **Volunteer Opportunities:** Many local organizations offer volunteer opportunities that serve as practical, hands-on learning experiences for homeschoolers. For instance, participating in a community garden project teaches about botany and ecology, while volunteering at a local animal shelter offers lessons in biology and responsibility. These activities not only enrich the homeschool curriculum but also foster a sense of community involvement and real-world skills.

- **Join a Co-op:** Joining a homeschooling co-op can be a great way to find low-cost activities and materials. Co-ops are groups of homeschooling families who come together to share resources, expertise, and support. They can offer group classes, music classes, field trips, and social activities at a reduced cost. Plus, they provide an opportunity for kids to make friends and for parents to connect with other homeschooling families.

ENTERTAINMENT—DIY FRUGAL FUN AND GAMES

Turn everyday items into a treasure trove of entertainment and laughter, and prove that the best classroom might just be your living room (or kitchen or backyard)—and the best supplies are those you probably already have.

- **The Great Science Experiment Bake-Off:** Combine culinary prowess with scientific curiosity by hosting a bake-off where your kids must explain the chemical reactions that occur as they whip up their treats. Don your best mad scientist persona, and watch the kitchen transform into a laboratory filled with delectable (and educational) concoctions!

- **DIY Game Show:** Produce your own educational game show! Customize popular game show formats like "Jeopardy!" or "Who Wants to Be a Millionaire?" to cover topics you're teaching. Make it as wacky as you want—bonus points if you include dramatic music and an overly enthusiastic host!

- **Re-Create Iconic Artwork with Household Items:** Channel your inner Monet by transforming everyday objects into replicas of famous artwork. Assign each family member a well-known masterpiece to re-create using only items found at home. Let the hilarity commence as you unveil your budget masterpieces!

- **History's Mysteries, Home Edition:** Transform your living room into a time machine! Spring into history by assigning each family member a different historical figure. Create costumes from items around the house (bedsheets for togas, anyone?) and have each person present a monologue as their character. The result? A comically immersive history lesson.

- **The Silly Scavenger Hunt:** Design a neighborhood scavenger hunt with a twist: each clue must be solved through educational riddles, puns, or wordplay. Form teams, and let the shenanigans begin as you race against the clock to find the treasure hidden right under your noses.

EVERYTHING ELSE—THE DISCOUNT DETECTIVE

Navigating the homeschool shopping maze without overspending is akin to a masterful game of chess—strategic and rewarding. Here are some clever tips to turn educational shopping into an adventure of savings rather than a budgetary black hole!

- **Ask for Memberships for Holiday Gifts and Birthdays:** Instead of traditional gifts for holidays and birthdays, consider asking for memberships to museums, zoos, or other attractions that offer homeschooling discounts. It's the gift that keeps on giving, providing unlimited access to resources and activities at a reduced cost. Plus, it's a great excuse to get out of the house and make some memories with your family.

- **Give Educational Toys as Gifts:** Who says that gifts have to be all fun and no learning? Why not kill two birds with one stone by giving your child an educational toy as a gift? Consider gifting them something educational, like a science kit, puzzle, or board game that promotes learning and development. For example, a chemistry set can be a fun and educational gift that teaches kids about chemical reactions and laboratory experiments. Not only will you be gifting something fun, but you'll also be promoting learning and development. Plus, when they outgrow it, you can always hand it down to younger siblings or donate it to a charity.

- **Use Services You Are Already Paying For:** You're already paying for a lot of services, so why not use them to supplement your homeschooling curriculum? Services like Netflix, Amazon Prime, or your local library offer a wealth of educational materials like documentaries, movies, and books that can be incorporated into your homeschooling routine. For example, you can watch educational shows like "Planet Earth" or "Bill Nye the Science Guy" to teach your kids about science and the natural world. It's a cost-effective way to add some variety and fun to your homeschooling curriculum

- **Ask for Homeschool Discounts:** Many attractions and retailers offer homeschool discounts, but they might not always advertise them. Don't be afraid to ask if there are any homeschooling discounts available, and be sure to bring your homeschooling ID, teacher ID card, or registration documents to show proof of homeschooling. You might be surprised at the discounts that are available to homeschooling families! (See Homeschool Buyers Co-op's website about getting a free ID card, or make your own).

- **Join Local Email Lists:** Joining local homeschooling email lists can be a great way to find out about low-cost activities and resources in your area. These lists often share information about co-ops, field trips, and other homeschooling events that you might not hear about otherwise. Plus, they provide an opportunity to connect with other homeschooling families and have a laugh about the joys (and occasional struggles) of homeschooling.

- **Public Libraries:** Mere mortals call them libraries; we homeschoolers know them as enchanted treasure troves of free knowledge. Armed with a library card and a sense of adventure, explore their sacred halls to uncover not only books but also programs, classes, movies, music, workshops, and access to online resources. Whew! Go get a library card!

- **Online Freebies:** Consider the internet as your treasure trove of free educational riches, primed to make your budget homeschooling as smooth as a well-oiled machine. Digital platforms like YouTube, Khan Academy, Scholastic, and an array of blogs and online communities are filled to the brim with awesome (and free) content covering subjects as diverse as algebra and zoology.

- **Scavenging for Deals:** To homeschool on a budget, you must embrace the art of the deal. Immerse yourself into the swirling chaos of garage sales, discount stores, and homeschool swaps. Keep an eye on online marketplaces like eBay, Craigslist, or Facebook Marketplace for deals on used homeschooling materials.

- **Frugal Innovation:** The principles of 'Reduce, Reuse, Recycle' become more than just eco-friendly slogans—they're a way of life. Embrace your inner MacGyver (look it up) and repurpose household items into educational tools. Got a cereal box? Voila, you have a canvas for an art project.

Empty egg carton? Perfect for a budding biologist's insect collection or a math counting game. Commonplace materials like jars, socks, and paper towel rolls can transform into exciting science experiments, puppets for storytelling, or arts and crafts projects. Just add a splash of creativity (and perhaps a little bit of tape).

- **Homebrewed Chemistry and Botanical Wonders:** Transform your kitchen into a science lab with simple, everyday items. Create a home-made volcanic eruption using baking soda and vinegar, offering both a fun experiment and a great photo opportunity. Then, switch to botany by planting seeds in eggshells or pots, watching them sprout and grow, turning your kitchen into a live demonstration of plant life cycles.

- **Math with Everyday Objects:** Utilize colorful buttons or beads from your craft drawer to demonstrate counting, sorting, and basic arithmetic operations. Children can engage with these vibrant objects, making math both visually appealing and interactive. Also, bring math into the real world by using a measuring tape or ruler around the house. Have kids measure furniture, windows, or even themselves to learn about units of measurement, area, and perimeter. This not only saves money but also grounds math concepts in everyday life, making them more understandable and fun for children.

- **Click, Print, Learn:** A variety of websites provide a wealth of free printable worksheets and activities to complement your homeschool curriculum. Two popular websites for free educational printables are:

  - **Education.com:** This site offers a wide range of free printable worksheets covering various subjects and grades, from math and science to reading and writing.

  - **Teachers Pay Teachers (Free Section):** Although known for paid resources, Teachers Pay Teachers also has a free section where educators share printable worksheets and activities at no cost. These online platforms are perfect for finding diverse and engaging materials for your educational needs.

- **Use Peer Tutoring:** Peer tutoring is a great way to encourage collaboration and help older children reinforce their own learning while teaching younger siblings. This approach not only saves you time but also helps your children develop communication and leadership skills. Older children can teach younger children subjects they have already mastered, and younger children can learn from their older siblings.

- **Multi-Person Tutoring Sessions:** Hiring a private tutor can be expensive, but organizing a multi-person tutoring session can be a more affordable option. You can split the cost of a tutor with other homeschooling families and have your kids learn in a small group setting. This can be a great way to get personalized attention for your kids without breaking the bank. It's like a mini classroom but without the chalk dust and creaky chairs.

- **Use Free Educational Apps:** Many free educational apps can be used to supplement your homeschool curriculum. Here's a list to get you going (Updated summer 2023).

  - **Khan Academy:** Offers a wide range of subjects and grade levels with interactive lessons, practice exercises, and quizzes.

  - **Duolingo:** A popular language-learning app that provides interactive lessons for a variety of languages.

  - **Coursera:** Provides access to online courses from top universities and educational institutions around the world.

  - **TED-Ed:** Offers a collection of educational videos on various topics, accompanied by quizzes and discussion prompts.

  - **Scratch:** A platform for learning and creating interactive stories, animations, and games through coding.

  - **Quizlet:** Helps children create and study flashcards, practice quizzes, and play educational games across different subjects.

  - **Libby by OverDrive:** Allows users to borrow e-books and audiobooks from their local library for free.

  - **Photomath:** Helps children solve math problems by using their smartphone's camera to scan and solve equations.

- ◦ **Khan Academy Kids:** Specifically designed for young learners, this app offers interactive activities and games covering various subjects.

- ◦ **Seesaw:** A digital portfolio app that allows students to document their learning, share work with teachers, and receive feedback.

- ◦ **GoNoodle:** Offers fun movement and exercise videos to help children stay active and energized throughout the day.

Please note that while these apps are free to download and use, some may offer additional premium features for a price or in-app purchases.

ADVENTURES IN BARTERING AND TRADING

Homeschooling on a budget requires creativity, especially when it comes to teaching materials. Think of your resources as a set of ingredients, and dare to experiment. Substitute your math curriculum for free online programs, and trade your literature textbooks for e-books from the library. Your homeschooling kitchen will be brimming with flavors you never knew existed. *Pro tip: Form a secret society with other homeschooling parents and trade homeschooling resources.*

- **The Swappening:** In the realm of the thrifty homeschooler, trading is king. Gather your fellow budgeteers and organize swap meets to exchange everything from textbooks to art supplies. Never underestimate the power of collective thriftiness, and watch the magic of the free market unfold in your living room, a park, or a library.

- **Skill Swapping:** There's no need to master every subject yourself. Collaborate with other parents and share your expertise. You can teach your neighbor's kids how to split atoms while your neighbor unravels the mysteries of Shakespearean iambic pentameter to yours.

- **Bargain Book Fairs:** As they say, one homeschooler's last year's curriculum is another homeschooler's treasure. Keep your eyes peeled for local book sales, thrift stores, and online bargains.

CENTS AND SENSIBILITY—THE GAINS OF PLANNING AHEAD

I've shared numerous saving tips and tricks that are highly beneficial, but there's one overarching piece of advice I'd like to emphasize: starting early really pays off. There's truth in the adage, "The early bird catches the worm," and it certainly applies to supercharging your savings. But what if you're beginning homeschooling mid-year? No problem—first concentrate on establishing your homeschool routine. Once you're set, you can start applying these savings strategies. By getting acquainted with these tips early, you will be ready to fully capitalize on your savings as the next school year commences, truly becoming that proverbial early bird! Let's explore how to put this into practice.

Summer Beginnings—Setting Sail on Your Homeschool Voyage

Starting your homeschool journey with ample preparation is like unlocking a treasure chest of savings. The key is starting early (as I've mentioned earlier) —not just for the financial benefits, but also for the rich opportunities it brings. By giving yourself time to strategize, you'll tap into second-hand markets, uncover elusive online coupon codes, and leverage community resources like a pro. You'll also reel in those early bird rewards everyone seems to be posting on Instagram or YouTube. The real prize, however, is the peace of mind that comes from knowing your planning is solid. So, while the carnival clown of last-minute stress might haunt others, you'll sail smoothly ahead, your bank account all the happier for it.

Spring's Touch: Refreshing Your Homeschool Plan

As winter fades away and spring's gentle touch reinvigorates the world, allow this seasonal shift to refresh your homeschool approach. With a significant part of your curriculum now behind you, it's the perfect moment to assess the hits and misses—what succeeded and what fell short. Be ruthless with your assessment!

The Pitfalls of Premature Purchases

Finally, be mindful of the dangers of premature purchases. While early planning is a fantastic way to save money, it comes with a warning—don't buy too soon before your plans take shape! Resist the urge to empty the store in one go. Instead, pace yourself throughout the year, buying what you need when you need it. This allows you to grab sales and discounts as they appear and prevents you from wasting money on resources that just collect dust.

---------- **Summary** ----------

Budget-friendly homeschooling isn't just achievable; it's an adventure. With these clever tips in your pocket, you're stepping onto the runway of becoming a successful cost-conscious homeschooling maestro. And this is about more than just lessons—you'll be molding your kids into adaptable, innovative, dollar-wise dynamos. Tackle this task with gusto, and you'll find yourself magically transforming a modest budget into a rich educational banquet. And here's the kicker: the secret ingredient of budget homeschooling isn't buried in your wallet but hidden in your imagination. With this touch of educational alchemy, you'll be enriching your family with skills that extend beyond the classroom and you'll be teaching them to find value in simplicity and imagination.

10

Teaching Multiple Children
The Fun of Herding Cats

It goes without saying that you should never have more children than you have car windows.

— Erma Bombeck

HOMESCHOOLING MULTIPLE KIDS CAN feel like trying to nail jelly to a wall, but don't panic—I've got some clever tricks up my sleeves. This chapter is all about turning that chaos into a smooth, harmonious symphony of learning. We'll dive into creating independent stations, setting up personalized learning plans, using technology without turning your home into a screen-time battle zone, and fostering some good old-fashioned teamwork among your kids. By the end of this chapter, you'll be armed with practical tips and tricks to make multi-grade homeschooling not just manageable, but downright enjoyable. Ready to tame the homeschool jungle? Let's go!

The Magic of an Independent Station

Creating an independent station is a game-changer! Whether it's a permanent setup or a portable one, this space is crucial. Whenever you need to work with one child, the others can head straight to the station—no questions asked.

- **Little Learners:** Put together a "busy box" filled with favorite toys, dollar store trinkets, playdough, etc. Sensory bins, stacking toys, picture books, and simple puzzles are also great choices. Add a tablet with age-appropriate educational apps for variety.

- **Elementary Learners:** Stock the station with items that encourage independent exploration and creativity. Provide a stack of engaging books, fun math puzzle books, and simple science kits. Math manipulatives, writing prompt dice, paper, pens, markers, art supplies, a small whiteboard, a globe, hands-on science materials, and engaging books are additional options to include.

- **Middle/High School Learners:** This could contain more advanced resources. Equip it with research materials, reference books, classic novels, art supplies for projects, physical logic games, a computer for research, literature books with reading guides and assignments they can tackle independently.

Organize the station with bins and shelves or a mobile cart for easy access. Make it inviting with colorful posters, a schedule board, and a cozy reading corner (not necessary, but nice-to-haves). This setup not only keeps your kids engaged while you work with another child, but also makes learning fun and accessible.

Staggered Routines

It's essential to create staggered routines that accommodate different ages and learning levels. This way, each child gets the attention they need without overwhelming you.

Example: Start your day by giving your older child a head start with an independent activity, like reading a book or working on a project. Meanwhile, spend 20-30 minutes with your youngest, perhaps reading a story or doing a craft together. Once that time is up, settle the youngest into an independent activity such as building with blocks, watching an educational show, or coloring. Then, transition to working one-on-one with your older child on more complex subjects.

Encourage Independent Work

Encouraging independent work is crucial for managing multiple children. Teach your kids to work independently on certain tasks, freeing you up to focus on another child.

- **All Learners:** Create a learning/independent station or cart/box/shelf where each child has specific tasks to complete independently (see above). For instance, while your older child is reading a chapter book or working on a math worksheet, your younger child can play with educational toys or watch an educational video. Rotate items in these stations to keep things fresh and engaging.

- **Little Learners:** Focus on activities that require minimal supervision. Set up play dough stations, simple puzzles, and coloring books. While your older child is working on a science project, your little one can play with blocks or work on a simple puzzle.

- **Elementary Learners:** Provide tasks that build on their growing independence, such as reading chapters from a book, completing fun worksheets, or working on art projects.

- **For Middle/High School Learners:** Assign more complex tasks that they can manage alone, such as research projects, essays, and advanced math problems.

Best Subjects to Group Teach

Some subjects naturally lend themselves to group teaching, allowing you to teach multiple children simultaneously:

1. **Science:** Conducting experiments, exploring nature, and discussing scientific concepts can be done as a group. Adapt the depth of the content to suit different ages.

2. **History:** Telling stories, watching documentaries, and doing timeline

activities can be engaging for children of various ages. Younger kids can draw pictures while older ones write summaries.

3. **Art:** Art projects can be easily adapted to different skill levels. Provide a range of materials and let each child create their own masterpiece based on a common theme.

4. **Physical Education:** Group activities like yoga, dance, or outdoor games can be done together, promoting physical health and teamwork.

5. **Music:** Singing, rhythm exercises, and learning about different musical instruments can be enjoyed by all ages. Older children might even help teach younger ones.

- **Example:** Organize a family science experiment where everyone has a role to play. The older kids can handle more complex tasks like measuring and recording data, while the younger ones can assist with simpler tasks like mixing ingredients or observing changes. Another option is a family read-aloud session, where you read a book that appeals to all ages and then discuss it together.

Flexible Learning Spaces

Designate different areas of your home for different activities to help manage multiple children. This way, everyone has their own space to work and play.

Example: Set up a quiet reading corner for older kids and a play area for younger ones. Use the kitchen for messy science experiments and the dining table for group projects. This not only keeps things organized but also minimizes distractions and conflicts.

Be Tech-Savvy

Technology can be a fantastic ally in your homeschool journey. From educational apps and online courses to virtual field trips and interactive learning games, there are countless resources available to enrich your child's education. Let's go over a few of them.

- **Interactive Learning:** Interactive learning tools can make subjects come alive. Use apps and websites that offer interactive simulations, quizzes, and games to engage your children and reinforce what they're learning.

  - **Little Learners:** Use an app like ABCmouse for preschool and kindergarten learning, where your child can engage with interactive lessons in reading, math, and art through fun games and activities.

  - **Elementary Learners:** For history, use an interactive timeline app like Kids Discover Online to explore different historical periods with videos and quizzes. For science, try an app like Mystery Science, which offers interactive lessons and virtual experiments.

  - **Middle/High School Learners:** Use Khan Academy for more advanced subjects like algebra or biology. For history, utilize an app like History Channel's History Here, which provides interactive maps and historical facts. For science, try Labster, which offers virtual labs and experiments.

- **Balance Screen Time:** While technology offers incredible opportunities, it's important to balance screen time with offline activities. Too much screen time can lead to burnout and reduced physical activity.

  - **Daily Schedules:** Create a daily schedule that includes specific times for using technology and times for screen-free activities. For instance, you might start the day with an hour of online learning, followed by a hands-on science experiment or outdoor play. In the afternoon, you could use educational videos to supplement your history lesson, but then transition to a creative arts and crafts project.

Peer Teaching & Role Reversals

Encourage older children to help teach younger ones. This reinforces the older child's knowledge and gives you a moment to focus on other tasks. Also, encourage little learners to teach or share something with an older sibling which can be a delightful and mutually beneficial experience. Here are some ideas:

Older Siblings Teaching Younger Siblings

- **Reading Together:** The older sibling can read a book to the younger one, pausing to ask questions about the story or explain new words. This can be a daily or weekly activity, fostering a love for reading in the younger child.

- **Math Help:** The older sibling can help the younger one with basic math concepts, such as addition and subtraction, using visual aids like counting blocks or drawing diagrams.

- **Science Experiments:** The older sibling can conduct simple science experiments with the younger one, such as creating a volcano with baking soda and vinegar or making slime. They can explain the science behind the reactions in a fun and engaging way.

- **Art and Crafts:** The older sibling can teach the younger one how to draw, paint, or create simple crafts. For instance, they can show how to make paper airplanes, origami, or basic painting techniques.

- **Cooking/Baking:** The older sibling can involve the younger one in cooking or baking projects. They can teach them how to measure ingredients, follow a recipe, and understand basic kitchen safety.

- **Music Lessons:** If the older sibling plays an instrument, they can give basic lessons to the younger sibling. For example, teaching simple piano scales or guitar chords.

- **Language Learning:** If the older sibling is learning a new language, they can teach basic words and phrases to the younger sibling. They can practice together through songs, flashcards, or simple conversations.

- **Technology Skills:** The older sibling can teach the younger one how to use educational apps or basic computer skills, such as typing, using a mouse, or navigating educational websites.

- **Sports and Physical Activities:** The older sibling can teach the younger one how to play a sport or engage in physical activities like riding a bike, swimming, or practicing yoga. They can demonstrate proper techniques and encourage physical fitness.

- **Homework Help:** The older sibling can assist the younger one with their homework, providing explanations and guidance on difficult subjects or assignments. This can include going over spelling words, helping with reading assignments, or explaining math problems.

- **Board Games and Puzzles:** The older sibling can teach the younger one how to play board games or solve puzzles, explaining the rules and strategies. This promotes critical thinking and problem-solving skills.

- **Chores and Responsibilities:** The older sibling can show the younger one how to complete household chores, such as making the bed, folding laundry, or setting the table. They can explain the importance of responsibility and teamwork.

- **Social Skills:** The older sibling can teach the younger one about manners, sharing, and communication through role-playing or real-life interactions. They can model positive behavior and encourage empathy and cooperation.

By involving older siblings in teaching and mentoring their younger siblings, families can create a supportive and collaborative learning environment that benefits both age groups.

Younger Siblings Teaching/Sharing With Older Siblings

- **Teach Simple Concepts:** Have the younger sibling explain basic concepts they are familiar with, such as colors, shapes, or counting. For example, they can use colorful toys to teach their older sibling about different colors.

- **Storytelling:** Encourage the younger sibling to "read" a picture book to the older sibling. Even if they can't read yet, they can describe the pictures and make up stories, which fosters creativity and confidence.

- **Show and Tell:** Let the younger sibling choose a favorite toy or object and explain why they like it, how it works, or tell a story about it. This helps them practice communication skills.

- **Art Projects:** Pair them up for an art project where the younger sibling can instruct the older sibling on what to draw or which colors to use. This can be as simple as finger painting or making a collage.

- **Gardening:** Involve both children in planting a small garden. The younger sibling can share their excitement about planting seeds, watering them, and watching them grow, while the older sibling assists with the more complex tasks.

- **Building Projects:** Use building blocks or a simple DIY craft kit. The younger sibling can suggest what to build, while the older sibling helps bring the vision to life. This fosters teamwork and creativity.

- **Educational Games:** Choose games that are suitable for both ages. The younger sibling can take the lead in explaining the rules of a simple game or suggesting ways to play.

- **Cooking/Baking:** Involve them in cooking or baking a simple recipe. The younger sibling can measure ingredients, stir, or decorate cookies while explaining their actions. The older sibling can handle more complex tasks and ensure safety.

- **Science Experiments:** Simple science experiments, like mixing baking soda and vinegar, can be led by the younger sibling with guidance. They can share their observations and excitement with their older sibling.

- **Emotional Sharing:** Encourage the little learner to share their feelings or daily experiences. This can help them develop emotional intelligence and build a stronger bond with their older sibling.

By engaging in these activities, the younger siblings gain confidence and communication skills, while older siblings practice patience and empathy. This dynamic also promotes a supportive and collaborative learning environment at home.

Involve Your Kids

Get feedback from your children about your homeschool routine. Their input can provide valuable insights and make them feel more involved in their education.

- **Little Learners:** During a weekly or monthly family meeting, ask your younger child simple questions about their favorite parts of the day and any new activities they might want to try. For example, they might say they love story time or playing with building blocks. Use this feedback to incorporate more story time sessions or creative building activities into their daily routine, ensuring they feel involved and excited about their learning experience

- **Elementary Learners:** During weekly or monthly family meetings, ask your elementary learner what subjects they enjoy the most and which projects they find exciting. Use their feedback to plan more of those activities, like incorporating more science experiments or art projects into their schedule.

- **Middle/High School Learners:** At a weekly or monthly meeting ask your middle/high school learner about their goals and challenges. Get their input on project ideas or subjects they want to delve deeper into. Adjust their schedule to include more self-directed projects or research based on their interests.

Think of managing multiple children like conducting an orchestra. Each instrument (or child) has its part to play, and with a little coordination, you can create a harmonious symphony of learning. Just remember, it's okay if there's the occasional off-note or solo—embrace the chaos and enjoy the music!

---------- **Summary** ----------

As we wrap up, you'll find that juggling the diverse needs of multiple children is more about strategic harmony than chaotic improvisation. From the magic of independent stations to the wonders of staggered routines and group teaching, you've gathered a treasure trove of practical tips to make multi-grade homeschooling not just feasible, but genuinely enjoyable. Remember, it's about creating a rhythm that works for your unique family dynamic, leveraging technology wisely, and fostering collaboration among siblings. With these strategies in your toolkit, you're well on your way to turning the potential chaos of homeschooling multiple children into a well-orchestrated, joyous learning adventure. Ready to continue this journey with renewed confidence and a smile? Let's keep moving forward!

11

The First Day of School

Grand Opening! Grand Closing?

If Plan A doesn't work, the alphabet has 25 more letters – 204 if you're in Japan.

— Claire Cook

G ET READY TO KICK off your homeschool adventure with a bang! This chapter is your guide to starting off on the right foot. We'll cover everything from the night-before preparations to morning routines, engaging afternoon activities, and wrapping up the day with a sense of accomplishment.

Let's get started with the cornerstone of a great homeschool day: the day-before preparations. Trust me, a little prep work tonight will make tomorrow morning feel less like herding cats and more like a well-orchestrated symphony (or at least less chaotic).The day before the first day of homeschooling is like the calm before a wonderfully chaotic storm. This is your golden time to set the tone for the entire school year.

THE DAY BEFORE—GETTING READY

Organize Your Supplies and Learning Materials

Gather and organize your supplies and learning materials. Everyone gets their stash of notebooks, pens, colored pencils, folders, textbooks, novels, etc. Let each kid spend some time with their materials. For younger kids, this could mean flipping through picture books, stacking counting blocks, or sorting through craft supplies. The elementary/middle school children can flip through their new books, label their notebooks/folders, and preview chapters. The high schooler can organize their digital assignments, practice logging into class, or look through the syllabus for each subject. Confirm that all children have all the necessary textbooks and technology charged and ready to go. Familiarizing themselves with the materials can help reduce anxiety and boost their confidence.

Prep Your Space

Set up your learning zone. Ensure everything your preschooler needs is within easy reach and safe. Create an engaging workspace for your elementary child with a dedicated desk or table, making sure they have all the supplies they need organized and accessible. For middle school and high school students, design a more structured study area that includes space for their textbooks, notebooks, and digital devices. Personalize each space with your children's input, adding elements like motivational posters, favorite colors, or comfortable seating to make the area inviting. Good lighting, a quiet environment, and minimal distractions are key to creating an effective learning space. By setting up their own special area, children can feel more motivated and ready to start their homeschool journey

Introduce the Routine to Your Kids

Starting a homeschool journey can be exciting and overwhelming for both parents and children. One of the most effective ways to ensure a smooth transition is to introduce a clear and engaging routine or schedule. Here's how to make the introduction process seamless and enjoyable for everyone involved.

- **Create a Visual Representation of the Routine:** This could be a colorful chart, a whiteboard layout, or even a digital format. Use images and icons to represent different activities, making it appealing and easy for younger children to understand. For example, a sun icon could signify morning preparations, a book icon for lesson slots, and a playground icon for break times. The visual aid serves as a constant reminder and helps children grasp the flow of their day. See Chapter 6, "Homeschool Routines" for more details on how to do this.

- **Explain Each Part of the Day:** Go through the routine step-by-step. This is an excellent opportunity to set clear expectations and build excitement for the learning journey ahead. Discuss what happens first thing in the morning, how lessons transition, and what the afternoon activities will entail. This structured approach helps children understand what to expect and when. For instance, you might explain that the morning lessons will start with a 30-minute reading session followed by a short 5-minute break, then a 45-minute math lesson followed by a 10-minute break, and then continue with a science activity before lunch. The afternoon might include creative projects and physical activities.

Encourage Input and Feedback

Ask for your children's input and feedback. Encourage them to share their thoughts on the routine and suggest any adjustments they might like. This could be as simple as changing the order of activities or adding a new one they are interested in. Involving them in the planning process not only makes them feel valued but also increases their buy-in and commitment to the schedule.

Gather Everyone for a Quick Pep Talk

Finally, the night before your homeschool journey begins, round up the crew for a meeting. Discuss the expectations for the year, and make it sound as exciting as possible. For your preschooler, "We're going to paint and sing!" For your elementary kid, "We're going to explode volcanoes!" For middle school, "We're going to solve mysteries!" And for the high schooler, "We're going to prep for real-world domination (or at least college)." You get the point. End the session on a positive note.

Documentary/Movie Night

End the pep talk with a light educational documentary, a board game, or a fun movie, something to spark curiosity or laughter without overwhelming them—keep it light and engaging.

ESSENTIAL START-UP QUESTIONS

With all this homeschool excitement in the air, let's address a few key start-up questions to ensure your beginning is as epic as it can be.

When to Start Our First Day of School?—The Midweek Launch

Why not kick things off in the middle of the week? Hear me out: starting on a Wednesday or Thursday gives everyone a taste of school without the full bite. It's like dipping your toe in the pool to check the temperature—it's better than a cannonball dive to the deep end. This allows for a shorter first week, easing the transition for everyone and giving you the weekend to adjust plans based on how the first couple of days go.

Tick-Tock: How Long Should Our Day Last?

So, you're figuring out how long your homeschool day should be. Good news: it's flexible! No need to mimic a traditional school's marathon day. Instead, tailor the duration to match your kids' attention spans and educational needs, keeping in mind your state's homeschooling requirements. Here's a guide to get you started:

- **Preschoolers:** Aim for 1-2 hours of playful learning. Think of it as fun school—short, sweet, and full of giggles.

- **Elementary Kiddos:** They can handle 3-4 hours, covering various subjects with plenty of breaks. Keep it interesting to prevent those wandering minds.

- **Middle Schoolers:** With their newfound curiosity, they can manage 4-5 hours. Jump into more in-depth subjects and sprinkle in some project-based learning to keep them engaged.

- **High Schoolers:** Plan for 5-6 hours. This includes a brief overview of each course and some electives, giving them a taste of everything without overwhelming them.

Author's note: Remember, these are just guidelines. Adjust to fit your family's unique rhythm and watch your homeschool day flow smoothly! (Check your state laws on instructional hours, if required.)

Should We Start a Family Tradition?

Alright, you've got your supplies sorted, spaces prepped, routines introduced, and essential questions answered. High fives all around! Now, let's kick things up a notch and talk about something that'll make your homeschool journey unforgettable: family traditions. Think of these as the secret sauce that'll spice up your homeschool life, creating memories that'll last longer than a never-ending math lesson. Here are several ideas to get you started:

- **First-Day Photos:** Take a photo in a specific spot every year. Have your kids hold a sign with their grade. It's a great way to see how everyone grows and changes.

- **Memory Jar:** Decorate a jar together and start it off with notes about what everyone is excited to learn this year. Add to it throughout the year with fun memories and achievements.

- **Special Dinner:** Have a "back-to-school" dinner where each family member gets to pick a favorite dish. Celebrate the day's accomplishments and discuss the highlights.

- **New Book Celebration:** Gift each child a new book that they can jump into at their own pace. It's a little treat they can anticipate.

HOMESCHOOL KICKOFF—READY, SET, LEARN!

Let's finally talk about the first day! This isn't just any day; it's THE day. The day where you set the tone, establish the vibe, maybe start a family tradition, and show your kiddos that learning at home can be as awesome as pizza on a Friday night.

On the first day of homeschool, introduce your children to a few core subjects to set the tone for the year while keeping things light and engaging. These introductory lessons should be brief and enjoyable, providing a positive and exciting glimpse into the learning journey ahead without overwhelming them on the first day. Let's look at a sample first day of homeschool. Note: I deliberately did not include times because I want you to focus on the teaching and learning, not the clock.

Rise and Shine!

- **Wake Up.** Your alarm goes off. Resist the urge to hit snooze—this isn't a drill, it's the first day of homeschool! Roll out of bed, stretch, and put on something that isn't pajamas. Sure, you could teach in your PJs, but let's start strong.

- **Breakfast Time.** Make it special. Pancakes, anyone? Or maybe some fun-shaped waffles. Get the kids involved—cooking is science and math, after all. While flipping those pancakes, have a casual chat about what they're excited about for the day. No pressure, just excitement.

Morning Routine

- **Kickoff Meeting.** Gather in the living room, around the kitchen table, or wherever is comfortable. It's like a mini assembly, but without the boring announcements. Go over the plan or routine for the day. (Hopefully, you did this yesterday, so this should be brief). Keep it light, keep it fun.

- **Icebreaker Activity.** A fun little game to get everyone in the mood. Maybe a quick round of "Two Truths and a Lie" or a scavenger hunt around the house. This isn't just for the kids; it's for you too. Get those creative juices flowing.

- **Morning Basket Time.** This special basket is filled with captivating read-aloud books, engaging puzzles, inspiring Bible/religious stories or devotionals, educational magazines, and poetry books to name a few. Spend some time exploring these treasures, setting a calm and enriching tone. After enjoying the morning basket, take a quick break and then transition seamlessly into your core subjects or other planned activities, energized and focused.

Quick Break Time

Learning Blocks (choose your subjects/electives and order; below is just a sample)

- **Reading Adventure:** Create a cozy reading nook with pillows and blankets. Let kids choose a book or read aloud to them. Incorporate themed days, like "Mystery Monday" or "Fantasy Friday," to keep things exciting.

- **Nature Exploration:** Take a nature walk and collect leaves, rocks, or flowers. When you get home, research and categorize your findings. It's science, exercise, and fun all rolled into one.

- **Math Quest:** Offer scavenger hunts that involve solving math problems to find the next clue. Or, use math card games or board games like Sudoku, puzzles, logic grids, ClumsyThief, Monopoly, or Payday.

- **Storytelling Session:** Encourage kids to create their own stories. They can illustrate them or even act them out. It's a fantastic way to boost imagination and narrative skills.

- **Cultural Exploration:** Choose a country to explore each week. Learn about its culture, language, food, and traditions. You can even cook a meal from that country together.

Lunch and Relaxation
- **Lunchtime:** Make it fun. Maybe a picnic in the backyard or a build-your-own sandwich bar. While eating, chat about what they liked about the morning. This is a great way to get feedback without making it feel like a performance review.

- **Chill Time:** After lunch, give everyone some free time. Whether it's playing outside, drawing, or just lounging with a book, it's important to have some downtime. And yes, this includes you. Take a breather. You've earned it.

Afternoon Adventures
- **Project Time:** Dive into a fun project. Maybe it's a craft, building a fort, or starting a garden. The idea is to work together on something tangible.

It's hands-on learning and bonding time rolled into one.

- **Poetry Picnic:** If weather permits, go outside with a blanket and snacks (if not full from lunch). Enjoy reading poetry together. Each person can choose a favorite poem to share.

- **Wrap-Up Session:** Gather everyone back together. Reflect on the day. What did they love? What was challenging? Share what everyone is looking forward to tomorrow. Keep it positive and light. This isn't the time for critiques, just observations. Celebrate the victories, no matter how small.

End the Day Early

Kick 'em out early (from the school table, not the house). Let them absorb the shock or thrill of learning at home while they decompress with their favorite activities. Conclude lessons by lunchtime or shortly after to ensure the first day isn't overwhelming and leaves your kids eager for more. This would be a great time to instill character traits by having everyone clean up. Teach them that part of learning at home is taking care of your space. Make it a game—who can tidy up the fastest? Teamwork makes the dream work.

---------- **Summary** ----------

Well, look at that—you've survived the first day of homeschool! Take a deep breath and reflect on what you've accomplished. The goal of this first day was to ease into the homeschooling routine, set a positive tone, and foster an environment where curiosity and learning thrive. By ending the day early and keeping activities light, you've hopefully left your children feeling enthusiastic and curious about what's to come.

As you move forward, use the insights gained from today to tweak your plans and schedules as needed. Celebrate the day's end as a family. Share a special dinner, take a walk together, or enjoy a family game night. These moments of connection are just as important as academic success, reinforcing the joy and the shared journey of learning at home.

Keep the lines of communication open, remain adaptable, and continue to nurture the love of learning that today has sparked. With the day's activities behind you and a sense of achievement in the air, let's move on to making homeschooling a lifestyle for you and your family. This will help you maintain this positive momentum and ease into a consistent routine for the future. Here's to many more days of discovery, growth, and joy in your homeschooling adventure!

P.S. Don't forget to take pictures!

PART III -
THE HOMESCHOOLING
LIFESTYLE

Welcome to the heart and soul of homeschooling! Part III dives into the everyday rhythm of homeschool life, from finding your teaching mojo to busting the myth that homeschoolers lack social lives (trust me, their social calendars are packed!). We'll explore the artistry of teaching, proving that passion trumps degrees any day. Plus, get ready to navigate the bustling, fun-filled world of homeschool conventions—where victory and sore feet often go hand in hand. We'll also share tips on assessing progress in engaging and practical ways. These chapters celebrate the vibrant, dynamic nature of homeschooling, showing how it seamlessly integrates with family life and community connections.

12

Teaching & Learning Styles
Teacher, Know Thyself (and Your Student)

If a child can't learn the way we teach, maybe we should teach the way they learn.

— Ignacio Estrada

As a homeschooling parent, you're not just a teacher; you're a guide, mentor, and sometimes, a fellow explorer. One of the trickiest riddles you'll encounter is figuring out how your child learns best. Understanding your child's learning style is like having the ultimate decoder ring—it unlocks the secret to making learning enjoyable and effective. Whether your child learns best by seeing, hearing, or doing, I've got strategies to help you tailor your approach to their unique needs. And let's not forget about you—the teacher. Knowing your teaching style is just as important. It helps you create a homeschooling experience that's not only educational but also fun and fulfilling.

With so many options and paths to choose from, it can feel like you're navigating an ocean of lesson plans, learning materials, DIY projects, and educational philosophies. Rest assured, this chapter serves as your trusty compass, helping you steer through the waves and chart a course through the vast sea of teaching and learning styles.

KNOW YOUR CHILD'S LEARNING STYLE

Have you ever found yourself scratching your head, trying to decipher how your child learns best? You're not alone. It's like a big mystery sometimes. Every child has their own unique approach to picking up new stuff, and it's up to us to uncover their learning style and help them shine. Are they a visual learner—captivated by images and colors, or perhaps an auditory learner—their ears perked and focused while absorbing every word of a gripping story? Or maybe a kinesthetic learner eager to touch and manipulate objects to better understand them? Or a combination of these? What about intelligences?

Are your eyes glazing over yet? Don't worry—you don't need a PhD in psychology to understand how your child learns best. With a little know-how, some determination, and a dose of good old-fashioned elbow grease, you can unlock their full potential. Howard Gardner's theory of multiple intelligences tells us that every child has a unique way of learning, whether it's through words, numbers, music, movement, or even social interaction. So let's dive in and discover your child's learning style once and for all!

Seeing is Believing—The Vibrant World of Visual Learners

Is your child captivated by vivid paintings and illustrations? Does she have a talent for recalling images, diagrams, or color-coded information? Is he gifted with an eye for detail and a strong ability to process information visually? They might be a visual learner. Visual learners benefit significantly and process information more effectively from a curriculum rich in videos, graphs, diagrams, charts, illustrations, and images. Opt for textbooks, workbooks, or other learning materials filled with visual aids to support their learning style. Visual learners also prefer to read and write down notes or instructions, as seeing them helps with comprehension. They tend to think in pictures and often use visualization techniques to remember information. Try these examples:

- Use story maps to visually organize characters, settings, and plot points.

- Use color-coded diagrams to illustrate different geometric concepts, such as the relationships between angles or the properties of different shapes.

- Create infographics or mind maps that highlight key historical events, figures, and timelines to see connections and grasp the broader context of historical developments.

Sound Minds—Tune into the Auditory Learning Experience

Can your child easily discern different notes in a melody or recall intricate conversations? They might be an auditory learner, their ears finely tuned to the symphony of sounds. Auditory learners prefer to learn through spoken instructions or lectures. They tend to process information better when it is presented to them in an auditory format, such as podcasts, speeches, or debates. Opt for learning resources that emphasize audio elements, like audiobooks, recorded lectures, or engaging discussions, to help them absorb information and excel in their studies. Look at these examples:

- Learn mathematical concepts through songs that explain operations, such as addition or division, or use rhythmic patterns to solve problems.

- Understand historical events by listening to documentaries or recordings of famous speeches.

- Engage deeply with literature by participating in group readings where each member reads a part aloud and discusses it afterward.

Move to Mastery—The Kinesthetic Connoisseur Learner

Does your child gravitate towards building intricate structures or find themselves tapping out a beat with their fingers? Introducing the kinesthetic learner, who thrives on connecting with the world through touch and movement. Kinesthetic learners excel in hands-on activities that allow them to physically interact with the material they are trying to understand. They tend to learn by doing, touching, moving, and experiencing the information first-hand. These learners tend to process information better when it is presented to them in engaging, interactive formats that involve physical activity or manipulation of objects. Choose educational materials that focus on hands-on learning, manipulatives, role-playing, teamwork, lab experiments, interactive workshops, field trips, group projects, and real-life problem-solving situations. Consider these examples:

- Understand geometry using manipulatives like pattern blocks or geoboards.

- Grasp physics principles by building and testing structures like bridges, catapults, or roller coasters.

- Improve writing skills by practicing on different surfaces, such as whiteboards while standing or use large movements, like writing with sidewalk chalk or in the air.

Tactile Treasures—Learn by Feeling and Doing

Does your child enjoy crafting, building models, or working with their hands? Introducing the tactile learner, who learns best through touch and manipulating objects. Tactile learners benefit from hands-on activities that involve creating, building, and exploring with their hands. These learners understand and remember information better when they can physically interact with it. Choose educational materials that incorporate tactile experiences, such as arts and crafts, model building, clay sculpting, tactile games, puzzles, and sensory activities. Consider these examples:

- Learn math concepts using tactile tools like counting beads, blocks, or abacuses.

- Understand history by creating dioramas, models, or timelines with physical materials.

- Improve spelling and vocabulary by forming words with letter tiles, clay, or sand.

- Enhance reading comprehension by reading a story using finger tracking or textured bookmarks.

Word Wizard—Unleash the Power of Verbal Learners

Does your child flourish when words, both spoken and written, take center stage? Do they revel in dissecting text, putting pen to paper, and engaging in animated debates? These language enthusiasts are masters of processing information through the spoken and written word. To satisfy their linguistic cravings, seek out learning resources that focus on reading, writing, and discussion-based activities.

For instance, they might benefit from reading aloud, participating in heated debates, sharing gripping narrations, or crafting stories and essays that showcase their understanding of concepts. Look for learning resources that emphasize rich, engaging texts, opportunities for written and oral expression, and collaborative, discussion-based activities to stimulate and challenge verbal learners. Here are a few more examples:

- Join a book club or discussion group and interpret themes found in literary masterpieces.

- Explain mathematical concepts or problems by talking through the steps out loud.

- Memorize scientific concepts using mnemonic devices, catchy rhymes, or clever acronyms.

- Conquer new vocabulary or grammar rules by playing word games, or exploring language apps designed to hone linguistic prowess.

Math Magician—Solve the Puzzle of Logical-Mathematical Learners

Got a little problem solver on your hands? Logical-mathematical learners are those who excel at reasoning, logic, and playing with numbers. Consider focusing on developing their logical and mathematical abilities by incorporating puzzles, strategy games, and real-world conundrums to flex their intellectual muscles. They tend to be interested in patterns, sequences, and the subtle dance of relationships. Choose learning resources that emphasize problem-solving, critical thinking, and a healthy dose of number-crunching to captivate these cerebral champions. They relish solving problems and dissecting information to reach mind-blowing conclusions. Learning resources to integrate into the curriculum can include Sudoku puzzles, chess, and brain teasers that dare them to deploy their analytical prowess. More challenges for our logical-mathematical heroes include:

- Explore the mysteries of probability and statistics through engaging experiments, like simulating coin tosses, dice rolls, or card games.

- Read mysteries or detective novels to practice critical thinking skills by following characters as they use logic and deduction to solve complex cases.

- Write brainteasers or riddles. Craft puzzles, riddles, or logic problems to help express analytical abilities through language.

- Engage with non-fiction books on mathematics, logic, or science. Read favorite subjects to build vocabulary and comprehension skills.

Nature's Classroom—Foster the Growth of Naturalistic Learners

Is your child captivated by the natural world, showing a keen interest in plants, animals, or ecosystems? They might be a naturalistic learner with a deep connection to nature and an innate curiosity about the living world. Adopt a curriculum that embraces nature-based learning, hands-on environmental studies, outdoor exploration, and observing natural phenomena. Mix in nature walks, gardening projects, and studying local flora and fauna to foster their connection with the natural world. For example, a naturalistic learner might better understand the concept of photosynthesis by observing the way plants grow in different environments. Think about these examples:

- Go to zoos and nature centers.

- Visit natural habitats and record observations on the plants and animals found there.

- Learn about the water cycle by observing the effects of evaporation, condensation, and precipitation in their local environment.

- Understand plant biology by growing a garden, observing changes, and recording data over time.

Deep Thinkers Unite—The Journey of Existential Learners

For the young philosopher, consider a teaching approach that fosters deep discussions, pondering the big questions of life, and exploring various cultural and religious perspectives. Existential learners are those who are interested in life's significant questions, such as the meaning of existence and the purpose of human life. They tend to learn best through exploring philosophical and spiritual concepts. For example, an existential learner might better understand the concept of free will by reading philosophical treatises on the subject or engaging them in activities such as discussing philosophical dilemmas, exploring ancient wisdom texts, and comparing various belief systems. Consider these examples:

- Debate ethical issues like climate change and its impact on future generations.

- Study philosophical concepts through classic literature that tackles existential themes.

- Analyze historical events from multiple ethical perspectives to understand their broader impact.

- Participate in meditation or mindfulness exercises to explore inner thoughts and self-awareness.

Mastering the Self—Inside the Mind of Intrapersonal Learners

Does your child exhibit introspection and self-awareness? Adopt a teaching method that encourages self-reflection, journaling, and independent exploration of emotions and thoughts. Incorporate activities like mindfulness exercises, reflective writing prompts, and opportunities for self-directed learning. Intrapersonal learners are those who prefer to work alone and introspectively. They tend to learn best through self-reflection, meditation, and introspection. They are interested in understanding their own emotions, motivations, and goals. Here are some examples:

- Set personal goals and track progress through journaling or using a goal-setting app.

- Understand their own decision-making process by reflecting on their experiences.

- Deepen self-awareness by practicing mindfulness meditation and reflecting on emotions and thoughts.

Social Superstars—The Landscape of Interpersonal Learners

Does your child thrive in group settings, displaying strong communication skills and empathy towards others? They might be an interpersonal learner with a gift for understanding and connecting with people. Interpersonal learners excel in social settings and prefer to learn through interaction and collaboration with others. They often have strong leadership qualities and can easily adapt to different roles within a group. Collaborative projects, group discussions, and interactive games are ideal for these learners. Encourage activities that involve teamwork, such as organizing a community service project or participating in group challenges, to develop their ability to work effectively with others. Try some of these examples:

- Develop negotiation skills by participating in group activities that require compromise and consensus-building.

- Strengthen public speaking skills by joining a debate club or presenting a topic of interest to a group.

- Gain a deeper understanding of a subject by participating in group projects or forming study groups with peers.

- Develop conflict resolution skills by engaging in role-playing scenarios or participating in team-building activities.

Picture Perfect—Unlock the Potential of Visual-Spatial Learners

Visual-spatial learners have a talent for understanding the world through images, maps, and spatial reasoning. They benefit from using diagrams, illustrations, and multimedia presentations to grasp complex ideas. Try incorporating graphic organizers, mind mapping, or educational videos to help them visualize concepts and relationships between ideas. For example, a visual-spatial learner might better understand a complex engineering design by looking at a detailed blueprint. Here are some examples:

- Bolster spatial reasoning by working with 3D models or virtual simulations and engaging with three-dimensional puzzles, like the Rubik's Cube or geometric dissection puzzles that defy the ordinary.

- Grasp historical events and timelines by examining detailed maps and visual timelines.

- Enhance reading comprehension through the use of storyboards or comic strips to visualize narrative elements.

Melodies of the Mind—Tap into Musical-Rhythmic Learners

For the young Mozart in your family, consider a teaching approach that integrates music, rhythm, and sound into the learning process. These learners excel when they can use melodies and rhythms to comprehend and retain information. Encourage activities such as creating musical parodies to remember facts, using mnemonic devices with rhythm or rhyme, or exploring the connections between music and math or language. Musical-rhythmic learners are those who have a strong sensitivity to rhythm, melody, and sound. They tend to learn best through musical activities, such as listening to music, singing, or playing an instrument. Examples include:

- Understand the structure of a song by analyzing its melody and rhythm.

- Improve memory by creating songs or rhymes to remember historical dates or scientific facts.

- Explore mathematical concepts through musical patterns and rhythms.

- Enhance language skills by singing songs in different languages or creating rhythmic poetry.

LEARN YOUR TEACHING STYLE

Deciding on your homeschooling approach starts with uncovering your unique teaching style. Do you thrive on the order of a structured curriculum with lesson plans that leave no stone unturned, prefer the freedom of an adaptable curriculum that dances to the beat of your daily rhythms, or find yourself comfortably perched somewhere in between? To make this choice a bit more fun, I've whipped up a tongue-in-cheek profile of different teaching styles. Spot one that sounds like you? Take note—it could be the secret sauce to your homeschooling success.

Types of Teaching Styles

1. Structured Instructor (Captain Plan-It)

- **Catchphrase:** *"If it's not in the lesson plan, it's not in the homeschool room!"*

- **Profile:** Captain Plan-It loves order and structure, resembling a librarian's passion for the Dewey Decimal System. Their homeschool room runs like a well-oiled machine, complete with schedules and syllabi. They use a grade book like a knight wields a sword, ready to conquer educational challenges with meticulous planning.

- **Look for:** A curriculum with clear lesson plans, assessments, and traditional grading systems, including extensive teacher guides that require active teaching roles. Pre-planned, pre-assessed, and pre-graded materials are essential.

- **Avoid:** Educational equivalents of jazz improvisation. Unschooling, self-taught programs, or overly independent study materials are not suitable.

2. Tech Whiz Teacher (Professor Pixel)

- **Catchphrase:** *"In the digital realm, we're all A students."*

- **Profile:** Professor Pixel transforms history lessons into immersive virtual reality journeys and math problems into exciting coding adventures. Their tech proficiency is so advanced, they might as well have programmed this profile themselves.

- **Look for:** Cutting-edge, digital-first platforms offering interactive lessons and rich multimedia content, leveraging the latest technological advancements.

- **Avoid:** Traditional, static teaching methods lacking interactivity and engagement, akin to relying on an old dial-up connection in a high-speed internet world.

3. Kinesthetic Captain (Sergeant Learn-a-Ton)

- **Catchphrase:** *"All hands-on deck and all minds in motion with our math manipulatives!"*

- **Profile:** Sergeant Learn-a-Ton believes learning is a tactile and kinesthetic journey. Every student is a vital crew member, navigating knowledge through hands-on exploration, with curricula full of interactive guides, manipulatives, and dynamic teaching tools.

- **Look for:** Engaging, interactive learning experiences encouraging physical involvement, and resources rich in manipulatives, laboratory experiments, and real-world applications.

- **Avoid:** Pedagogical approaches favoring isolated, sedentary learning.

4. Last-Minute/Lazy Maestro (Queen of the 11th-Hour)

- **Catchphrase:** *"Why plan ahead when you can improvise with flair?"*

- **Profile:** The Queen of the 11th-Hour is the champion of creative chaos, relying on last-minute inspirations. Their toolkit includes a whirlwind of spontaneous ideas, with minimal organization and impromptu lesson plans.

- **Look for:** Resources labeled "open-and-go," "no prep," or "low prep." Materials should be as straightforward as a microwave dinner—minimal fuss, maximum efficiency.

- **Avoid:** Curricula demanding extensive prep time. Steer clear of resources requiring significant customization, complex planning, or lots of manipualtives. If there's no pacing guide or a sample teaching week, run.

5. The Minimalist Mentor (Professor Just-Enough)

- **Catchphrase:** *"Less is more, except when it comes to coffee."*

- **Profile:** Professor Just-Enough embodies efficiency, with an uncluttered homeschooling space, lean lesson plans, and a simple grading system. They find shortcuts, pave them, and put up street signs for others to follow.

- **Look for:** Lesson plans or curricula labeled "open and go," "no-prep," or "low prep."

- **Avoid:** Teaching methods requiring more than two steps or complex project-based learning needing extensive supplies and planning.

6. The Free-Spirit Educator (Professor Whimsy-Wind)

- **Catchphrase:** *"Where the curriculum is made up, and the lesson plans don't matter."*

- **Profile:** Professor Whimsy-Wind is unpredictable, with a teaching space resembling a blend of a jungle gym and a bohemian art studio. Every lesson is an adventure, guided by spontaneous tangents rather than conventional plans.

- **Look for:** Lesson plans with phrases like "It's a surprise!" or "Let's see where the wind takes us!" Embrace materials that allow for spontaneous learning adventures.

- **Avoid:** Rigid structures or schedules. Traditional textbooks and standardized test prep materials are likely to be repurposed or ignored.

These examples should give you a clearer idea of what to look for or avoid in homeschool curricula based on your teaching style. Each teaching style and curriculum has its unique flavor, so it's all about finding the right recipe that suits your educational taste!

---------- **Summary** ----------

In this chapter, we've navigated the intricate maze of teaching and learning styles, uncovering the unique ways your child absorbs and processes information. Whether your child is a visual learner captivated by vivid imagery, an auditory learner tuned into the world of sounds, a kinesthetic learner thriving through touch and movement, or any combination of these, you've now got the tools to decode their learning preferences.

Understanding these styles isn't just about making your homeschooling journey smoother; it's about unlocking your child's potential and fostering a love for learning that lasts a lifetime. By tailoring your educational approach to match your child's strengths, you're setting the stage for success and ensuring that learning remains engaging and effective.

We've also touched on the importance of knowing yourself as a teacher. Recognizing your own teaching style and adapting it to fit your child's needs is the secret sauce that turns homeschooling from a daunting task into a delightful adventure.

So, as you move forward, keep this chapter as your guide. Embrace the diversity of learning styles, experiment with different approaches, and most importantly, stay flexible. Remember, if Plan A doesn't work, the alphabet has plenty more letters to try out. Happy homeschooling!

13

The Art of Teaching

Degrees Don't Make the Teacher

The essence of teaching is to make learning contagious, to have one idea spark another.

— Marva Collins

LIFE HAS A FUNNY way of taking us down roads we never expected to travel, and sometimes, it leads us to become teachers even if we didn't pursue a formal education in the field. The truth is, teaching is an art, and like any art, it doesn't always require a degree or a wealth of knowledge to be good at it. In this chapter, we'll explore why teaching is more of an art than a science and how passion, empathy, and adaptability are the real keys to being an effective educator. Don't believe me? Let me give you some examples to help prove my point.

Take the story of Angela. She's a stay-at-home mom who was suddenly thrust into the role of a teacher when her children's school shut down due to the worldwide pandemic. Angela had no formal training in education, but she knew her kids better than anyone. She took it upon herself to teach them in a way that made sense to them. By incorporating their interests into her lessons, she made learning engaging and enjoyable. Even without a degree, Angela discovered that teaching is about understanding your children and adapting your methods to their unique needs.

Another great example is Marcus, a young entrepreneur who found himself mentoring aspiring business owners in his community. With no prior teaching experience, Marcus relied on his first-hand experience and passion for entrepreneurship to guide his lessons. By sharing his successes and failures, he was able to provide a real-world perspective that resonated with his students. They appreciated his honesty, and his informal teaching style helped them gain confidence in their abilities. Ultimately, Marcus's ability to connect with his students and share valuable insights made him an effective teacher, regardless of his lack of formal qualifications.

And let's not forget about Tasha, a retired professional dancer who decided to share her love of dance by teaching classes at her local community center. Tasha had never set foot in a classroom as a teacher, but she was a master of her craft. She understood the importance of breaking down complex steps into simple, manageable parts and demonstrated patience and kindness with her students. As a result, Tasha's classes flourished, and her students found joy in the art of dance. It wasn't her formal education that made Tasha an exceptional teacher, but rather her passion, empathy, and ability to communicate effectively.

So, what do these examples tell us? They illustrate that the true art of teaching lies in an individual's ability to connect with their students, communicate effectively, and adapt to their specific needs. While a degree in education or a wealth of knowledge may be helpful, it isn't the be-all and end-all of successful teaching.

What's essential is a teacher's ability to inspire, engage, and guide their students in a way that encourages growth and development. It's the emotional connection, patience, and understanding that fosters a love of learning and leaves a lasting impact on students' lives. I highly recommend watching the movie *The Marva Collins Story* to see how she truly embodies the art of teaching. You can watch it for free on YouTube.

So, if you ever find yourself in a position to teach, don't worry about whether you have the right qualifications or the most in-depth knowledge. Instead, focus on getting to know your children, understanding their needs, and adapting your approach accordingly. The art of teaching lies in your hands—you just need to believe in yourself and be open to the learning process. Here are some strategies to incorporate.

HOW TO TEACH STUFF—TRICKS OF THE TRADE

Make Learning Fun with Humor

Children respond well to laughter and playfulness, so don't be afraid to incorporate jokes, funny stories, and light-hearted activities into your lessons. One way to do this is by creating silly mnemonics to help your child remember new information, such as wacky acronyms or funny phrases. Not only will this make learning more enjoyable, but it will also increase the likelihood of the information sticking.

Encourage Curiosity and Exploration

To foster a spirit of curiosity in your homeschooling, encourage your child to ask questions, explore new subjects, and dive deep into their interests. One effective technique is to have your child lead their own learning journey. For example, if they express an interest in a particular topic, let them research it, ask questions, and guide the direction of their studies. This will instill a sense of ownership and excitement about their education.

Develop Critical Thinking Skills

Encourage your child to think critically about the world around them, questioning assumptions and considering multiple perspectives. To build these skills, incorporate activities like debate, essay writing, and discussing current events in your lessons. Giving your child the opportunity to form and defend their own opinions will help them grow into thoughtful, well-rounded individuals.

Nurture Emotional Intelligence

Fostering emotional intelligence in your child is just as important as developing their academic skills. Encourage your child to express their feelings, listen actively, and empathize with others. Role-playing scenarios, journaling, and discussing characters' emotions in books or movies are all great ways to help your child develop emotional intelligence. This will equip them with the tools they need to navigate relationships and understand themselves better.

Set Realistic Goals—Shoot for the Moon (but Don't Get Lost in Space)

Designing a homeschool lesson plan is akin to plotting a route to the moon. You've got a destination in sight, but how do you get there without losing your way? Simple. Set waypoints or manageable goals. Consider the budding astronaut who aims to land on the moon. She doesn't just hop into a spaceship; first, she needs to learn the basics of physics and advanced mathematics, study astronomy, and maybe learn a thing or two about piloting. Now, imagine your child is that astronaut. Want him to master calculus? First, he needs to know arithmetic, then pre-algebra, and then algebra and so on. Each step is a manageable goal that eventually leads to the moon.

Celebrate Personal Growth

As a homeschooling parent, it's essential to recognize and celebrate your child's growth, both academically and personally. Regularly acknowledge your child's accomplishments and progress, no matter how small. This will boost their confidence and reinforce the idea that learning is a lifelong journey filled with ups and downs.

Make Space for Creativity

Encourage your child to develop their own creative skills by providing ample opportunities for artistic expression, writing, and other creative outlets. Some ideas to foster creativity include setting up a designated arts and crafts area, participating in local theater or writing workshops, and encouraging your child to create their own stories or poetry.

Embrace the Power of Storytelling

Storytelling is a powerful tool for teaching, and it can bring concepts to life in a memorable and relatable way. Use stories, both fiction and non-fiction, to explore new subjects and ideas with your child. Incorporate story-based activities in your homeschooling routine, such as reading aloud, watching educational films or documentaries, and discussing the themes and lessons found in various stories. This will not only help your child retain information but also develop critical thinking and communication skills.

Foster a Love of Learning

A cornerstone of homeschooling is nurturing a love of learning that lasts a lifetime. Encourage your child to take ownership of their education and view learning as an exciting adventure rather than a chore. You can do this by following their interests, allowing them to set their own goals, and celebrating their achievements. Remember to keep a positive attitude toward learning and model the joy and curiosity you wish to instill in your child.

Emphasize the Importance of Resilience

Teaching your child the value of resilience is crucial for their success in both homeschooling and life in general. Discuss with your child the importance of learning from mistakes, embracing challenges, and developing a growth mindset. Share your own experiences and model resilience in your daily life, showing your child that setbacks can lead to growth and new opportunities.

Cultivate a Supportive Community

Homeschooling can be a solitary experience, but it doesn't have to be! Build a supportive community of fellow homeschoolers, educators, and friends who share your values and approach to teaching. Join local homeschooling groups, attend workshops or conferences, and participate in online forums or social media groups. This will provide you and your child with valuable connections, resources, and inspiration to help you succeed on your homeschooling journey.

Encourage Independent Learning

Encouraging your children to work independently on certain subjects can also save you time and money. For example, older children can work on math or language arts while younger children work on art projects or reading. This approach not only allows you to focus on teaching the subjects that require more attention but also helps your children develop their own independent learning skills.

Laughing Through Literature

One way to foster a love of reading while incorporating humor is to introduce your child to funny books and authors. There's no shortage of hilarious literature out there, from the absurd adventures of Roald Dahl to the witty wordplay of Lemony Snicket. Not only will your child develop their reading skills, but they'll also learn that literature can be as entertaining as it is enlightening. Who knows, they might even be inspired to pen their own comedic masterpiece!

THE ART OF TEACHING IN ACTION—TIPS AND TRICKS

As we continue discussing how to homeschool, it can be helpful to see examples of how these strategies and techniques can be implemented in real-life situations. Let's take a look.

Real-Life Example #1—Foster Creativity

Meet Maria and her daughter Isabella, who have been homeschooling for two years. Maria noticed Isabella's passion for storytelling, so she decided to incorporate creative writing into their homeschooling routine. They set up a cozy writing nook in their home, complete with colorful stationery and inspirational quotes on the walls. Each week, Maria and Isabella explore a new writing prompt, allowing Isabella to express her thoughts and ideas through stories and poems. This creative outlet has not only helped Isabella improve her writing skills but also boosted her confidence and love of learning.

Real-Life Example #2—Embrace the Power of Storytelling

John is a single father homeschooling his son, Noah. John decided to use storytelling to teach Noah about historical events. They began a project where they would read historical fiction novels and watch films based on true events. After each story, they would discuss the events, characters, and themes to help Noah understand the broader historical context. Through this storytelling approach, Noah developed a deep interest in history and improved his critical thinking and communication skills.

Real-Life Example #3—Cultivate a Supportive Community

Diane and her two children recently started homeschooling. To build a supportive network, Diane joined a local homeschool co-op, where families gather to share resources, participate in group activities, and support each other in their homeschooling journey. Through the co-op, Diane's children made new friends while she connected with other homeschooling parents who shared her educational philosophy. The co-op's collaborative and supportive environment had enriched their homeschooling experience and helped them navigate any challenges they might have faced.

Real-Life Example #4—Teach Resilience Through Life Lessons

When nine-year-old Jevon struggled with his math lessons, his homeschooling mother, Yvette, saw it as an opportunity to teach resilience. Rather than becoming frustrated or discouraged, Yvette encouraged Jevon to see his mistakes as learning experiences. Together, they discussed the importance of perseverance and how setbacks can lead to personal growth. Yvette shared her own struggles and successes, emphasizing that everyone faces challenges at some point. With this mindset, Jevon began to approach his math lessons with a more positive attitude, viewing each obstacle as an opportunity to learn and improve.

BUILD YOUR TEACHER TOOLBOX

Use Pop-Culture References

Embrace today's trending topics. When teaching geometry and discussing parallel lines, you might say, "Parallel lines are like Tom and Jerry. They run side by side but never meet, no matter how long they chase each other!" By likening concepts to familiar stories, your child can grasp and recall information with ease.

Movie Magic for the Win

While discussing ecosystems in biology, you could mention, "Just like the various districts in 'The Hunger Games', each ecosystem has its own set of rules and inhabitants that thrive in those conditions." Using films or tv shows help make abstract ideas tangible and relatable.

Tap into Chart-Topping Hits

During a lesson about poetic structures, consider saying, "Remember how Michael Jackson's (or any popular artist) songs have a unique rhythm and style? Poets, too, have their distinctive patterns and beats!" This can help your child understand and appreciate the rhythm and beauty of poetry.

Sports Analogies Work Wonders

If teaching about momentum in physics, you might say, "It's just like when Lionel Messi gains speed with the ball; the momentum makes it hard for defenders to stop him!" Using well-known sports figures can make theoretical concepts feel more real and approachable.

Popular Video Games to the Rescue

When discussing urban planning or civilization building, you could draw a parallel with, "It's similar to constructing and managing your city in 'SimCity'. Every choice impacts the growth and health of your virtual population!" This can foster understanding by relating to games your child might be familiar with.

Celebrate the Small Stuff

Whether it's your child mastering a tricky math problem or the entire family surviving a hectic science experiment gone awry, celebrate the small victories. Turn these moments into cherished memories, laugh about the mishaps, and give yourself credit for being a resilient, creative, and dedicated homeschooling parent.

Introduce Friendly Competitions

Add a dash of playful rivalry to your homeschooling routine with friendly competitions that encourage humor and creativity. For example, hold a poetry contest where the objective is to create the funniest limerick or haiku, or organize a storytelling challenge where each person has to improvise a short, silly story based on three random words. The person with the most laughs wins, and the "loser" might have to wear a goofy costume during the next lesson.

As we explore more examples of homeschooling finesse, let's once again see how these techniques can be applied in everyday situations to create engaging and memorable learning experiences.

TEACHING IN ACTION—MORE REAL-LIFE EXAMPLES

Real-Life Example #5—Math Word Problems

Instead of using typical word problems to teach math, Carol decided to incorporate her son Langston's love for superheroes. She created math problems involving superheroes planning daring rescues, like "If Batman needs 15 gadgets for each mission and he has 4 missions this week, how many gadgets does he need in total?" Langston found these scenarios exciting and engaging, leading to a newfound appreciation for math.

Real-Life Example #6—Vocabulary Lessons

Shen wanted to make vocabulary lessons more enjoyable for her daughter, Mei. Instead of using traditional flashcards, Shen challenged Mei to create silly sentences using the new words they learned. By adding humor to these sentences, Mei found it much easier to remember the meanings and use of the words in her daily conversations.

Real-Life Example #7—Science Experiments with a Twist

When teaching her children about the solar system, Julie decided to add a touch of whimsy by using fruit to represent the planets. They created a fruit solar system, with watermelons as Jupiter, oranges as Mars, and strawberries as Earth. This amusing and hands-on approach helped her children better understand the relative sizes and distances of the planets, and it certainly made for a tasty learning experience!

Real-Life Example #8—Witty Spelling Bees

For their weekly spelling bees, Elizabeth added a humorous twist to keep her kids engaged. Instead of just spelling the words, they were required to use them in a funny sentence or even sing them to a familiar tune. The sillier, the better! This light-hearted approach to spelling made the activity far more enjoyable and memorable for Elizabeth's children.

MORE TEACHING FUN—EXTRA TIPS AND TRICKS

Building a homeschooler's toolkit with clever strategies can be a game-changer, especially for parents who need to keep lessons lively and flexible. Here are five more tips and tricks to boost your homeschooling game.

1. **Learning through Games:** Incorporate educational games (especially board games) into your lessons. Board games like 'Scrabble' can boost vocabulary and spelling skills, while 'Monopoly' introduces kids to basic math and financial concepts. 'Catan' teaches strategic thinking and resource management, and 'Trivial Pursuit' can enhance general knowledge. Games like these make learning enjoyable and can be very effective in reinforcing material in a dynamic way.

2. **Incorporate Real-World Skills:** Use everyday tasks as teaching moments. Cooking can teach measurements and fractions; shopping can help with budgeting and math skills; and gardening can introduce concepts of biology and ecology. This method helps children see the practical application of their studies and keeps them engaged with hands-on learning.

3. **Theme Days:** Spice up your teaching schedule with themed learning days. For example, have a "NASA Day" where all subjects revolve around space exploration, or a "Back in Time" day focusing on a specific historical period. This not only makes learning more fun but also allows for deep dives into particular subjects.

4. **Multi-Age Projects:** If you're teaching multiple age groups, design projects that each child can contribute to at their own level. For instance, while working on a family newsletter, younger children can draw or dictate stories, and older children can type and edit the content. This encourages teamwork and helps children learn from each other.

5. **Mystery Subject:** Add a dash of excitement to your routine by introducing a 'mystery subject' once a week or month, where your children won't know what they're learning until the lesson starts. This could mean a surprise guest speaker (perfect if you're part of a co-op or charter

school), an unexpected virtual field trip, a brand-new documentary, or a hands-on project they didn't see coming. You can also try themed cooking lessons, spontaneous science experiments, surprise scavenger hunts, or impromptu art workshops. The element of surprise turns these lessons into thrilling and unforgettable learning adventures

---------- **Summary** ----------

The essence of teaching transcends formal qualifications, relying instead on the ability to inspire, connect, and adapt to children's needs. By incorporating humor, fostering curiosity, encouraging critical thinking, and nurturing emotional intelligence, educators can create an engaging and supportive learning environment. Celebrating personal growth, promoting creativity, and emphasizing resilience further enrich the educational experience. Ultimately, the true art of teaching lies in cultivating a love of learning and guiding children on their unique educational journeys with empathy, passion, and adaptability. Keep it fun, keep it creative, and you're not just teaching—you're inspiring a lifelong love for learning in your child. And that is the art of teaching!

14

The Socialization Myth

Yes, My Homeschooled Kids Have Friends

True socialization is not about being surrounded by people, but about connecting deeply with the ones who matter.

– Unknown

ALRIGHTY, SO LET ME just, you know, adjust my lovely monocle and read this stoic dictionary definition of socialization:

"Socialization is the process by which we learn and internalize the norms, values, and behaviors needed to be accepted in society."- Oxford English Dictionary

Wow, that's a tall order. I mean, have you met people? Sometimes, it feels like no matter what you do, you're bound to offend someone, especially these days. Confusing, right?

In this chapter, we're busting the myth of the unsocialized homeschooler wide open. We'll explore what socialization really means, tackle common misconceptions, and share practical tips for ensuring your homeschooled kids have plenty of social interactions. Spoiler alert: Homeschoolers aren't just socialized—they often thrive socially in ways traditional school settings can't always match.

So, let's really deconstruct the "S" word.

What is Socialization, Anyway?

The answer is not as simple as grabbing that Oxford dictionary or consulting a panel of experts. Socialization, my dear friend, is the wondrous art of navigating the perilous waters of awkward small talk, deciphering the cryptic meanings behind text messages (with no facial expressions or tone to guide you), and facing your fears as you attempt to master the rare skill of recognizing sarcasm without offending your peers. It's about avoiding getting cornered by that overly chatty neighbor who can't take a hint and, most importantly, not forgetting to unmute yourself during a video call as you passionately present your brilliant ideas to a bewildered audience.

So, now that we have a realistic (although quite long) operational definition of socialization to work with, let's talk about some of these myths surrounding it.

The Myth of the Unsocialized Homeschooler

One of the biggest myths about homeschooling is the so-called "bubble" effect. Critics claim homeschoolers are isolated and cut off from real-world interactions. But the reality is quite different. Homeschooling families often seek out diverse social opportunities, actively participating in community events, sports teams, and cultural activities.

Consider the Johnson family, who live in a rural area but keep a packed social calendar. They attend local 4-H meetings, participate in a regional homeschool soccer league, and organize monthly field trips with other homeschooling families. These activities give their kids plenty of chances to interact with peers and adults, ensuring a well-rounded social experience.

Another myth is that homeschoolers lack social skills. However, research consistently shows that homeschoolers often excel in social competencies. They tend to engage with people of various ages, fostering a broader range of social interactions. Many homeschoolers are deeply involved in their communities, volunteering, participating in public speaking clubs like Toastmasters, and even engaging in local politics.

Picture this: while conventionally schooled kids are stuck in their age-specific classrooms, learning the art of social interaction through the lens of a single grade, homeschoolers are on a grand adventure. They're exploring the social jungle beyond their own age bracket, befriending both the wise old owls and the eager young squirrels. They're not just bound to people who share their favorite pastimes but get the chance to dip their toes into a medley of hobbies and skills.

From teaming up with fellow soccer enthusiasts to joining a local chess club or even serving up a steaming bowl of community service, homeschoolers have an entire social smorgasbord at their fingertips. So, let's raise a toast to homeschooling and socialization, for they are truly the unlikeliest of homies!

Now that we've established the possibility and advantage of socializing homeschooled kids, let's investigate some effective strategies to get your homeschooled children to intermingle and enjoy the company of others.

CREATE SOCIAL OPPORTUNITIES

Ensuring that homeschooled kids are well-socialized requires some creativity and planning, but it's totally doable. One great strategy is leveraging community resources. Libraries, museums, and community centers often offer programs specifically for homeschoolers. For example, many libraries host book clubs, science workshops, and art classes tailored for different age groups. These programs provide educational enrichment and help kids make new friends.

Homeschool co-ops are another fantastic resource. These parent-led groups organize regular classes, field trips, and social events, creating a supportive community where kids can learn and socialize together. Co-ops cover a wide range of subjects, from STEM to the arts, allowing kids to explore their interests while making friends.

Virtual socialization is also a big deal, especially nowadays. Online platforms offer interactive classes, discussion forums, and virtual meet-ups that connect homeschoolers from around the world. These platforms can broaden their social horizons and introduce them to diverse perspectives.

Family and neighborhood involvement can further enhance socialization. Simple activities like family game nights, neighborhood playdates, and community events offer valuable opportunities for kids to develop social skills in a familiar and supportive environment.

By being proactive and resourceful, homeschooling parents can ensure their kids meet and exceed their socialization needs. The key is to embrace the flexibility that homeschooling offers and to seek out diverse and enriching social experiences.

OVERCOME CHALLENGES IN SOCIALIZATION

While homeschooling offers tons of benefits, it's not without its challenges. Socialization can be trickier for families in remote areas or those with kids of different ages. But don't worry—these hurdles are totally surmountable with a little creativity and effort.

Dealing with Isolation in Remote Areas

For families living in rural or isolated areas, finding social opportunities can be tough. However, technology and a bit of ingenuity can bridge these gaps. Online communities and virtual co-ops offer great resources for connecting with other homeschoolers. Platforms like Zoom and Outschool.com facilitate virtual classes, group projects, and social hangouts, giving kids the interaction they need.

Take the Pelfrey family from a remote farming community. They initially struggled with socialization but found a solution by joining an online home-school co-op. Jane, who loves science, enrolled in a virtual biology class. She learned a lot and made friends from different states. Tom joined a virtual drama club and got to perform in online plays and connect with like-minded peers. These experiences boosted their confidence and social skills.

The Pelfrey's also started a local nature club, inviting neighboring families to join bi-weekly nature walks and educational outings. These activities not only provided social interaction but also enriched their learning experiences.

Managing Diverse Age Groups

Homeschooling multiple kids of different ages can be a logistical challenge, but it also offers unique social opportunities. Mixed-age interactions can foster mentoring relationships, teamwork, and empathy. Older kids can help teach younger siblings, reinforcing their own knowledge and developing leadership skills. Younger kids can learn new skills and concepts more quickly by observing and interacting with their older siblings, who may introduce them to more advanced ideas and activities. See Chapter 10 on "Teaching Multiple Children" for more information.

The Colby family, with children ranging from toddlers to teenagers, found success by integrating mixed-age activities. They organized weekly family read-aloud sessions where everyone participated. The older kids took turns reading and discussing the stories, which improved their reading and leadership skills. The younger ones contributed by asking questions and sharing their thoughts, fostering a collaborative learning environment.

The Colby's also incorporated multi-age projects like gardening and cooking, which encouraged teamwork and skill-sharing among siblings. These activities taught valuable life skills while providing plenty of social interaction.

ONE SURPRISING (BUT TRUE) REASON WHY HOME-SCHOOL KIDS STRUGGLE WITH SOCIAL SKILLS

Alright, listen up. I know we've been talking about how the idea of homeschoolers lacking social skills is a big fat myth. And for the most part, it is. But let's not pretend there's zero truth to it.

This claim that homeschool kids struggle with social skills may be tough to accept, especially when homeschooling parents assert that their children are either social maestros or introverts who don't desire interactions with others. While this may be their truth, it could potentially lead to a lax attitude that might cause issues such as loneliness, social anxiety, or even depression in the long run. The positive portrayal of homeschooled children's social skills is often due to proactive parents who actively arrange social activities for their children, not just confining them to home-based learning.

So, what's the plan? Send our kids back to public school? Stuff their schedule with every social event under the sun? Certainly not. Instead, it's about finding a balance. My concern is that new homeschooling parents might believe that their children's social lives will naturally fall into place with little to no effort on their part.

So, I suggest keeping an eye on things. For example, how much free time is your kid spending with other kids? I'm talking about unstructured, fun time where kids can be kids. How hard are you working to ensure your child has this kind of time? Are social activities considered as important as academic stuff in your homeschool?

Also, do you make sure your kids have time to build and nurture close friendships, just like you ensure they have the best curriculum? Who are their best friends? If they had a birthday party, who would they invite first? If these questions make you squirm, don't sweat it. But, we have to be honest with ourselves about the self-imposed challenges we place on our children's socialization experiences. So, let's talk about it.

SOCIALIZATION CHALLENGES (WITH SOLUTIONS!)

I understand if you're feeling annoyed with me right now. Believe me, setting up frequent social activities for your children is no easy task. Been there, done that. I'm here to offer you some incredibly useful advice to simplify this whole situation. First, go through the listed "challenges" below (with solutions), select the top three that resonate with your life, and then aim to put at least ONE solution into practice. Give it a try—you're fully capable of this!

Common Excuses Used to NOT Socialize

1. Baby-Napping Dilemma

"We prefer to do schoolwork in the morning, but the baby naps in the afternoon. So, when do we meet friends?"
- **Solution:** How about arranging playdates during the baby's nap time at your place? This way, your older kid gets to socialize, the baby gets their nap, and you get a breather. Or, homeschool during naptime and socialize in the morning. The baby can nap on you in a baby carrier or in the stroller.

2. Ghost Neighbors
"People drive into their garages, and you never see them again. How can we make friends in the neighborhood?"
- **Solution:** If people are disappearing into their garages, take the initiative. Bake some cookies, take them over, and introduce yourself (Introverts: get a gift basket or something you can safely leave at the front door with a note). Or, organize a block party or a neighborhood kid's day in a local park. This could be a great way to build connections.

3. Soccer Practice Silence
"Everyone is on their phones during practice!"
- **Solution:** Be the initiator! Start a conversation with other parents. Propose a rotating schedule whereby parents take turns organizing snacks or activities after practice. This fosters interaction among kids and parents.

If you're an introvert, position yourself near the loudest, most out-going, or friendliest parent and wait patiently for them to engage you in conversation. Rest assured, they will—either soon or eventually.

4. Burnt Out From Homeschooling

"After homeschooling all day, the last thing I want to do is head to the park or a playdate."

- **Solution:** Why not try a cooperative approach? Team up with other homeschooling parents and take turns hosting playdates. This way, your kid gets to socialize, and you get some downtime.

5. Frequent Movers

"We move so often, it's hard to build a solid social circle!"

- **Solution:** Moving often can indeed make it hard to build lasting re-lationships. But joining local homeschooling groups or community activities in your new area can speed up the process. Also, main-taining friendships from previous places through online playdates or pen pal exchanges can provide a sense of continuity.

6. Bad Weather Blues

"The weather's terrible. All I want to do is stay in!"

- **Solution:** Virtual hangouts to the rescue! Organize an online trivia night, a book club, or even a craft session. Or use the time indoors to build deeper connections with family—game nights, cooking together, movie marathons, you name it!

7. Health Issues

"My child (or myself) has a health issue that makes frequent social outings challenging."

- **Solution:** Take advantage of online platforms for social interaction. Many forums, clubs, and virtual classes provide opportunities for children to engage with others. Outschool.com is a wonderful plat-form to find these outlets. If possible, arrange for friends to visit your home or have gentle outdoor activities. Keep communication open with your child about their social needs and comfort levels.

8. Scheduling Conflicts

"My child's friends have different school schedules. It's hard to find common free time."

- **Solution:** Use weekends and holidays to your advantage. Organize playdates, sleepovers, or fun outings during these times. Additionally, participating in community or extracurricular activities that take place after traditional school hours can provide a consistent opportunity for socialization.

9. Stigma of Homeschooling

"People tend to stereotype and isolate homeschooled children."

- **Solution:** Make it a point to join homeschooling groups in your community, where your child can meet other homeschooled kids and engage in group activities. Also, open up dialogue with people who have misconceptions about homeschooling to educate them on your choice.

10. Differing Age Groups

"My children are of vastly different ages. How can they all socialize together?"

- **Solution:** Look for activities that cater to a wide age range, like community service projects, family game nights, or nature hikes. Encourage your older children to include the younger ones in their activities. This promotes bonding while teaching valuable leadership skills to the older kids. Many organized homeschool groups recognize this and offer services/classes for multiple ages for this very reason.

11. Social Anxiety

"My child (or me) is introverted or has social anxiety.

- **Solution:** Gradually introduce your child to new social situations. Start with smaller, less intimidating gatherings before gradually moving up to larger events (if desired). This experience could help your child find that one friend they truly bond with on a deeper level. Seek professional help if necessary, and always ensure that your child feels heard and supported.

12. Lack of Local Homeschool Groups

"There aren't any homeschool groups nearby."

- **Solution:** Consider starting one! You might be surprised by how many homeschooling families are in your area feeling the same way. Use social media to reach out and create your group. If starting a group isn't feasible, try reaching out to online homeschool communities. These can provide support, resources, and virtual socialization opportunities.

13. Socialization, Why Bother?

"Everyone says socialization is no biggie for homeschoolers. Why bother?"

- **Solution:** If people keep saying socialization isn't a big deal for home-schoolers, remind yourself that social skills are just as vital as academics. They help your kid build relationships, communicate effectively, and handle social situations. So, it's worth the effort!

14. Where are the Kids?

"I never see any homeschooled kids in our area!"

Solution: Sadly, we live in a time where most kids are not outside ripping and running and being kids. It's common to find that many children, whether home-schooled or not, spend a significant amount of time indoors. Consider enrolling your children in afterschool activities, local clubs, or community sports teams. These settings are excellent for meeting other children, both homeschooled and those attending public or private schools. Additionally, participating in commu-nity events, library programs, or group classes can also provide valuable social interaction and help integrate your children into a broader social network.

Do these excuses sound familiar? If you're nodding your head, I'd urge you to stop buying into the idea that "Homeschool Socialization is a Myth!" For some people, it might be because they've already got a great system in place. For others, it could be an excuse to ignore their child's social needs. I'm just saying let's strive for excellence in our kids' social lives like we do with their academic lives. Ok, let's lighten things up and talk about what you can do to get your socialization fix on.

FOMO NO MORE!

The Secret Sauce to Master Socializing

One of the most important steps in fostering socialization is building your dream team. This is about assembling a solid support network for you and your kids. Who said homeschooling is a lonely business? Quite the contrary. We've got homeschooling groups, parent forums, online communities, and even that friendly, knowledgeable librarian down the street. Your dream team might be your homeschooling veteran neighbor, your childhood bestie who's also homeschooling, or the family across town with kids the same age as yours. Let's not forget the power of the Internet. Many homeschooling parents have blogs or YouTube channels (ahem... humbly raising my hand) where they share their experiences, advice, and resources. So, folks, don't be shy; find your peeps and stick together!

Next, we're going local. No, we're not talking about farmers' markets. We're talking about local homeschool groups, events, and playground takeovers. Many areas have established homeschooling groups that host various activities like co-op classes, field trips, and playdates. If your area doesn't have one, guess what? You can start one. These groups offer a great opportunity for your children to build lasting friendships and experience group dynamics similar to traditional school environments. *Pro tip: There are many Facebook homeschool groups or homeschool-related groups. Find one in your neck of the woods and join.*

Getting involved in your community is an enriching experience that can provide numerous benefits. Volunteering is a prime example of this, serving as a wonderful way to meet new people and provide your children with an opportunity to interact with individuals from various age groups. Potential volunteering opportunities abound in places like hospitals, libraries, or animal shelters, all of which could benefit from an extra set of hands. In addition, community events such as festivals and parades offer fun social time and a chance to strengthen ties with local residents.

On a more personal level, exploring your child's passions can prove highly beneficial. One way to do this is by finding a team, club, or creative collective that aligns with their interests. This not only gives your child the chance to mingle with like-minded youngsters, but it also helps them grow in their chosen field. Encourage them to participate in local theater or drama clubs, which provide a platform for homeschooled virtuosos to unite, perform on stage, and forge lifelong friendships and memories.

Moreover, you can jump into various fields of interest, such as robotics, gardening, or chess, by seeking out local clubs and meetups. These platforms can spark new interests and allow your child to make friends who share their curiosity. Homeschooled children can also embark on linguistic and cultural adventures by joining language groups or cultural clubs. By exploring the rich tapestry of human diversity together, they can build friendships while broadening their perspectives.

Lastly, encourage your children to tap into their inner Hemingway, Ansel Adams, or Julia Child by enrolling in workshops, camps, or classes tailored to their specific interests. This not only sharpens their skills but also provides them an opportunity to make friends and partake in social activities. As your child navigates through these experiences, they'll find not only academic growth but also social development and friendship.

DIGITAL DIALOGUES

Build Connection in the Digital Classroom

In this techno-tastic age we find ourselves in, social media and online forums are the perfect vehicles for homeschoolers to ride the wave of virtual connection. Social media platforms are also ideal for sharing triumphs, commiserating over challenges, and reveling in camaraderie—with vetted peeps.

Whether they're bonding over the latest Minecraft creation or swapping sonnets in a poetry group, there's a world of online interaction at their fingertips. Online forums open the door to lively discourse, fresh perspectives, and the occasional meme-slinging battle. Virtual clubs and study groups let kids collaborate on projects, swap ideas, or indulge in friendly competition. But be warned. The digital dance floor isn't without its perils. Keep a watchful eye on your child's online escapades, ensuring that their internet interactions remain safe and sound. Equip them with the skills to sidestep unsavory characters and dodge the dastardly pitfalls lurking in the depths of cyberspace.

LEARN IN THE WILD—FIELD TRIPS, SPORTS, AND ARTS

Field Trips and Frolics

The world's your oyster! Or, in this case, your classroom. Museums, nature reserves, factories, farms, you name it. Educational group field trips can be a fantastic way for kids to learn about different topics while socializing with each other. Plus, it's a blast! Think of it like this: it's not just learning; it's an adventure, an expedition into the wild unknown of knowledge. Just imagine your kids' faces when they see that dinosaur skeleton after studying the Jurassic period.

P.E. and Sports: The Great Escape

Remember dodgeball and relay races from your own school days? Well, home-schooling doesn't mean your kids will miss out. There are many local sports teams, dance classes, and martial arts dojos that welcome homeschoolers. Some communities and churches even have P.E. days specifically for homeschool groups. See? Your kids will still get their fair share of friendly competition and team spirit!

Arts and Enrichment

Homeschooling offers a unique opportunity to let your kids dive deep into their passions. Are they showing signs of a budding Picasso or Mozart? Do they have the makings of a future game designer? Or maybe they've got a flair for fashion design? You can nurture these talents through targeted homeschooling activities, local classes, online courses, and more. Unleashing your child's inner artist, programmer, or designer can make learning engaging, relevant, and fun.

So, next time your friends raise their eyebrows at your homeschooling decision, you'll know what to say. Your kids aren't missing out; they're gaining a tailored, engaging, well-rounded education—school dances and cafeteria lunches are not required!

INTROVERTS UNITE! . . . SEPARATELY

Six Homeschool Tips for Introverts

Calling all introverts and bookworms! If the idea of exchanging pleasantries at crowded playgrounds or navigating large gatherings sends a shiver down your spine, you're in the right place. You see, the world of homeschooling is not exclusively reserved for the social butterflies and extroverted powerhouses among us. Oh, no. In fact, it can be an introvert's paradise. Let's explore six ways to make homeschooling work for your introverted personality and how to create a learning experience that is both fulfilling and enjoyable.

Tip #1. Unleash the Power of Introversion! Contrary to popular belief, being introverted does not mean you lack social skills or can't thrive in the homeschooling world. In fact, your preference for quiet and thoughtful interactions can be a secret weapon when it comes to teaching. So, put on your thinking cap (we know you have one), and let's hatch a plan that highlights your unique strengths.

Tip #2. Get crafty with co-ops. The secret society of introverted homeschoolers is vast and thriving. Connect with like-minded parents through intimate online forums or support groups. You'll discover opportunities to join or form local homeschool co-ops that cater to your preferences. Sharing resources, planning events, and even coordinating classes can all be done without the razzmatazz of large social gatherings.

Tip #3. Embrace field trips—with a twist. Homeschooling allows you the freedom to explore the world on your own terms. Curate bespoke field trip experiences with visits to local museums, historical sites, or natural wonders at off-peak times or even virtually. By choosing less crowded settings, you can offer a more intimate, focused, and enjoyable learning experience for your child and yourself.

Tip #4. Foster social connections—the introvert way. Forget the pressure to sign up for every club, activity, or sports team in the neighborhood. Introverted parents can arrange playdates with one or two children at a time rather than large group activities. Similarly, introverted children might benefit from the quiet focus of one-on-one learning and smaller social engagements. So, seek out meaningful social interactions for your child by encouraging playdates with compatible peers, participating in smaller group activities, or enrolling them in clubs that align with their passions.

Tip #5. Celebrate the introvert in you and your child. Remind your mini-me that introversion is a gift, not a flaw. Emphasize the value of introspection, thoughtfulness, and creativity, which are often associated with introverted personalities. Foster a home environment that promotes self-awareness, self-acceptance, and resilience in the face of a world that often prioritizes extroverted traits.

Tip #6: Create a script. Sometimes kids are introverted or shy because they don't know how to enter or exit a conversation or gathering. Create a script and role play different common scenarios that your child would find themselves in and practice what they can say or do. Practice until they feel comfortable doing this in public.

As you stride boldly (or rather quietly and thoughtfully) into the realm of homeschooling, don't let your introverted nature hold you back. You've got the power to create a stimulating, engaging, and personalized learning experience for your child that even the most extroverted social butterflies will envy. Just remember: your introversion is your superpower, and with it, you can shape your homeschooling adventure to be as unique and extraordinary as you are. Now, go forth and conquer the educational landscape, one cozy, introspective step at a time!

DISARM THE DOUBTERS

Here's where you get to flex your witty repartee when naysayers enter your sphere of existence, saying that socialization will be problematic.

- **Mention Famous Homeschoolers:** Famous homeschoolers include Abraham Lincoln, NBA star Blake Griffen, NFL player Tim Tebow, Thomas Edison, and C.S. Lewis. Say something like, "Abraham Lincoln was homeschooled, and last time I checked, he did pretty well for himself." (On second thought, perhaps C.S. Lewis would be a better example given Lincoln's tragic end).

- **Use Dry Humor to Defuse the Situation:** "I'm just doing my best to make sure my kids don't end up like some of the people I went to school with."

- **Use Sarcasm:** "Yeah, because nothing screams 'socialization' like a bunch of kids sitting in a classroom for 8 hours a day, only interacting with their peers."

- **Flip the Script:** "Actually, I'm more concerned about the negative socialization that can happen in traditional schools—bullying, cliques, and social pressure to conform. By homeschooling, we can create a positive social environment for our kids."

- **Talk About the Benefits**: "Homeschooling actually allows us to expose our kids to a wider variety of people and experiences. They can interact with people of all ages, from different backgrounds and cultures, and develop social skills that will serve them well in the real world."

- **Share Success Stories:** "Did you know that homeschoolers often perform better academically and socially than their traditionally schooled peers? There are plenty of examples of homeschoolers who have gone on to successful careers and fulfilling social lives."

- **Make a Joke:** Flash a knowing grin, nod sagely, and tell them you're considering starting an underground fight club to ensure the kids get their daily dose of social interaction.

Just kidding! Please don't start a fight club.

Instead, remind the naysayers that socialization for homeschoolers is not only possible, but it can be fun and fulfilling. Tell them about the co-ops, community events, and clubs that your children participate in. And don't be afraid to share your own positive experiences with homeschooling and socialization.

---------- **Summary** ----------

Remember, socialization is all about finding what works best for you and your family. As long as your kiddos are happy, healthy, and learning, you are absolutely WINNING. So, there you have it: the myth of the unsocialized homeschooled kid gets a well-deserved boot. Forget the outdated notion that socialization means surviving high school hallways; it's about cultivating genuine connections and diverse experiences. Homeschoolers often shine in social settings, thriving in a mix of community events and activities that break the age barrier. By tapping into local resources, co-ops, and both virtual and real-world opportunities, you can ensure your child's social life is anything but boring. With a bit of creativity and planning, you'll find that homeschooled kids can be as socially savvy as they come.

15

Homeschool Conventions

The Thrill of Victory, the Agony of the Feet

The poignant taste of victory is sweetest when it comes after the struggle.

— Unknown

HOMESCHOOL CONVENTIONS. THEY'RE LIKE the Coachella for homeschoolers, only instead of rock stars and flower crowns, you get history textbooks, protractors, keynote speakers, and a plethora of workshops. Picture a sea of enthusiastic parents and curious children, buzzing with ideas and a shared love for learning. It's a place where seasoned homeschoolers, wide-eyed newcomers, and the homeschool-curious come together for a grand jamboree of networking, resource shopping, and workshop attending. These conventions, also called conferences, offer everything from sage advice from homeschool veterans to the latest and greatest in educational resources. And yes, there's usually coffee—thank heavens! In essence, a homeschool convention is an epic one-stop-shop and idea factory for anyone delving into the riveting world of homeschooling.

I'll show you 3-day scenarios of attending a convention solo and attending a convention with your gremlins, I mean kids. I'll also spill the secrets to making the most of a convention, even if you've only got a single day or just an afternoon to play with. By the end of this chapter, you'll be cruising through the homeschool convention scene like a surfer on a perfect wave. You'll have the know-how to research and compare conventions without blowing your entire homeschool budget on, let's be honest, a glorified guess.

BENEFITS OF HOMESCHOOL CONVENTIONS

Homeschool conventions offer more than just free pens and tote bags, I assure you. They're like a theme park, with different rides and attractions waiting for you. Prepare to encounter sessions and workshops ranging from curriculum reviews to inspirational guest speakers. Beyond the allure of freebies, there are priceless connections to be made. Here's how you can maximize your homeschool convention adventure:

- **Networking:** Homeschool conventions are like a big potluck, with each family bringing their unique homeschooling experiences to the table. Meeting other people who are on the same journey can inspire new ideas and create lasting friendships. Imagine a friendly chat with a seasoned homeschooler who shares their tried-and-tested system for staying organized or a dad describing how he turned his garage into a thrilling science lab.

- **Resources:** These conventions are like a homeschooling shopping mall. Rows and rows of curriculum materials, textbooks, and online courses are at your fingertips in the vendor hall. You might come across that math program you've been considering and get to flip through it in person. And who can resist those educational games, art supplies, and science kits that make learning so much fun?

- **Workshops:** Not to forget, the convention's workshops are your golden ticket to learning from the best in the homeschooling world. Picture a session on "how to teach math to kids who aren't fond of numbers" or one about setting up a homeschool routine that fits your family like a glove.

Now that we know what a homeschool convention entails and its benefits, check out these seven tips to help you quickly benefit from attending one.

HOMESCHOOL CONVENTION HACKS—READ THIS BEFORE YOU GO!

- **Follow the Buzz, But Don't Get Stung:** As with any big decision in life, like choosing the right streaming service or deciding between ordering pizza or sushi, research is key. Start by asking around in your homeschool communities, checking out online reviews, and keeping an ear out for convention buzz. Remember, you're looking for a Goldilocks convention—not too big, not too small, but just right for you.

- **Location, Location, Location:** Unless you possess Hermione Granger's Time-Turner or Doctor Who's TARDIS, consider the convention's location before you sign up. A convention on the other side of the country might sound adventurous, but unless you enjoy road-tripping more than the Griswolds, you might want to stick with something closer to home.

- **Show Me the Money:** Conventions can vary significantly in cost, from 'steal-of-a-deal' to 'maybe-we-don't-need-to-eat-this-month.' When considering your budget, don't forget to factor in extras like travel, accommodations, meals, and whether you'll be tempted to buy every shiny new curriculum that smiles at you from the vendors' hall.

- **The Star-Studded Line-Up:** Check out the speaker line-up. If the keynote speaker is a homeschooling legend you've admired since the dawn of time (or at least since you started homeschooling), this might be the convention for you. However, if the most exciting name on the list is that of a renowned snail breeder, unless you're really into mollusks, you might want to reconsider.

- **The Curriculum Conundrum:** If you're looking for a fresh curriculum, see which vendors will be present. But beware—you don't want to end up in a predicament where you're bartering your car for a full set of materials, promising yourself it's an investment in your child's future.

- **Themes and Schemes:** Some conventions have specific themes or focus on certain educational philosophies. If you're a Montessori maniac or a Classical education crusader, make sure the convention matches your style. If the convention is titled "Unleash Your Child's Inner Caveman: The Stone Age Approach to Homeschooling," and you're not keen on using flint tools for your next art project, it's probably not the one for you.

- **The Size of the Prize:** Some parents love the buzz of a big convention, with its smorgasbord of workshops and city-sized vendor halls. Others prefer a smaller, more intimate setting where you don't need a map and a compass to find the bathrooms. Decide what environment you'll thrive in before signing up.

CHOOSE YOUR CONVENTION ATMOSPHERE

Now that you have an idea of what a homeschool convention entails let's figure out what type of convention you might wish to attend. Believe it or not, these gatherings are not just about swapping curriculum tips or rushing your kids into algebra. There's so much more to discover! Each type of convention has its own distinctive vibe and character. So, let's tune in to find the perfect frequency for you.

Heavenly Halls, Secular Spots, or Something in Between?

- **The "Rise and Shine at 5:00 a.m." Convention:** These are the conventions run by homeschool parents who not only have their lives together but have them together before most of us even have the courage to peek out from under the blanket. Their children have already studied Latin, built a replica of the Roman Empire, and made breakfast...all before 8:00 a.m. The convention lectures start bright and early, and the vendor hall looks like a Black Friday sale by 7:00 a.m. Be prepared; if you're not an early bird, you may find yourself trampled in the stampede of eager homeschooling parents in their race for the newest curriculum.

- **The "Old-School, One-Room Schoolhouse" Convention:** Attendees at this convention can't resist the allure of chalkboards, McGuffey readers, and vintage desks. The workshop topics range from "How to Make Your Own Quill Pen" to "Why Suspenders Should Be Mandatory for All Students." Your modern tablet may feel a bit out of place here, but that's okay. There's something quite charming about watching children learn how to churn butter during recess.

- **The "Homeschooling is a Competitive Sport" Convention:** You can feel the intense energy in the air as parents discuss whose six-year-old is already at a college reading level and who has a toddler who can identify all the countries on a globe. Workshops include "Turn your Science Fair Project into a Nobel Prize Contender" and "Prepping your Pre-K for the SATs". Remember to wear your game face and bring your list of your kids' accomplishments. It's like the Olympics but with more Latin and less running (the sister to the "Rise and Shine at 5:00 a.m." convention).

- **The "We're Just Hanging on by a Thread" Convention:** This convention feels like a giant group therapy session. Parents swap stories of curriculum mishaps, spilled paint disasters, and just how many times a child can ask "why?" before a parent's brain officially implodes. There's camaraderie in the chaos, and everyone leaves with the comforting knowledge that they're not alone in this wild homeschool ride.

- **The "Higher Calling" Convention:** These are the conventions steeped in religious tradition. Scripture is seamlessly woven into subjects, from art to zoology, and the vendor hall is full of faith-based curriculums. If your faith plays a significant role in your homeschooling approach, a religious convention could be your bread and butter (or loaves and fishes). You'll find resources aligned with your values, workshops tackling faith-based education, and speakers who can quote scripture while explaining algebra. The workshops are a mix of pedagogy and prayer meetings, offering spiritual support along with educational guidance. If you're seeking a more worldly perspective or follow a secular homeschooling approach, you might feel like a fish out of holy water at a religious convention.

- **The "Secular Scholars" Convention:** These conventions leave religion at the door, focusing on secular approaches to learning. Evolution is a given, and critical thinking is the holy grail. Some secular conventions pride themselves on being inclusive, embracing a wide range of homeschooling philosophies, ideologies, and curricula. If your homeschooling approach is as eclectic as a hipster's vinyl collection, this could be a good fit for you. If, however, your homeschooling philosophy is more defined, you might feel like you're in a melting pot that's bubbling over with too many ingredients. Don't be surprised to see a booth devoted entirely to Darwin or a workshop titled "Teaching Ethics Without Religion." Keep an eye out for guest speakers who might include renowned scientists, historians, or philosophers.

Your tribe, your vibe. Whether you choose a religious or secular convention or something in between, what's most important is that you feel comfortable, accepted, and inspired. If you find your tribe in a crowd of prayerful parents, that's great. If you feel more at home among secular scholars, that's equally awesome. In the end, the best convention is the one where you can be yourself, meet like-minded parents, and enrich your homeschooling journey.

As we leap into this grueling yet exhilarating event, we equip ourselves with a sense of humor, buckets of patience, and an arsenal of essential supplies. It's a triathlon of the mind, a mental marathon stretching over three nonstop days.

Let's get ready for our Day 1 journey titled 'Freaky Friday,' where we'll face the daunting early morning wake-up calls, the meticulous packing of a survival kit, and a whole lot more. Buckle up, and let's go!

TRIATHLON OF THE MIND—SURVIVING A 3-DAY HOMESCHOOL CONVENTION

Day 1: Freaky Friday

Morning:

- **Rise and Shine, But Mostly Panic:** The harsh blare of your alarm at 5:00 a.m. reminds you that, today, the familiar comfort of your living room teaching corner is being swapped for a crowded convention center buzzing with over-caffeinated parents. Remember, no amount of coffee is too much today.

- **Packing Survival Kit:** You pull out your oversized 'Homeschooling: Because I love my kids' tote bag, packing it with the precision of a seasoned mountaineer. Inside, you place an assortment of granola bars to quell unpredictable hunger pangs, a 32-oz water bottle for hydration, your favorite pair of running shoes for the inevitable discomfort of formal footwear, and a notebook. In this notebook, you record everything from new strategies for teaching fractions to epiphanies about the parallels between homeschooling and running a small circus.

Afternoon:

- **Workshop Wandering:** As you scan the complex workshop timetable, reminiscent of an overly complex Sudoku puzzle, the variety of options is overwhelming. Titles range from "Decoding the Da Vinci Code of Algebra" to "Calm Parenting: Myth or Reality?", making the selection process seem almost Herculean. You opt for "The Art and Science of Patience"—a fitting choice. Faced with a schedule more convoluted than a Christopher Nolan plot, you aim for workshops that offer realistic outcomes rather than overnight prodigies. With options as perplexing as quantum physics, finding the right sessions feels like a maze. A simple rule guides you: promises of effortless genius are likely illusions.

- **Vendors' Hall Hustle:** The vendors' hall challenges your patience and haggling skills. At one stall, a "revolutionary" curriculum claims to merge Montessori, Waldorf, and Jedi training. You acknowledge the creativity with a polite smile and continue on. This hall, akin to navigating Mordor for homeschool convention attendees, is filled with stalls eager to sell you on curricula that will supposedly transform your child into a scholar in less than seven days. Amidst this chaos, you steel yourself for the onslaught of sales pitches, navigating through a maze of curriculum providers, tutors, and educational tools. This epicenter of persuasion tests your resolve as you sift through the myriad of educational resources.

Evening:

- **Sneaky Snooze:** After a day so packed it felt like a year's worth of learning and networking, you find a serene nook with a chair that invites comfort. Using your tote bag as a makeshift pillow, you settle in and gently shut your eyes. This isn't sleeping; it's merely 'resting your eyes'—or, even more aptly, 'strategic recharging.

Day 2: Socialization Saturday

Morning:

- **Breakfast and Morning Prep:** The day starts with an improvised breakfast—a granola bar and a cup of coffee. You also manage to squeeze in some preparation for the upcoming breakout sessions, jotting down a few questions and rehearsing them under your breath like an actor before the big performance. You skim through your convention guide, pinpointing the most interesting breakout sessions.

- **Breakout Blitz**: You've picked "Physics for the Phobic," and as the speaker begins explaining how rocket science isn't actually rocket science, you can't help but wonder if this is what Neil Armstrong felt like when he first stepped on the moon. Overwhelmed but intrigued. You head to your next chosen breakout session. If your chosen speaker starts suggesting that the Bermuda Triangle is actually a portal to an alternate dimension used by historical figures to escape the public eye, it's probably time to take a 'critical' washroom break- or grab some popcorn. Pro tip: if the speaker looks as lost as you feel, it's definitely a good time for a snack break.

Afternoon:
- **Lunch and Linger:** Mingle over lunch. Yes, that means talking to other adults about non-homeschooling related topics. Scary, we know. This is your chance to finally connect with another parent over your shared love for sci-fi novels or 1980s TV shows during the lunch hour. Did you just make a friend? Mission accomplished!

- **Book Sale Scramble:** Armed with a half-eaten sandwich and determination, you join the crowd swarming the book-sale tables. With a fierce look, you dive into the fray and resurface, breathlessly clutching a well-preserved copy of "To Kill a Mockingbird" and an illustrated edition of "Moby Dick", all under four bucks. Victory! Remember, in the wild realm of discount literature, the early bird gets the classic novels.

Evening:
- **Evening Evasion:** With an Oscar-worthy performance you escape the evening session, citing an urgent call from your dog's therapist. Your bathtub and the latest thriller novel have never looked so inviting.

Day 3: Survival Sunday
Morning:
- **Coffee, Lots of Coffee:** The bags under your eyes are now suitcases. You mentally prep yourself for the day ahead. It's the final stretch! The triple-shot espresso you've been saving for the apocalypse? Now's the time. This is the way.

- **Keynote Kraziness:** The keynote speaker, a celebrated homeschooling veteran, shares some inspiring wisdom about the importance of "letting your kids steer their own ship of learning." You can't help but chuckle—that sounds suspiciously like your go-to phrase to justify binge-watching documentaries on Netflix with the kids.

Afternoon:
- **Vendor Victory Lap:** You take one last stroll through the vendors' hall. As you approach that intriguing curriculum booth from Day 1, the vendor recognizes you and throws in a last-minute 30% discount on the "Montessori-Waldorf-Jedi" curriculum. You give it a shot—after all, who doesn't want their kid to have a bit of Jedi training?

Evening:
- **Wrap-Up Rally:** As you rush towards the exit, someone from the organizing committee smiles at you, "Same time next year?" You respond with a grin, "Absolutely!"—secretly relieved for the year-long break ahead. Congratulate yourself. You've survived. Now get out of there before they rope you into helping out with next year's convention!

Home Sweet Home!

You are back to the calm and tranquility of your home. Revel in the silence. Enjoy it because, in no time, you'll be hearing the delightful clamor of homeschooling again. But this time, in the comfort of your favorite pajamas. And that's it. You've successfully navigated the wild, wonderful whirlwind of a 3-day homeschool convention. Now, put on your favorite pajamas and promise yourself you'll never do this again—until next year, of course. The freshly purchased books are calling your name, but so is the inviting softness of your couch. You kick off your shoes, collapse into the cushions, and promise yourself a well-deserved break. After all, you've survived the 3-Day Homeschool Convention!

But wait! "What if I have to bring my kiddos to the convention?" you ask.

You thought we were done?

Let's go...

GUMMY BEARS AND LOST SHOES—TAKING KIDS TO HOMESCHOOL CONVENTIONS

Pack your patience and an artillery of snacks. This is the way. Just kidding. But if you're taking your children to a 3-day convention, here's a handy guide to kickstart your journey!

- **Mission: Inconspicuous:** Ever played a round of hide-and-seek in a convention hall? Neither have most parents until they bring their kids along. Your little Houdinis can disappear faster than you can say "curriculum." To prevent your own live-action version of "Where's Waldo," set clear boundaries and meeting points. ***Example:*** *"Stay by the Land of Lego displays, and if lost, meet by the giant stuffed dinosaur."*

- **Cardio Convention:** Forget the gym subscription; trailing your energetic five-year-old through aisle after aisle of book displays will have you sweating like you're running a Zumba class in a sauna. By the time you're done, you'll be wondering why you didn't just sign up for American Ninja Warrior. ***Pro Tip:*** *Wear comfortable shoes (sneakers or memory form sandals are good choices), pack a hand towel to mop your sweaty forehead, and consider this your workout for the week...or maybe even the month.*

- **Are We There Yet?:** The car ride to the convention can feel longer than a Lord of the Rings marathon. Be ready to answer existential questions like, "Why do we have to learn anyway?", "Can we grow burgers in the garden?", and my fav, "Are we there yet?" about a hundred times. ***Pro Tip:*** *Audiobooks and car games are your allies here.*

- **Snack-Pocalypse Now:** Think of snacks as your lifeline. Pack enough to feed a miniature battalion. When the yawn of boredom approaches, snacks are your ultimate shield. But remember, handing out sugar-laden gummy bears could turn your convention day into a scene from 'Fast & Furious'. Instead, try easy-to-carry, mess-free snacks like carrot sticks or whole-grain crackers. The idea is to keep them fueled, not ricocheting off the convention walls like pinballs. ***Pro Tip:*** *Try to include protein-rich snacks like nuts, cheese cubes, or hummus with veggies. Not only do they* *keep hunger at bay longer than simple carbs, but they also help prevent the sugar highs and subsequent crashes that can come from overly sweet snacks.*

- **Bathroom Bingo:** Just as the keynote speaker starts unveiling the secret to effortless homeschooling, your youngest will need the bathroom. It's practically a law of nature. Try to choose seats near the exits, identify restroom locations in advance, and maybe even have a "bathroom break" schedule. Think of it as an unplanned game of "Beat the Clock." ***Pro Tip:*** *Ask a nearby parent (BEFORE the workshop/keynote begins) to share any tips/notes you might miss while answering nature's call. Just screenshot their notes with your phone, if possible.*

- **Gadget Give and Take:** To iPad or not to iPad, that is the question. Whether to bring gadgets is the modern-day parental dilemma. On the one hand, you'll have a peaceful workshop session while they're engrossed in "Math Bingo," "Stack the States," or Blue's Clues. On the other hand, monitoring screen time and prying the tablet from your stubborn child's candy-sticky hands later can be more challenging than negotiating a peace treaty between rival siblings. The compromise? Timer set, headphones on, educational game, audiobook, or show/movie chosen, peace brokered! ***Pro Tip:*** *If you decide to bring gadgets, remember to load them with educational apps/movies/audiobooks BEFORE your arrival! And don't forget the chargers.*

- **Make it Fun:** Amid the stress and chaos, try to make the experience fun for your kids. Conventions often have activities for children. Before the event, have a look at the convention's schedule and highlight the kid-friendly activities. Discuss these with your children and let them choose a few they're particularly interested in. This will give them something to look forward to and feel more involved in the convention process. Let them enjoy the experience and make new friends, and maybe, just maybe, they might start looking forward to these events as much as you do.

But, what if my schedule allows for only one day at the convention?

THE ONE AND DONE—A TURBOCHARGED GUIDE TO ROCKING A ONE-DAY HOMESCHOOL CONVENTION

- **The Early Bird Catches the Goodies:** Set your alarm early. A day at the convention will fly by quicker than your child's sudden interest in algebra. You want to be there bright and early to maximize your time.

- **Convention Bag for Holding Stuff:** Pack smart—a water bottle to stay hydrated, snacks to keep energy levels up, a notepad and pen for capturing all the juicy insights, all the freebies from the vendor hall, and a pair of comfortable shoes for when the convention floor starts to feel like a hike up Everest.

- **Agenda Attack:** Look at the convention's schedule ahead of time and plan your day meticulously. Prioritize what's most important to you—keynotes, workshops, vendors, networking. You'll barely have time, if any, to do it all, so focus on what will benefit you and your family the most.

- **Workshop Whizz:** Choose your workshops wisely. You don't have time to sit through a dull talk. Pick the ones that resonate most with your homeschooling style and challenges, and don't be afraid to leave mid-session if it's not meeting your needs. This is about getting the most value for your limited time.

- **Vendor Hustle:** Vendors' hall can be overwhelming. Do your research beforehand to know which vendors you definitely want to visit. Be ready for sales pitches, but also be ready to ask hard-hitting questions about how a product can serve your family's specific needs.

- **Networking Ninja:** You only have one shot at making connections. Don't be shy—approach other parents, exchange contacts, and share experiences. Who knows, your new homeschooling best friend could be just one conversation away!

- **The Keynote Chase:** Keynotes are often the highlight of a convention. Make sure to secure a good seat for soaking in the wisdom of homeschooling veterans. It's not just about the talk—this is also a great time to observe and connect with the larger homeschooling community.

- **Bookstore Browsing:** If there's a bookstore or a book sale, make a beeline for it. Great resources can often be found at discounted prices. Just remember, your goal is not to recreate the Library of Alexandria at home, so choose wisely.

- **Escape Plan:** At the end of the day, don't linger. You've absorbed a ton of information, made connections, and, hopefully, scored some great resources. Now, it's time to head home, digest all that you've learned, and, most importantly, take off your shoes. After all, you've earned it!

Remember, even though it's just one day, a homeschool convention can offer a wealth of inspiration, resources, and connections. Plan wisely, stay focused, and make the most of your day.

DECOMPRESS AND DIGEST—A POST-HOMESCHOOL CONVENTION GUIDE

Attending a homeschool convention is often just the first part of the journey. It's crucial to effectively process everything you've learned and gathered afterward. Here's a quick cheat sheet to help you navigate the post-convention journey.

- **Rest and Rejuvenate:** It might sound counterproductive, but the first thing you should do after a convention is to rest. Give yourself a day or two to recharge, physically and mentally, before attempting to tackle the mountain of new information and resources you've gathered.

- **Organize and Reflect:** Once you're well-rested, start by organizing all the materials you've collected—notes, brochures, business cards, etc. As you do this, reflect on the key messages and insights you remember from the convention. Jot these down as they come to mind.

- **Review and Evaluate:** Now comes the task of going through your notes in detail. Review each session, workshop, or keynote you attended. Highlight the key takeaways and evaluate how these insights can be incorporated into your homeschooling practice. This can range from new teaching methods to resources that could augment your existing curriculum or even entirely new subjects to explore.

- **Follow-ups and Connections:** Remember the parents and speakers you connected with? Now is the time to follow up. Send a quick email or message expressing how much you enjoyed meeting them and discussing your shared interests. This is a good way to establish ongoing connections and build a support network.

- **Implementation Plan:** Based on your review and evaluations, develop a plan for how you'll implement new ideas or resources into your homeschooling. Don't try to change everything at once—prioritize and phase in the changes gradually.

- **Sharing and Discussing:** Share your experiences and insights with your homeschooling family. Discuss the new ideas you've encountered and get their thoughts. After all, these changes will affect them too.

- **Revisit and Refresh:** Finally, keep your convention notes and resources in a place where you can revisit them regularly. Every now and then, take a look back and see if there's something you missed or a great idea you haven't implemented yet.

---------- **Summary** ----------

Surviving a homeschool convention can feel like an epic quest, but with the right preparation and mindset, it can be incredibly rewarding. By planning ahead, prioritizing must-see sessions, and packing comfy shoes, you'll navigate the sea of resources, workshops, and networking opportunities like a pro. Embrace the chance to meet fellow homeschoolers, share experiences, and gather fresh ideas to enrich your homeschooling journey. Each convention offers a unique opportunity to connect, learn, and grow, so go forth, homeschool warrior! May your convention experience be filled with inspiration, new friendships, and maybe a few too many free pens. Happy homeschooling!

16

Assessing Progress

Are We There Yet?

Assessing progress is not about measuring how far you still have to go,
but about recognizing how far you've already come.

– Unknown

T RACKING YOUR CHILD'S PROGRESS is crucial, but it's not all about grades and tests. Spotting their strengths and weaknesses is like finding the treasure map that shows you where to dig deeper or when to offer a little extra help. We're diving into both the tried-and-true methods and some off-the-beaten-path ways to assess your homeschoolers. Plus, I'll throw in some savvy tips to make assessments work for you instead of against you. And yes, we're also tackling record-keeping—don't worry, I'll keep it as painless as possible. No stuffy jargon here, just clear, friendly advice. So grab a seat and let's get practical about homeschool assessments with some straight talk and useful tips!

TYPES OF ASSESSMENTS

- **Curriculum-Based Assessments:** These are assessments that are based on the curriculum the student is using. These assessments test the student's knowledge of the subject matter covered in the curriculum. They are great for seeing how well children are grasping the material. For example, let's say your children are learning about the American Revolution. A curriculum-based assessment might include questions about key events, people, and causes of the war. By checking their answers, you can see if they really get what happened during that time and if they might need a little more help with certain topics. It's like a sneak peek into their brain to see what's sticking and what might need more attention.

- **Parent Evaluations:** So, what are parent evaluations all about? It's you, the parent, assessing how your child is doing. You can use rubrics or checklists to evaluate your children's understanding of a subject. Is this approach helpful? Absolutely! For example, your child just finished learning about the water cycle. You could create a checklist to see if they understand concepts like evaporation, condensation, and precipitation. You might even ask them to explain the process in their own words. This way, you can see where they're shining and where they might need a little extra help. These evaluations give you insights into your child's progress, but keep in mind that they can be a bit subjective.

- **Peer Assessments:** Peer assessments involve students evaluating each other's work. This collaborative approach can be beneficial for homeschooling families with children of different ages. It facilitates learning from one another and assists parents in identifying where extra support may be needed. If you have multiple children you could have them exchange science experiment observations and assess each other's conclusions. They could spot any oversights and learn from their siblings' analytical skills. Additionally, it provides you with valuable feedback on areas that may require more in-depth exploration.

- **Standardized Testing:** Standardized Testing offers a consistent metric for evaluating student knowledge and skills, with assessments such as the Stanford 10, Iowa Test (ITBS), SAT, ACT and others providing a snapshot for easy performance comparison. These tests can illuminate areas where a student excels or may need further support, such as distinguishing between a flair for mathematics and a struggle with reading comprehension. While these insights are valuable, it's crucial to maintain balance and remember that these tests are but one piece of your child's broader educational tapestry.

- **Portfolios:** Portfolios are an excellent tool for assessing a student's educational progress, particularly in a homeschooling environment. They act as a cumulative record, showcasing a range of work that illustrates skill development and learning depth over time. Through portfolios, you can trace your child's improvement in areas such as writing, where initial drafts and final essays lay side by side, or in complex subjects like science, where early experiments can be compared with more advanced projects. This visual and tangible record captures not just the end results, but the learning process itself, highlighting your child's evolving understanding and the application of feedback. The key to their effectiveness, however, lies in regular and careful curation to ensure they serve as an accurate and reflective measure of a child's journey.

RECORD KEEPING—CAN'T WE JUST HIRE A SECRETARY?

If you've ever lost that very important math test your kid aced between the couch cushions, or your state requires you to report grades or turn in work samples, pay attention to this section! We'll talk about keeping track of grades, transcripts, and all that fabulous student work without breaking a sweat. For now, let's look at some traditional ways to keep track of your child's work.

The Good Ol' Binder System:

- **How it Works:** Just grab a binder for each of your kids and throw in some tabs for different subjects. Toss in those clear plastic sleeves to keep the really cool stuff, like art or that science project they rocked.

- **Quick Tip:** Make it fun and let the kids deck out their binders with whatever floats their boat (unless they're at that age where everything's just 'meh'). It'll be a blast, and hey, maybe the binder won't vanish into the black hole of their room.

Digital Portfolios with Google Drive:

- **How it Works:** Create a folder for each child and then sub-folders for each academic year or subject. Scan or snap photos of their work, save it, and bam! Everything's in one place.

- **Quick Tip:** Share the folder with grandparents, aunts, uncles, and whoever else wants to ooh and aah over your child's work. Or, just keep it as a backup in case of a juice spill on the original.

Excel or Google Sheets for Grades:

- **How it Works:** Each kid gets their own sheet. Columns for subjects, rows for assignments/tests, and a handy formula to calculate the average. Here's a simple formula for how to calculate unweighted grades.

Steps to calculate your average grade:
Average Grade = Sum of All Grades/Number of All Grades
1. **Add up** all your grades.

2. **Count** how many grades you have.

3. **Divide** the total sum of your grades by the number of grades.

Example:
~ If you have three grades: 85, 90, and 80, the formula would look like this:

Average Grade = 85 + 90 + 80 = 255. Divide 255 by 3 (total # of grades). Answer is 85.
So, the average grade is 85.
For weighted grades, see the notes section in the back of the book.
Quick Tip: Color-code passing grades as green and ones that need improvement in orange (or whatever colors you wish). At a glance, you'll know where to high-five or where to help out.

Online Tools for Transcripts:

- **How it Works:** Websites like Homeschool Tracker or My School Year are designed just for homeschoolers to keep grades, produce report cards, and even generate transcripts.

- **Quick Tip:** These often have a free trial. Test drive a few to find the one that makes you feel more like a superhero and less like you're herding cats.

Memory Boxes for Sample Work:

- **How it Works:** Grab a sturdy box for each academic year. As the year progresses, drop in standout essays, art projects, and science reports.

- **Quick Tip:** At the end of the year, have a "review day." Look back at all the awesomeness and reminisce about the highs and lows of the year.

The Calendar Method:

- **How it Works:** Get a big wall calendar. Every time your child completes a task, jot it down with a grade or note. At the end of the month, transfer this data to your more 'official' record-keeping system.

- **Quick Tip:** Make it a ritual! End of month = pizza night + grade transferring. Win-win!

UNCONVENTIONAL HOMESCHOOL ASSESS-MENTS—THINK OUTSIDE THE BOX

Sometimes, traditional assessment methods might not capture the full extent of your child's learning experience. That's where unconventional assessments come in! They can make the learning process fun and memorable while still providing insights into your child's progress. Here are some creative and out-of-the-box ways to conduct assessments in your homeschool.

- **Project-Based Assessments:** These are about letting students embark on hands-on projects to showcase their understanding. Take, for instance, your child building a model solar system to delve into astronomy or creating a stop-motion animation about a historical event. This method doesn't just display their grasp of a topic; it also promotes creativity and problem-solving.

- **Game-Based Assessments:** Turn the peer review process into a game, where your children earn points for providing constructive feedback on each other's work. This can be gamified further by adding levels, badges, or rewards for comprehensive and helpful reviews. Or, transform quizzes into competitive game-show-style formats. Tools like Kahoot! or Quizizz allow educators to create interactive quizzes where students compete against each other, earning points for speed and accuracy.

- **Interactive Assessments Using Technology:** The primary focus here is to integrate technology to make assessments more dynamic and interactive. For example, students might use digital tools for multimedia presentations or participate in online simulations. The advantage? It promotes digital literacy and offers instant feedback.

- **Performance-Based Assessments:** Provides children an opportunity to display their learning through actual demonstrations. This could be a persuasive speech on a significant topic or even a dance routine explaining a scientific concept. Beyond showcasing understanding, this approach fosters confidence and allows children to express themselves creatively.

- **Nature-Based Assessments:** Leverage the natural world as a classroom. Whether it's a scavenger hunt to identify local species or maintaining a nature journal, it's about harnessing the environment for learning. This method encourages outdoor exploration and sharpens observational skills.

- **Character Assessment:** Let's widen our lens beyond just quizzes, projects and the like. We're sculpting wholesome individuals here. How's their collaboration when they team up with siblings or neighborhood kids on a group project? Can they present their findings to the family at dinner confidently? How are they coping with setbacks? Do they demonstrate virtues such as honesty and empathy? Discussing moral narratives from books or movies can provide insight into their moral reasoning. It's these bits and pieces that give a complete picture and help in molding a well-rounded individual.

---------- **Summary** ----------

Keeping tabs on your homeschoolers isn't just about making sure they're acing their math—it's about checking in on who they're becoming along the way. You've got options, from the standard quizzes and tests to some creative approaches that keep things interesting. The key is to track their progress without turning into a drill sergeant, making sure home learning stays supportive and, dare I say, enjoyable. By doing this, you're not just managing their education, you're playing a big part in making sure their homeschooling journey is on track. Plus, you're setting them up for an amazing future.

PART IV - PHILOSOPHIES, APPROACHES, & METHODS

Part IV is your guide to the wildly diverse world of homeschooling philosophies. With nine major methods on the menu, I promise you won't be overwhelmed—just enlightened. Whether you're into structured schedules or free-form learning, traditional methods or avant-garde approaches, this section will guide you in finding the perfect fit for your family's style and your child's needs. Plus, you'll get the lowdown on making savvy curriculum choices, a topic that we tackled in Part II, Chapter 7, "The Curriculum Jungle."

17

Homeschooling Approaches

From Relaxed to Regimented

Going to school just for the degree is like going to the Grand Canyon just for a selfie.

— Unknown

S O, IF YOU'RE WADING into the world of homeschooling, you'll bump into a lot of terms that sound different, but really they're all buddies hanging in the same crowd. Whether folks are chatting about homeschool philosophies, methods, approaches, or educational philosophies, they're just talking about the cool and varied ways families teach their kids at home. And by the way, I'll probably interchange these terms throughout this section of the book. It's like everyone's using different words to describe their recipe for learning—some like it structured, some like it free-flowing, but in the end, it's all about cooking up an education that feels just right for them.

Think of picking a method as a whirlwind romance. Shall you tango with the brainy classical education, waltz with the whimsical eclectic style, or slow dance with the tender-hearted Charlotte Mason method? Or, if you already homeschool, does your homeschool resemble 'Dead Poets Society' inspiration or 'School of Rock' unconventional methods? Something in between?

Each approach comes with its own charms and eccentricities, so feel free to play the field, let loose, and uncover the perfect match for your family's happily ever after. In the quest to craft a dazzling homeschool curriculum, it's crucial to lean into a realistic educational philosophy that aligns with your family's core beliefs and your child's learning groove.

We'll review, in alphabetical order, nine major homeschool philosophies (plus two that aren't philosophies, per se) and their histories, definitions, key features, advantages, and disadvantages. We'll also explore examples of each homeschool philosophy in action. Ready?

18

The Charlotte Mason Approach

Embracing the Beauty of Nature and Literature

The question is not,—how much does the youth know? when he has finished his education—but how much does he care?

— Charlotte Mason

D O YOU LONG FOR an educational method that embraces nature, literature, and the arts? British educator Charlotte Mason, who lived from 1842 to 1923, revolutionized the educational landscape with her unique philosophy of education. Her belief that children are persons in their own right and deserve respect as individuals shaped the development of her approach. She placed a high value on nature, literature, and the arts and firmly believed in home-based education.

HOW DOES THE CHARLOTTE MASON APPROACH WORK?

The Charlotte Mason method emphasizes a broad and rich curriculum based on the belief that children are whole persons who should be educated with respect and dignity. This approach incorporates living books—engaging, well-written narratives—rather than dry textbooks to spark children's imaginations and interests. Daily nature walks, art appreciation, music study, and narration (children retelling what they have learned) are integral parts of this method. The Charlotte

Mason approach encourages short, focused lessons to keep children attention and foster a habit of excellence, promoting an education that cultivates curiosity, creativity, and a love for lifelong learning.

CHARLOTTE MASON KEY FEATURES

The Charlotte Mason approach can be described as a homeschooling technique that brings the coziness of a cabin nestled in the woods, a library abundant with books, and a lively art studio into your home. This method not only encourages a love for learning but also immerses children in enriching experiences like nature walks, fascinating literature, and artistic endeavors.

Underpinning the Charlotte Mason approach is a philosophy of gentle, nature-inspired education. This literature-rich approach advocates for the importance of nature, observation, and habit formation. Short lessons, nature study, copywork, dictation, narration, and exposure to quality literature are its mainstays, combined with a lot of outdoor exploration.

At the core of this method is the use of living books—texts that bring subjects to life penned by authors passionate about their topics. As opposed to dull textbooks, living books offer stories that engender enthusiasm and stimulate the mind. Whether your child delves into an exciting historical novel, an engaging marine biologist's memoir, or an adventurer's tale, the key to learning lies in narration. Instead of answering comprehension questions, children narrate or relay what they've read or heard, boosting information processing, memory, and communication skills. The Charlotte Mason approach, with its emphasis on making learning a part of everyday life rather than a detached activity, could be your ticket to a more engaging and meaningful homeschooling experience. The following examples demonstrate this approach:

Nature Studies

Here are a few examples of how nature studies can be used in your homeschool.

- **Observation and Journaling:** Let's say the focus of the study is on birds native to your area. Begin by taking a walk with your child in a nearby park or nature reserve, encouraging them to remain quiet and observant to notice the various birds around them. They could be instructed to pay attention to different aspects like the bird's colors, size, distinctive markings, behavior, and songs.

This is a basic nature studies example and can be adapted to study any other aspects of nature, such as trees, insects, weather patterns, etc., depending on your child's interest and the resources available in your location.

Living Books

Choosing living books for homeschooling is an exciting journey. Living books are written by authors who have a passion for the subject and write in an engaging and narrative way. These books make the subject come alive and are in stark contrast to the dry, factual presentation found in many textbooks. If you're new to homeschooling and would like to integrate living books into your curriculum, here are some steps and tips to consider:

- **Understand Your Goal:** Before diving into book selections, be clear about what you want to achieve with the living books approach. Do you want to enrich a particular subject, inspire a love of learning, or provide a more holistic view of a topic?

- **Know Your Child:** Each child is unique. Consider their interests, reading level, and maturity. What topics excite them? Are there particular areas they're curious about?

- **Quality Over Quantity:** A living book is rich in ideas, so you don't need as many of them. It's better to delve deep into a few books than to skim through many.

Seek Recommendations:
- Join homeschooling groups online or locally to ask for living book recommendations.

- Websites like AmblesideOnline, Simply Charlotte Mason, and The Baldwin Project have extensive lists and recommendations.

- Libraries can be an excellent resource. Talk to librarians about your goals and see if they have recommendations.

- Download the U.S. Newbury and Caldecott Awards book winners and honorable mentions lists. These are timeless classics going back to the early 1900s.

Preview Books:
- Skim or read through potential books to see if they fit your criteria.

- Look for books that are engaging, thought-provoking, and well-written.

- Avoid books that talk down to children or oversimplify complex topics.

Things to Consider:
- Ensure your book selection represents a wide range of perspectives, cultures, and voices. This helps children understand the world's diversity and complexity.

- **Mix Subjects:** Living books aren't just for history or literature. You can find living books for science, math, art, and more.

- **Consider Historical Fiction:** While it's fiction, well-researched historical novels can provide an immersive experience of a particular period.

- **Supplement With Other Resources:** Living books can be enriched with field trips, hands-on projects, documentaries, and other educational resources.

- **Record Your Progress:** Keep a reading log or journal. This will not only be a wonderful record of your homeschooling journey but can also serve as a resource for other books or topics you'd like to cover.

Remember, the key idea behind living books is that they should inspire and engage children, stirring their emotions and sparking their imaginations. What qualifies as a "living book" can vary between different families and children based on their unique interests and reading levels. It's always a good idea to pre-read books or read reviews to ensure they align with your educational goals and values. Refer to the appendix to discover how to obtain your complimentary homeschool planner, which includes a book log/journal for tracking your child's reading.

Narration

Children might be asked to relay the story in their own words after reading a chapter from a book. This active engagement helps them consolidate their understanding. Here are some examples to give you an idea of what that can look like.

- **History Narration:** After reading a chapter about the American Revolution from a living book, you could ask your child to narrate what they learned. They might talk about the causes of the war, key figures and their roles, significant battles, and the resulting impacts.

- **Science Narration:** After watching a documentary about animal adaptations, ask your child to narrate what they've learned. They might describe how polar bears are adapted to live in arctic conditions or how a chameleon changes its colors for camouflage and communication.

- **Literature Narration:** After reading a chapter of "Charlotte's Web" by E.B. White, your child might narrate the events of the story, the characters involved, their actions, feelings, and motivations.

- **Math Narration:** Narration can be used even in math. For example, after solving a problem, your child could narrate their process—how they approached the problem, the strategy they used, and how they knew their answer was correct.

- **Art Narration:** After studying a piece of art, your child might narrate what they see in the painting, the colors and techniques used, the mood of the artwork, and their interpretation of the piece.

- **Field Trip Narration:** If you've taken a trip to a museum, a farm, or a local business, ask your child to narrate their experience. They might discuss what they saw, what they learned, what surprised them, and their favorite part of the trip.

Remember, the goal of narration is not just to ensure the child remembers information but also to help them process, understand, and communicate their learnings effectively. For younger children, the narration will likely be oral, while older children can be encouraged to write down their narrations. You can also switch it up by having them draw or act out their narrations for a bit of fun and creativity!

Copywork

Copywork is a foundational element of the Charlotte Mason method that improves writing, grammar, and attention to detail. Students meticulously copy literature excerpts, historical documents, and other significant texts to enhance these skills.

- **Historical Documents:** Students copy excerpts from important documents like the Declaration of Independence, enhancing their understanding of historical context and legal language.

- **Literature Excerpts:** Children transcribe passages from classic novels such as *Pride and Prejudice,* fostering an appreciation for narrative structure and character development.

- **Poetry:** Copying poems like those by Robert Frost helps students grasp rhythmic patterns, enriching their literary and artistic senses.

Remember, the goal of copywork is to enhance students' writing skills by meticulously reproducing written texts. This practice reinforces grammar, spelling, and punctuation while expanding their appreciation of literary style and content.

Dictation

Dictation complements copywork by requiring students to write down a piece of text spoken aloud. This exercise tests their listening skills, grammar, punctuation, and spelling in a more challenging setting than copywork. It's typically introduced after a child has a solid grounding in copywork, gradually increasing in complexity to include richer and more intricate passages from literature, poetry, or scripture.

- **Classic Literature:** During a dictation session, students might write down passages from *To Kill a Mockingbird* as it is read aloud, helping them to improve their listening comprehension and attention to detail in punctuation and spelling.

- **Scientific Texts:** Students could transcribe parts of a scientific article on climate change, enhancing their understanding of scientific terminology and concepts while practicing accurate transcription.

- **Historical Speeches:** Dictating segments of famous speeches, such as Martin Luther King Jr.'s "I Have a Dream," allows students to engage deeply with powerful rhetoric and historical context while honing their listening and writing skills.

Remember, the goal of dictation is to enhance students' listening, writing, and cognitive skills by transcribing spoken words accurately. This reinforces understanding of grammar, spelling, and the deeper meanings within various texts.

Art and Music Appreciation

This involves studying a famous artist or composer's works, learning about their life, and trying to create art or music in the same style. A typical week could involve studying a famous artist or composer's works, learning about their life, and trying to create art or music in a similar style.

- **Artist Study:** Choose an artist to focus on for a month or a term. Provide your child with a book or prints of the artist's work. Spend time each week observing a different piece of art, discussing it, and perhaps trying to replicate it. For example, you might study Monet and spend time observing and discussing his famous painting "Water Lilies." Your child might try to use pastels or watercolors to create their own version of a water lily pond.

- **Composer Study:** Similar to artist study, pick a composer to study for a term. Listen to their music during mealtimes, in the car, or during quiet times. Talk about how the music makes your child feel, the instruments they can identify, and any patterns they notice. You could study Beethoven, listen to his Symphony No. 5, and try to identify and replicate the rhythm of the iconic beginning.

- **Sculpture Appreciation:** Visit a local sculpture park or use online resources to view and discuss different styles of sculpture. You could study Rodin's "The Thinker," discuss the emotions it evokes, and have your child create their own clay model based on the pose.

- **Architecture Study:** Teach your child to appreciate the beauty and function of buildings. Visit different architectural styles in your local area or use books and online resources. Look at gothic cathedrals, modern skyscrapers, and ancient pyramids. Discuss the characteristics, materials used, and purpose of the buildings. Your child could then build their own models with blocks or crafting materials.

- **Music Making:** Encourage your child to learn to play an instrument or sing. Regular practice and exposure to making music can increase their appreciation for the skill and creativity it takes to compose music. They could learn a piece of music from the composer they're studying.

- **Dance:** Study different forms of dance, from ballet to hip-hop to traditional cultural dances. Watch performances, learn about the history and technique, and encourage your child to try out some moves.

Remember, the aim is to expose children to a wide variety of art and music forms, helping them to develop an appreciation for the creativity and talent involved. It's not about becoming an expert in each artist or composer but rather fostering a lifelong love and respect for the arts.

Habit Training

This approach emphasizes nurturing positive habits, including attentiveness and kindness, which can be fostered through engaging in activities such as role-playing and open discussions.

- **Patience:** Encourage patience by setting up activities that require waiting. This could include planting seeds and waiting for them to germinate or baking a cake that needs time to rise and bake. Discuss the importance of patience during these activities.

- **Respect:** Habit training in respect might involve role-playing different scenarios where respect is important. You could role-play listening to someone else's opinion without interrupting or treating others' belongings with care.

- **Responsibility:** Assign your child a regular chore or responsibility, such as setting the table for dinner, feeding a pet, or watering plants. This can help establish the habit of taking responsibility and understanding the importance of fulfilling obligations.

- **Time Management:** Help your child develop a routine for their day, including time for study, chores, free time, and bedtime. Using timers or alarms can help reinforce the importance of keeping to a schedule and valuing time.

- **Healthy Eating Habits:** Involve your child in meal planning and preparation, discussing the importance of a balanced diet. Encourage them to taste a wide variety of foods and make healthy choices.

- **Gratitude:** Incorporate a daily or weekly gratitude practice, such as sharing one thing they are thankful for at the dinner table or keeping a gratitude journal. This helps to cultivate the habit of appreciating the good in life.

- **Reading:** Establish a regular reading time each day, cultivating the habit of reading for pleasure. This could be individual silent reading or family read-aloud time.

Remember, habit training is not just about enforcing rules but fostering positive behaviors that will become second nature to the child. It involves setting an example, providing guidance, and giving your child the opportunity to practice these habits regularly until they become a natural part of their behavior. And it's always important to remember that nobody is perfect—everyone has off days, and that's okay. The aim is progress, not perfection.

CHARLOTTE MASON ADVANTAGES

- **Holistic Educational Experience:** The Charlotte Mason method immerses children in living books rather than dry textbooks, engaging them with stories that fuel curiosity and a passion for learning. This approach views education as an integrated part of life, aiming to create meaningful connections with the world.

- **Natural World Engagement:** Prioritizes outdoor exploration, allowing children to learn through direct interaction with nature. This hands-on approach fosters a deep appreciation for the environment and stimulates scientific inquiry.

- **Development of Communication Skills:** Through narration, copywork, and dictation, children enhance their ability to express themselves, remember details, and pay attention, laying a strong foundation for effective communication.

- **Artistic Appreciation:** Incorporates art and music into the curriculum, encouraging children to appreciate and enjoy various forms of creative expression, enriching their cultural and aesthetic understanding.

- **Flexible Learning:** Offers a customizable learning experience, enabling parents to adapt the educational process to their child's unique interests and learning pace, making education a more engaging and personal journey.

CHARLOTTE MASON DISADVANTAGES

- **Potential for Learning Gaps:** The interest-led, flexible curriculum may result in uneven coverage of subjects, particularly in areas like math and science, which are less emphasized compared to literature and history.

- **Accessibility Concerns:** Heavily reliant on reading, this method might be less effective for children with learning differences. The lack of a structured curriculum could also hinder some families' ability to fully implement the approach.

- **Not One-Size-Fits-All:** May not suit every child or family, especially those who prefer a more structured or traditional educational model. It's essential to consider the child's needs and family resources when choosing this method.

---------- **Summary** ----------

Remember, the primary goal is to find an approach that works best for your individual child and your family situation. Feel free to adjust, blend, or change methods as needed. The essence of the Charlotte Mason approach is to make learning an integral part of everyday life rather than a disconnected activity. If you're looking for an educational experience that feels less like a factory assembly line and more like a tailored craft, the Charlotte Mason method may be the perfect fit for you. All it requires is your explorer's hat, a classic book, and a readiness to embark on a grand adventure of lifelong learning!

For Further Research:

A leading educator on the Charlotte Mason method, Sonya Shafer offers a range of resources, including books, curricula, and insightful articles to help implement this educational philosophy. Key publications and comprehensive resources are available at Simply Charlotte Mason. You can visit them here at: https://www.simplycharlottemason.com.

19

The Classical Approach

Socrates & Co. - Schooling With the Ancients

Education is the kindling of a flame, not the filling of a vessel.

— Socrates

THE CLASSICAL METHOD OF education is a rich, historically rooted system that nurtures the mind through structured stages of learning steeped in tradition and intellectual rigor. Drawing from the educational traditions of ancient Greece and Rome, it is organized around the trivium, a sequence of three phases called Grammar, Logic, and Rhetoric, tailored to coincide with a child's cognitive development.

HOW DOES THE CLASSICAL APPROACH WORK?

In the Grammar stage, young children focus on foundational knowledge, memorization, and the basics of reading, writing, and arithmetic. As your children progress to the Logic stage, typically in middle school, they develop critical thinking and analytical skills, learning to understand and articulate complex concepts. Finally, in the Rhetoric stage, usually during high school, students refine their expressive abilities, engaging in persuasive writing, speaking, and in-depth study of classical literature and philosophy. Parents guide their children through this structured framework, emphasizing the importance of classical texts, Socratic dialogue, and the development of a well-rounded intellectual foundation.

CLASSICAL KEY FEATURES

The core tenets of the classical approach to education, often associated with the Trivium, are grounded in a structured progression of learning that emphasizes critical thinking, eloquence, and a deep understanding of the Western intellectual tradition. Here are the key principles:

The Trivium-This is the foundation of the classical approach, consisting of three stages that correspond to a child's cognitive development:

1. **Grammar Stage (Knowledge):** Focuses on absorbing facts and establishing the building blocks of learning. Children at this stage are excellent at memorization and learning the fundamental "grammar" of subjects.

2. **Logic Stage (Understanding):** Corresponding with adolescence, this stage emphasizes reasoning and analysis. Students learn to think critically, argue effectively, and make connections between different subjects.

3. **Rhetoric Stage (Wisdom):** In the final stage of the Trivium, students learn to express themselves persuasively and eloquently, applying the knowledge and analytical skills they have developed.

Here are additional components of the classical approach:

- **Integration of Learning:** Classical education often stresses the interconnectedness of different disciplines, believing that this integration helps children develop a coherent and holistic view of the world.

- **Development of Virtue:** Classical education seeks to cultivate not only intellectual skills but also moral virtues. The aim is to shape students into well-rounded individuals with a strong sense of ethics and civic responsibility.

- **Emphasis on Western Tradition:** The curriculum usually has a strong emphasis on the literature, philosophies, and historical events of Western civilization, believing that understanding the past is crucial to understanding the present and shaping the future.

- **Language-Centered:** The approach is language-centered, not im-age-centered; it demands that students use and understand words, not video or photographs, as the primary symbols for communicating and thinking.

- **Socratic Teaching:** The use of Socratic dialogue or questioning is common to promote critical thinking and depth of understanding.

- **Great Books:** Many classical educators advocate for the reading and understanding of the "Great Books," a collection of works considered foundational to Western scholarship and thought.

- **Latin and Greek:** The study of classical languages, particularly Latin (and sometimes Ancient Greek), is considered important for understanding the roots of Western language, thought, and culture.

These tenets work together to support a view of education that is not only about academic development but also about the formation of character and the appreciation of the richness of human intellectual heritage. Remember, the goal of the classical approach is not just to fill students with knowledge but to teach them how to think critically, reason logically, and communicate effectively.

CLASSICAL ADVANTAGES

Structured and Disciplined Foundation: Emphasizes memorization in the early years, instilling an invaluable foundation of knowledge that enables deeper understanding and creativity in later stages.

- **Preparation for Complex Thought:** The rigor of the curriculum prepares students for complex thought and innovation, providing a solid base of facts and concepts.

- **Critical Thinking and Analytical Skills:** Developed through classical literature, philosophy, and languages, these skills are transferable to contemporary fields, fostering adaptability and problem-solving abilities.

- **Cultivation of Work Ethic and Resilience:** The intensity of the curriculum demands a high level of commitment, cultivating a strong work ethic, resilience, and a profound sense of achievement.

- **Questioning, Analyzing, and Synthesizing:** Children learn to not just absorb information but to question, analyze, and synthesize, developing invaluable skills for any discipline or profession.

- **Global Perspective:** Focus on Western tradition is complemented by the development of a global perspective, encouraging critical examination of texts and comparative studies.

- **Community of Learning:** Requires significant time and effort from children and parents, fostering a unique community of learning that often forms lifelong bonds and a shared love of learning.

While the classical approach has its definite merits, it's not without its downsides. Here are a few potential drawbacks:

CLASSICAL DISADVANTAGES

- **Straightjackets & Sonnets:** Classical education is structured and disciplined, and it tends to be heavy on memorization, especially in the early years. This approach may not work well for children who thrive in more flexible, experiential learning environments. If your kid prefers learning about the world by getting their hands dirty rather than reciting Latin verbs, they might find the classical approach a bit of a drag.

- **Limited Focus on Modern Subjects:** From Hieroglyphics to HTML? Sadly, no. Classical education is like time traveling, but it's not always a joyride. Diving deep into ancient literature, philosophy, and languages can be fascinating, but it might not float every kid's boat. This means subjects like modern sciences, technology, and social studies might not get as much emphasis. If your child dreams of becoming a coding whiz or a cutting-edge biologist, they might need some supplemental education to fill in the gaps.

- **It's Heavy Lifting:** This method is like a hefty tome of ancient philosophy—rich and rewarding but requiring considerable effort to lift. It demands a high level of commitment from both parents and children.

The rigorous curriculum and the expectation for children to master complex subjects at a young age can be overwhelming.

- **Missing the Forest for the Trees:** The classical approach's focus on details and mechanics can sometimes lead to missing out on the bigger picture. The risk is that in the pursuit of grammatical perfection or logical precision, students may lose sight of creativity and innovation.

- **Not Always a Crowd Pleaser:** If you aim to prepare your child for standardized tests or a typical school environment, the classical approach might not be the best fit. Its focus on classical subjects and critical thinking skills might not align perfectly with mainstream education's expectations.

- **Time and Effort:** The classical approach requires a significant time investment from both students and parents. There's a lot of reading, writing, and discussing involved, which can be quite demanding. And if you're not naturally inclined toward the philosophical debates of ancient Greece or the linguistic complexities of Latin, guiding your child through their classical education can feel like you're the one back in school!

- **The Socratic Blindspot:** Classical education struggles with global perspectives. Some critics argue that the classical approach, with its focus on Western civilization and literature, may not provide a broad enough perspective on global cultures, histories, and ideas.

---------- **Summary** ----------

In the end, the classical approach is like a grand old symphony—it's sophisticated, structured, and deeply rewarding, but it might not be everyone's cup of tea. And that's perfectly okay. Education is not about finding a one-size-fits-all solution but about finding the approach that fits your child best. As with any educational method, what works best will depend on the child's individual needs, learning style, and interests, as well as the resources and commitment level of the parents or educators.

For Further Research:

Well-Trained Mind: A leading resource in Classical education, offering guides, curriculum advice, and support for those following the classical model of education. You can visit them here at: https://www.welltrainedmind.com.

20

The Eclectic Approach

A Fusion of Learning Styles

When you know better, you do better.

— Maya Angelou

E DUCATION IS NOT ONE-SIZE-FITS-ALL; Think of schooling like a wardrobe. You wouldn't wear the same outfit as everyone else, right? That's what's up with learning these days. More and more parents are catching on to the fact that kids learn in their own unique ways. Enter the eclectic homeschooling approach—it's like being a DJ for education, mixing a bit of this and a bit of that to craft the perfect learning groove.

HOW DOES THE ECLECTIC APPROACH WORK?

Eclectic homeschooling is a flexible and personalized approach that combines elements from various educational philosophies and curricula to tailor learning to the individual needs and interests of each child. Parents act as facilitators, selecting resources and methods from traditional, classical, Montessori, Reggio Emilia, Charlotte Mason, and other approaches to create a customized educational experience. This method allows for adaptability, enabling parents to adjust the curriculum as the child's interests and learning styles evolve. With eclectic homeschooling, the focus is on creating a dynamic and engaging learning environment that incorporates a mix of structured lessons, hands-on activities, and real-world experiences, ensuring a well-rounded and holistic education.

ECLECTIC KEY FEATURES

The eclectic homeschooling approach can be seen as a grand buffet of learning philosophies, where parents and children are empowered to select and combine the best parts of various methodologies. This model allows the creation of a bespoke curriculum that aligns with the learner's unique needs, interests, and learning style. It could involve a touch of Montessori's hands-on learning, a bit of Charlotte Mason's nature-based education, a slice of traditional schooling's structure, and a dash of unschooling's child-led exploration. The eclectic approach is fundamentally about flexibility, customization, and adaptability.

A key benefit of this approach is the ability to fine-tune the curriculum based on a child's progress and evolving interests. If a child shows an inclination towards science, parents can incorporate more science-based activities or experiments, even if they initially planned a literature-heavy curriculum. Similarly, if a child struggles with a particular teaching style, parents can adjust the teaching methods to better suit the child's learning style. This continual refinement is a cornerstone of the eclectic approach, ensuring the education process remains dynamic, engaging, and beneficial.

Let's consider an example of how the eclectic homeschooling approach might play out in a typical week. Here's a week in the life of Marcus, a 10-year-old homeschooled student.

- **Monday:** Marcus starts the week with a Montessori-style lesson. He uses tangible materials to learn about fractions. He cuts up an apple into halves, quarters, and eighths to better understand how these fractions relate to a whole.

- **Tuesday:** Today is a Charlotte Mason day. Marcus spends his morning reading a classic novel, "The Magician's Nephew". He then narrates what he's read, strengthening his understanding and memory of the story. In the afternoon, he paints a watercolor picture inspired by the new world of Narnia described in the book.

- **Wednesday:** Marcus's mom uses a more traditional homeschooling method. They use a structured curriculum for studying history, delving into the events of the American Revolution using a textbook and completing a worksheet to reinforce what he's learned.

- **Thursday:** Today is all about project-based learning. Marcus has been fascinated by space recently. He spends the day working on a model of the solar system, researching different planets, and painting and placing his planets in order.

- **Friday:** Marcus wraps up the week with an unschooling day. He's given the freedom to explore what he's most interested in. He chooses to bake a cake with his mom, measuring out ingredients (a bit of sneaky math practice) and learning about the science of baking.

This is just an example of how an eclectic approach could look like, and the structure could vary greatly depending on the family and the child's interests and needs. Remember, the eclectic approach is all about flexibility and adaptation.

ECLECTIC ADVANTAGES

- **Flexibility:** Eclectic homeschooling allows parents and children to adjust their schedules, curriculum, and learning methods to meet individual needs and learning styles. For example, a parent may use a structured curriculum for subjects like math and science while adopting a more child-led, project-based approach for subjects like history and art.

- **Variety in Resources:** Eclectic homeschoolers draw upon a wide array of resources. This might include traditional textbooks, online courses, educational apps, community resources like libraries and museums, and real-world experiences like field trips, internships, and travel.

- **Child-Focused Learning:** In eclectic homeschooling, the child's interests, skills, and pace of learning guide the educational process. For instance, if a child shows a keen interest in dinosaurs, parents might encourage in-depth learning across subjects, using this interest as a basis for reading (books about dinosaurs), writing (reports on different dinosaur species), science (paleontology), history (the Mesozoic era), and art (creating dinosaur models or drawings).

- **Integration of Life Skills:** Unlike more traditional educational approaches, eclectic homeschooling often includes practical life skills in its curriculum. This could involve cooking, budgeting, gardening, or home repairs. For example, a cooking session could double as a math lesson by measuring ingredients or a science lesson by observing the chemical reactions that take place during cooking.

- **Adaptability:** As children grow and develop, their needs and interests can change. Eclectic homeschooling provides the adaptability to change the learning plan as required. For instance, a child who has been struggling with a textbook-based approach to learning language arts may switch to a more interactive, hands-on method using story-telling, role-playing, and creative writing.

- **Emphasis on Critical Thinking and Creativity:** Eclectic homeschooling encourages children to think critically and creatively by allowing exploration and deep dives into subjects of interest. This could be through problem-solving activities, open-ended projects, and encouraging questions and discussions. For instance, a study on ecology might involve brainstorming and researching creative solutions for environmental problems.

- **Freedom to Experiment:** Eclectic homeschooling gives the freedom to try out different methods, resources, and approaches until the best fit is found. If a particular math curriculum isn't working, parents and children are free to try another one that might work better.

Remember, the goal of eclectic homeschooling is to foster a love of learning, encourage self-directed learning, and prepare the child for the future by building a broad range of skills and knowledge. It's a fluid, evolving approach that can be as unique as each child and family using it.

ECLECTIC DISADVANTAGES

Eclectic homeschooling can be a wonderful ride through the park of education, but like any walk in the park, there can be a few potholes along the way. Here are a few things that might trip you up: The eclectic homeschooling approach is not without its challenges. It requires a significant investment of time and effort from parents to research different educational philosophies, monitor their child's progress, and continually adapt the curriculum. However, for families that value a highly personalized and flexible approach to education, the eclectic model may be a perfect fit. It encapsulates the ethos of 'learner-centered education', where the focus is on nurturing a child's natural curiosity, fostering a lifelong love for learning, and promoting the development of well-rounded individuals.

- **The "Too Many Cooks" Dilemma:** With the freedom to choose from an array of methods, you might feel like a kid in a candy store. But remember, too much candy can lead to a stomachache. You might get overwhelmed with the wealth of options, leading to analysis paralysis or a curriculum that feels like a mish-mash rather than a coherent plan.

- **Time-Consuming Prep:** The eclectic approach can feel a bit like being a one-person show. You're not just the teacher; you're also the lesson planner, curriculum wrangler, and the school counselor. You'll need to spend time researching different educational philosophies, tweaking the curriculum, and making sure it all aligns with your child's learning style and interests.

- **Consistency, What's That?:** With so much flexibility, maintaining consistency can be a challenge. You might find that you're switching approaches so often that it's hard for your child to find a rhythm. Too much change can be as problematic as too little.

- **Jack of All Trades, Master of None:** While the eclectic approach can give a broad education, there's a risk of not going deep enough into any one area. It's like tasting a little bit of everything at a buffet but never really savoring any one dish.

- **The "Is This Enough?" Question:** Without a prescribed curriculum, it can be tough to know whether you're covering all the necessary academic ground. You might find yourself constantly worrying if your child is learning enough or the right things.

---------- **Summary** ----------

The eclectic homeschooling approach is like a custom-built education, mixing and matching learning styles to fit your child's unique needs and interests. It lets you create a lively, ever-evolving learning environment that grows right along with your child. But, just like with any educational path, it's important to keep your kid's learning style, your family's resources, and the commitment level in mind before diving in.

For Further Research:

Eclectic Homeschool Online: Provides articles, curriculum resources, and support for homeschoolers who adopt an eclectic approach, combining various educational philosophies to suit their unique needs. You can visit them here at: http://www.eclectichomeschool.org

21

The Montessori Approach
A Pathway to a Tidy Child's Room

Help me to do it myself.

— Maria Montessori

ONTESSORI IS FUNDAMENTALLY A child-centric method that promotes self-guided learning through practical activities and exploration. Developed by Maria Montessori, an Italian physician and educator, this method fosters independence and self-motivated exploration within a well-prepared learning environment. Maria Montessori's pioneering approach emphasized respect for a child's natural psychological development, as well as the importance of adapting the learning environment to fit the developmental needs of each child. However, an important note to remember: steering your child towards tidying their room might pose a challenge, even within a Montessori framework. Therefore, if you decide to adopt a Montessori-inspired curriculum, be ready to accept a certain degree of disorder and disarray. After all, the path to independence often navigates through a landscape of chaos!

HOW DOES THE MONTESSORI APPROACH WORK?

With focus on hands-on, self-paced, and collaborative learning, parents create a prepared environment with carefully chosen materials that encourage exploration and independent learning. Children are free to choose activities that interest them, allowing for personalized learning paths and the development of intrinsic motivation. Practical life skills are integrated with academic subjects, fostering holistic development. Parents act as guides, observing their children's interests and providing appropriate challenges to support growth, ensuring that learning is both engaging and meaningful.

In a traditional classroom setting, a teacher might lecture about the different continents, show pictures, or have students read from a textbook and memorize the names and locations. In contrast, a Montessori environment would approach this topic differently.

Here's how a Montessori classroom might introduce the concept of continents:

- **Prepared Environment:** The classroom is set up with various materials designed to aid learning through exploration. For this lesson, a Montessori globe, continent puzzle map, and individual continent boxes might be provided.

- **Hands-On Learning:** The teacher will first introduce the Montessori globe, encouraging the child to feel the different textures that represent land and water. This tactile activity helps the child understand the physical differences between land and sea.

- **Self-Directed Exploration:** Next, the teacher introduces the continent puzzle map. Each continent piece is a different color, and the child is encouraged to take out the pieces and put them back in, thereby learning the shape and location of each continent.

- **In-Depth Exploration:** Once the child has mastered the puzzle map, they can explore individual continent boxes. Each box contains items related to a specific continent, including animals, landmarks, and cultural items. The child can explore these boxes independently, choosing the ones they are most interested in.

- **Extension Activities:** Children can then participate in various extension activities, such as drawing their own maps, creating continent booklets, or researching specific countries or cultures within a continent.

In this example, the child has the freedom to learn at their own pace, to choose the activities they are most interested in, and to learn through hands-on, practical experience, all key elements of Montessori education. It's worth noting that throughout this process, the teacher acts more as a guide, stepping in when necessary but mainly observing and facilitating the child's learning process.

MONTESSORI KEY FEATURES

In a Montessori environment, children are treated as naturally eager for knowledge and capable of initiating learning in a supportive, thoughtfully prepared learning environment. One of the hallmark features of the Montessori method is its focus on mixed-age classrooms, which, in a homeschool setting, translates to activities that are designed to encourage older and younger children to learn from each other. This approach fosters not just academic skills but also social development, as children learn to help and be helped by their peers, promoting a sense of community and empathy.

Montessori emphasizes learning through discovery rather than through direct instruction, encouraging children to explore materials and activities at their own pace. This self-directed learning promotes a sense of independence and confidence, as children are allowed to choose their activities based on their interests and abilities. The materials used in Montessori homeschooling are specially designed to be aesthetically pleasing and to teach specific skills; they are often self-correcting, which means they provide immediate feedback that empowers children to learn through their mistakes without adult intervention.

Another key aspect is the prepared environment, which is carefully organized and tailored to facilitate independent learning and exploration. In a homeschool setting, this means creating a learning space that is orderly, child-sized, and filled with materials that meet the developmental needs of the child. This environment is designed to maximize independent learning and exploration.

The Montessori approach also places a strong emphasis on practical life skills, such as cooking, cleaning, and gardening. These activities are not only aimed at teaching specific skills but also at fostering a sense of responsibility, independence, and respect for the environment. Additionally, Montessori homeschooling encourages uninterrupted blocks of work time, allowing children to become deeply engaged in their learning activities without frequent interruptions. This approach respects the natural rhythms of the child's learning process, promoting concentration and depth of understanding.

Lastly, Montessori values the development of the whole child—physical, social, emotional, and cognitive. This holistic approach aims to cultivate not just academic abilities but also life skills, problem-solving abilities, and a lifelong love of learning. Through its emphasis on individualized learning, hands-on discovery, and respect for the child's natural development, the Montessori homeschooling approach offers a unique and effective educational experience that prepares children for both academic success and the practical challenges of everyday life.

MONTESSORI ADVANTAGES

- **Individualized Learning Pace:** The Montessori method allows children to learn at their own pace, fostering a deeper understanding of concepts. This individualized approach ensures that each child can spend more time on areas they find challenging and move ahead quickly in subjects in which they excel.

- **Hands-On Learning:** Montessori emphasizes hands-on, experiential learning, which can be particularly effective in a homeschool setting. By using a mix of physical materials and real-world activities, children can engage more fully with the subject matter. This approach helps in developing fine motor skills, critical thinking, and a love for learning.

- **Fostering Independence and Responsibility:** This method encourages children to take responsibility for their own learning and to develop independence. This can translate into children managing their own schedules, choosing their activities, and setting personal goals. This sense of ownership over their education can boost motivation, self-discipline, and confidence, preparing them well for future academic and personal challenges.

MONTESSORI DISADVANTAGES

While the Montessori education system has many benefits, like any educational approach, it also has some potential drawbacks, depending on the specific needs and circumstances of the child and their family. Here are a few:

- **Cost:** Montessori schools can be expensive, which may put them out of reach for some families. This is primarily due to the low student-to-teacher ratio and the cost of the specialized Montessori materials.

- **Limited Structure:** The free-form nature of Montessori education may not suit all children. Some kids thrive in a more structured environment with clear rules and instructions.

- **Transition to Traditional Schooling:** Children who transition from a Montessori school to a traditional education setting may face challenges. The self-directed, independent learning style of Montessori can be quite different from the structured, teacher-led approach in many traditional schools.

- **Academic Rigor:** While Montessori schools typically provide a rich learning environment, some parents and educators argue that they may not provide the same level of academic rigor as traditional schools, particularly in subjects like math and science.

- **Social Interaction:** Because Montessori education emphasizes individual work, some critics argue that it does not provide enough opportunities for social interaction and team collaboration.

- **Availability:** Not all communities have Montessori schools, and even in communities where they do exist, there may be limited availability due to high demand.

- **Adherence to Principles:** Not all schools that label themselves as Montessori adhere strictly to Maria Montessori's principles. This can lead to inconsistency in the quality and implementation of the Montessori method.

---------- **Summary** ----------

Keep in mind that Montessori education isn't a one-size-fits-all deal—it really comes down to whether it suits your child's unique learning style and your family's resources and preferences. Montessori has made a big splash in early childhood education by focusing on child-centered learning, hands-on exploration, and personalized guidance. It's got some serious perks, like encouraging independence, well-rounded growth, and a genuine love for learning. But it's not without its critics—some say it lacks standardized assessments and can be a bit pricey. Still, the undeniable benefits, like its emphasis on individuality, self-discipline, and nurturing environments, keep Montessori in the spotlight. By tackling its drawbacks and playing to its strengths, Montessori continues to be a go-to approach for educators and parents who want something a little different in early childhood education.

For Further Research:

To explore more about the Maria Montessori method and determine if it's the right fit for your child, visit the Montessori Foundation's website here at: http://www.montessori.org. Here, you'll find a wealth of resources including detailed articles, toolkits for parents, and a directory of accredited Montessori schools. Additionally, Maria Montessori's original writings provide profound insights into her educational philosophy and can serve as an invaluable guide for both new and seasoned practitioners.

22

The Reggio Emilia Approach

Where Curiosity Becomes the Curriculum

One child, one teacher, one book, and one pen can change the world.
— Malala Yousafzai

T HE REGGIO EMILIA APPROACH, named after the city in northern Italy from which it originated, is a unique educational philosophy centered on preschool and primary education in the classroom. It was developed by psychologist Loris Malaguzzi and the parents of the villages around Reggio Emilia after World War II. They sought to create a new approach to education based on the principles of respect, responsibility, and community through exploration and discovery in a supportive and enriching environment.

HOW DOES THE REGGIO EMILIA APPROACH WORK?

The Reggio Emilia method is an educational approach that emphasizes child-centered, experiential learning driven by the interests and curiosities of the child. In this method, the learning environment is seen as the "third teacher," and it is carefully arranged to encourage exploration and discovery. Parents act as facilitators, guiding their children through projects and activities that integrate art, science, literature, and other subjects. Collaboration and social interaction are key components, often involving group work with other homeschool families or community participation. Documentation of the child's progress through various mediums, such as photos and journals, is also a crucial aspect, allowing for reflection and deeper understanding of their learning journey. While the Reggio

Emilia approach was initially developed in a preschool setting, its principles can certainly be adapted for homeschooling.

REGGIO EMILIA KEY FEATURES

Key aspects such as encouraging child-led learning, viewing the environment as a 'third teacher', and documenting the child's learning journey can all be integrated into a homeschooling routine. The Reggio Emilia emphasis on experiential learning, creativity, and critical thinking is very much compatible with homeschooling. It also often emphasizes individualized learning and practical, real-world experiences.

Child as Protagonist

In the Reggio Emilia approach, the child is viewed as a protagonist—a strong, capable being full of potential and eager to interact with the world around them. Here's an illustrative example of this principle:

Let's imagine a group of children in a Reggio Emilia-inspired school have shown an interest in birds—they've been watching them from the classroom window, making birdlike sounds, and sketching images of birds during art time. Noting this interest, the teacher doesn't impose a preset curriculum about birds but instead facilitates an exploration driven by the children's curiosity.

The children might decide they want to build a birdhouse. The teacher supports this initiative, providing them with the necessary materials and guidance. But the children are the ones leading the project, deciding on the design, collaborating on the construction, and figuring out the best place to hang it. They might research different types of birds, study their characteristics, and learn about their habitats and behaviors to ensure their birdhouse is suitable. The children are also encouraged to document their projects. They might draw pictures, write about their observations, or even make a presentation to share with the rest of the school community.

Throughout this project, the children are the protagonists. They're actively involved in their learning journey, making decisions, solving problems, and exploring their interests. The teacher's role is to facilitate, guide, and scaffold their learning, but the children are the ones driving their educational adventures. In this way, the child's rights, individuality, and potential are respected and nurtured.

Teacher as Collaborator

Teachers work alongside children rather than leading them. They facilitate learning by providing resources, asking questions, and documenting progress. The role of the teacher in the Reggio Emilia approach is one of a collaborator. Rather than being the sole source of knowledge, the teacher collaborates with children, co-learning and co-constructing knowledge with them. Here's an example illustrating this principle:

Imagine a group of children expressing an interest in shadows during outdoor play. Instead of immediately providing a lecture about the scientific explanation behind shadows, the teacher, following the Reggio Emilia approach, might pose thought-provoking questions like "What do you think makes shadows?" or "Why do you think the shadow changes its shape and size?" The goal here is to encourage the children to think critically and express their initial thoughts and theories.

Next, the teacher might suggest an exploration activity—using various objects and a light source to create shadows and observe their properties. The children and the teacher engage in this activity together, making observations, discussing findings, and forming new questions. The teacher provides guidance and introduces scientific concepts in a conversational way as and when they naturally emerge in the exploration.

The learning journey might further unfold with children creating shadow art, writing stories about "the secret life of shadows," or exploring how shadows are used in different cultures or art forms. The teacher collaborates with the children throughout these activities, providing support, encouraging deeper thinking, and making connections to broader concepts, but always ensuring that the children's interests and ideas are at the forefront.

In this setting, the teacher is a facilitator, a guide, and a collaborator. They learn alongside the children, embracing moments of surprise and discovery and modeling the joy of lifelong learning.

Environment as the Third Teacher

The layout and decoration of the physical space are significant. Classrooms are designed to be beautiful, calming, and stimulating with natural light, plants, and displayed artwork. In the Reggio Emilia approach, the environment is seen as a crucial part of the learning experience and is often referred to as the "third teacher." It's not just a physical space but an interactive entity that provokes exploration, communication, and relationship-building. Here's an example of how this principle might come to life:

Let's imagine a classroom in a Reggio Emilia-inspired school. The room is bathed in natural light from large windows that offer a view of a lush, green outdoor space. This view itself serves as an ever-changing canvas that sparks curiosity and discussion about seasons, weather, and nature's cycles.

Within the room, different learning stations are set up to encourage exploration. There might be a nature table filled with a variety of leaves, rocks, and seashells. Magnifying glasses are available for children to examine these natural items up close, promoting scientific inquiry and discovery.

In one corner, there's a reading nook with comfortable cushions and a bookshelf holding a diverse collection of books. The area is inviting and encourages children to explore literature and language in a relaxed setting.

Another section of the room could be dedicated to art with easels, paints, clay, and a variety of craft materials. Children's artwork is prominently displayed around the room, validating their efforts and inspiring their peers. The setup encourages self-expression and creativity.

Every piece of furniture and material in the classroom is child-sized, emphasizing the child's importance and ownership in the learning process. The environment is designed to be flexible and responsive to children's changing needs and interests. The room's arrangement can be easily adapted based on children's ongoing projects or evolving interests. Through this carefully crafted environment, children are stimulated to learn through exploration, interaction, and observation. The environment is indeed a "third teacher," fostering children's autonomy, curiosity, and love for learning.

Documentation

Teachers document children's work and the learning process, often displaying it to allow children to see their own learning journey. Documentation is an integral part of the Reggio Emilia approach, and it serves multiple purposes. It makes children's learning processes visible, gives value to their work, allows for reflection and deeper understanding, and provides a historical record of children's learning journey. Here is an example of how documentation might work in practice:

Let's consider a scenario where a group of children are working on a project about recycling. They're exploring the importance of recycling, understanding the recycling process, and creating an art installation using recycled materials. The teacher might document this process through photographs and videos of children engaged in various activities—collecting recyclable materials, discussing their ideas, working on their art pieces, and so on.

In addition, the teacher might record verbatim quotes of children's dialogues and reflections, capturing their thought processes, discoveries, challenges, and solutions. Children's sketches, writings, and other work products related to the project would also be included in the documentation.

This collected documentation could then be organized into a display on the classroom wall or compiled into a portfolio. It tells the story of the children's work on the recycling project from inception to completion.

At various stages of the project, the teacher might refer back to the documentation with the children, prompting them to reflect on their learning, consider new questions, and plan the next steps. The final documentation also serves as a valuable tool for sharing the project and its outcomes with parents, other teachers, and visitors, demonstrating the children's learning journey and the value of their work.

In the Reggio Emilia approach, documentation is not just a method of record-keeping; it's a way of honoring children's work, promoting reflection and deep learning, and facilitating communication and collaboration among children, teachers, and parents.

REGGIO EMILIA ADVANTAGES

- **Child-Centered Learning:** The Reggio Emilia approach places the child at the center of the learning process, emphasizing their interests, ideas, and curiosity. This means that the curriculum can be tailored to the child's passions and questions, fostering a love for learning and encouraging deeper engagement with the material.

- **Collaborative and Social Learning:** Reggio Emilia promotes collaborative learning through social interaction and community involvement. For homeschoolers, this can be adapted by creating opportunities for group projects, interactions with other homeschooling families, and community-based activities. This collaborative approach helps children develop social skills, teamwork, and communication abilities, which are essential for personal and academic growth.

- **Emphasis on Creative Expression:** The Reggio Emilia approach strongly values creative expression through various forms of art, such as drawing, painting, sculpture, and drama. This emphasis on creativity allows children to explore and express their ideas in diverse ways. It nurtures their imagination, critical thinking, and problem-solving skills, while also providing a holistic educational experience that integrates multiple disciplines.

REGGIO EMILIA DISADVANTAGES

It's worth noting that applying the Reggio Emilia approach in a homeschooling context might require a fair amount of preparation and adaptability from parents, as they'll need to facilitate their children's learning, provide a stimulating environment, and find ways to document and assess their progress.

Additionally, the Reggio Emilia philosophy values social interaction and collaborative learning, which could be more challenging to provide in a homeschooling setting, particularly for an only child. However, parents can create opportunities for social interaction through community activities, play dates, extracurricular classes, and so on. Here are some more detailed potential drawbacks to consider:

- **Requires Skilled, Committed Teachers:** The teacher's role as a facilitator requires them to be very involved, responsive, and creative. It requires more planning and reflection than traditional teaching methods. Consider a classroom where the children express interest in building a miniature city. A teacher following the Reggio Emilia approach would need to facilitate this complex project, helping children to research different types of buildings, plan their city, gather materials, and construct their buildings. This requires a high degree of creativity, resourcefulness, and adaptability from the teacher, as well as substantial planning and reflection time.

- **Potential Lack of Structure:** The child-led nature of the Reggio Emilia approach might leave gaps in education if certain areas never become topics of interest. If a child or group of children never express interest in mathematics, for instance, their education might lack in this area. There's a risk that important topics might be overlooked or not explored deeply enough due to the child-led nature of this approach.

- **Inadequate Assessment Measures:** The absence of formal testing or grading might make it hard to assess a child's development and learning progress. If a child is learning at a slower pace or is facing difficulties in a particular area, it might be challenging to identify these issues without formal assessments. For example, without a standard reading test, a teacher might not realize that a child is struggling with reading comprehension.

- **Need for Resources:** The importance placed on the environment requires resources for creating and maintaining an enriching learning space. It could feature different learning stations like an art studio, a construction zone, a science lab, a library, and more, all filled with quality materials. Creating and maintaining such a rich, stimulating environment can be resource-intensive and might not be feasible for schools with tight budgets or large class sizes.

- **Not for Every Child:** Certain children tend to flourish in a setting characterized by structure, clear guidelines, and explicit rules. The unstructured nature of the Reggio Emilia approach, with which these children might struggle to engage, could present a challenging aspect for them. For instance, if a child is asked to explore a topic of their choice and present their findings, they might feel overwhelmed by the open-ended nature of the task and struggle to engage with it effectively.

---------- **Summary** ----------

The Reggio Emilia approach is an innovative and child-centric educational philosophy that places the learner at the heart of the educational process. It values the child's individuality, encourages their curiosity, and fosters a deep love for learning. With classrooms that buzz with creativity and teachers who act more like partners than instructors, this method offers a unique, hands-on learning experience. However, it's important to remember that this approach, like any educational philosophy, has potential drawbacks and may not be suitable for every child. But, as with any educational philosophy, it's not a one-size-fits-all solution. It's key to consider whether this approach aligns with your child's needs, interests, and learning style. At the end of the day, whatever path you choose, the goal is the same: helping your child develop a lifelong love for learning.

For Further Research:

North American Reggio Emilia Alliance (NAREA): Offers a wealth of resources including insights, training opportunities, and community connections for those interested in the Reggio Emilia approach. You can visit them here at: https://www.reggioalliance.org.

23

The Unit Studies Approach

Making School Subjects Play Nice Together

You teach what you are, you teach what you read, you teach what you tell children, but most of all you teach by example.

— John Taylor Gatto

DELVE INTO THE INTERCONNECTED realms of unit studies, where subjects are woven together around key topics. Unit Studies, in a nutshell, are thematic, interdisciplinary learning experiences that allow your child to explore a topic in depth by integrating various subjects. Think of it as the Swiss Army knife of homeschooling—a multipurpose tool that packs a lot into a neat little package. This approach encourages hands-on, experiential learning while providing enough structure to guide your child's educational journey. Eager to see the big picture and weave together threads of knowledge from different subjects? Well, hold onto your interdisciplinary hats, folks! We're about to freefall into the unified universe of Unit Studies.

HOW DO UNIT STUDIES WORK?

You start by selecting a topic or theme that interests your child, such as ancient Egypt, ocean life, or even chocolate. Then, you design a series of lessons and activities that incorporate different subjects—like history, science, math, language arts, and the arts—all centered around that theme. Here are a few examples:

- **Dinosaurs Unit:** If your child is fascinated by dinosaurs, you can create a unit that involves reading books about dinosaurs (literacy), exploring the eras in which different dinosaurs lived (history), understanding dinosaur anatomy (science), calculating the possible sizes of different dinosaurs based on their footprints (mathematics), and even creating a diorama of a prehistoric landscape (art).

- **Space Unit:** For a child interested in space, you can investigate the history of space exploration (history), learn about different celestial bodies (science), write a story about traveling to a different planet (creative writing), calculate the distance between different planets (math), and create a model of the solar system (art).

- **Ecosystem Unit**: If your child is interested in nature, you can study different ecosystems (science), read about animals that live in those environments (literacy), create a timeline of how those ecosystems have changed over time (history), calculate the populations of different species (math), and make a collage of an ecosystem (art).

- **Ancient Civilizations Unit:** For a history-loving child, you could explore an ancient civilization such as the Romans. You can learn about their daily lives (history), read Roman myths (literacy), experiment with building structures like aqueducts (science and engineering), understand Roman numerals (math), and create a mosaic or a toga (art).

- **Food and Nutrition Unit**: You can explore the journey of a vegetable from farm to table (science and social studies), read about different cuisines around the world (literacy), calculate the nutritional content of a meal (math), and prepare a dish from a different culture (home economics and art).

You see? All the subjects tie back to the central theme of ancient Egypt, creating a rich, interconnected web of learning. In each of these examples, the unit study approach brings together multiple subjects around the chosen topic, offering a multifaceted exploration. It's a great way to foster deep learning and see the interconnectedness of different areas of knowledge.

UNIT STUDIES KEY FEATURES

- **Integrated Learning:** Unit studies integrate multiple subjects around a central theme or topic, allowing children to explore connections and relationships between different disciplines. This approach promotes a holistic understanding of concepts and encourages critical thinking skills.

- **Interdisciplinary Approach:** Unit studies encourage the blending of subjects such as science, social studies, language arts, and math rather than teaching them in isolation. This enables students to see how different subjects are interconnected in real-life contexts.

- **Hands-on Experiences:** Unit studies often incorporate hands-on activities, experiments, field trips, and projects to deepen students' understanding and engagement. These hands-on experiences make learning more tangible and memorable.

- **Student Engagement and Choice:** Unit studies typically offer opportunities for student choice and voice, allowing learners to have input in selecting topics or designing aspects of their learning. This fosters a sense of ownership and motivation in students.

- **Depth and Breadth of Understanding:** By studying a topic in-depth over an extended period, unit studies promote a deeper understanding of concepts and encourage children to make connections beyond surface-level knowledge. This approach allows for more meaningful learning experiences.

- **Cross-Curricular Skills Development:** Unit studies provide ample opportunities for children to develop essential skills such as critical thinking, research, communication, and collaboration. These skills are integrated naturally within the context of the chosen theme or topic.

- **Personalization and Differentiation:** Unit studies can be tailored to meet the individual needs, interests, and abilities of students. Teachers can adapt and modify the curriculum to ensure that each student is appropriately challenged and supported.

- **Real-World Relevance:** Unit studies often emphasize the application of knowledge in real-world contexts. By exploring topics that are relevant and meaningful to students' lives, they develop a deeper appreciation for the practicality and value of what they are learning.

UNIT STUDIES ADVANTAGES

Unit studies are a bit like the Swiss Army knife of the homeschooling world—super versatile and ready to handle a family of learners, no matter their ages or grades. Imagine plopping down a theme or topic—let's say, the solar system—and then watching each of your kids orbit around it in their own unique ways. The older ones might be calculating the force of gravity like they're ready for NASA, while the littles are over there crafting papier-mâché planets or getting the lowdown on why Pluto isn't invited to the planet parties anymore.

This isn't just a win for the kids; it's a game-changer for you, the parent-teacher. Not only do you get to cut down on planning time (because who doesn't love a one-theme-fits-all approach?), but you also get front-row seats to the coolest collaboration show—your kids teaching each other! Big brother explains asteroid belts, little sister shares a star-shaped cookie, and just like that, you're not just building brains—you're building bonds. Plus, watching how each child approaches the same material? It's like being a talent scout in your own home, picking up on clues to help you tailor the learning experience to fit each budding brainiac's style.

UNIT STUDIES DISADVANTAGES

Now, a word of warning: unit studies aren't just a walk in the educational park. They do require a bit of planning. Imagine being the mastermind behind a grand-themed party—you've got to think about the decorations, the food, the games, all linking back to the theme. Similarly, you'll need to creatively intertwine various subjects with the chosen theme, ensuring it's an engaging, enlightening romp and not just a theme park ride that goes around in circles. Here are a few to consider:

- **Time-Consuming Preparation:** Unit Studies can be labor-intensive to prepare. To create a truly integrated study, parents often have to scour multiple resources and curate materials themselves, which can be time-consuming.

- **Potential for Knowledge Gaps:** Since Unit Studies often delve deep into specific topics, there's a risk of skipping over or glossing past other important subjects or subtopics. It can be challenging to ensure a comprehensive education that covers all necessary areas evenly.

- **Difficulty in Tracking Progress:** Traditional subject-based curriculums often come with clear benchmarks and assessment tools. However, with the Unit Studies approach, it can be more challenging to assess a student's progress and mastery of various subjects.

- **Not Ideal for Every Learner:** Some Children thrive on deep dives into topics of interest, but others may prefer a more structured approach to learning with clear separations between subjects. Unit Studies require a certain level of curiosity and self-direction that might not suit every learner.

- **Can be Overwhelming:** Since Unit Studies integrate multiple subjects, they can sometimes feel overwhelming for both the parent and the child. Balancing depth with breadth can be a tricky line to tread.

- **Flexibility can Lead to Procrastination:** The flexibility of Unit Studies is generally a plus, but for some families, it can lead to procrastination or lack of structure. Without a clear plan, it's easy to keep pushing fewer desirable topics to the side.

---------- **Summary** ----------

The beauty of unit studies is the flexibility it offers. It's like being the director of your own educational movie, where the central theme is the star, and all the subjects are the supporting cast, making the star shine brighter. Your child can take the lead in choosing the unit study topic and in guiding her own exploration. You can provide a variety of resources—books, videos, field trips, art supplies—and let your child's curiosity dictate the direction of their learning. With this approach, unit studies provide a framework that encourages self-directed, hands-on exploration while still offering some structure. So, give unit studies a try, and watch as your child's education takes flight in the fascinating world of themed, interdisciplinary learning!

For Further Research:

Dive deeper into the lovely world of unit studies by visiting this website here: http://www.homeschoolhelperonline.com/unitstudies. This resource offers a wide array of free unit study plans, activities, and guidance on how to effectively integrate different subjects around compelling themes. Whether you're looking for ideas on historical events, scientific discoveries, or artistic pursuits, you'll find comprehensive tools to help you craft engaging educational experiences that spark curiosity and foster learning.

24

The Unschooling Approach

Free-Range Scholars

The teacher is the most important member of our society. He or she is building the nation and its future.

— Martin Luther King, Jr.

I MAGINE A DAY FREE of textbooks and strict schedules, where curiosity is the compass guiding your child's learning adventure. With this homeschool approach, you'll encounter a lot of hands-off teaching and learning, allowing your kids to take charge of their own education. Remember that scene in "Jurassic Park" when Dr. Ian Malcolm says, "Life, uh, finds a way?" Well, so do unschooled kids.

HOW DOES THE UNSCHOOLING APPROACH WORK?

Unschoolers typically follow a more relaxed schedule, giving their kids the freedom to learn at their own pace and choose the topics that interest them. There's less emphasis on structured lessons and more focus on creating a nurturing environment that fosters creativity, critical thinking, and a love for learning. Parents act as facilitators rather than instructors, providing resources and opportunities for discovery based on the child's curiosities and developmental readiness. This method emphasizes autonomy and experiential learning, where children learn through everyday life experiences, play, and exploration.

UNSCHOOLING KEY FEATURES

If this sounds like a dream, unschooling might be the perfect fit for your family, allowing your child to follow their interests and explore the world around them organically. Here are some areas of focus for unschoolers:

- **Nature Exploration:** Unschooling often involves spending time outdoors and exploring the natural world. Children might have the freedom to observe plants and animals, go on hikes or nature walks, and learn about ecology and conservation through hands-on experiences.

- **Pursuing Personal Interests:** Unschooling encourages children to follow their passions and get lost into subjects that genuinely interest them. For example, if a child shows a keen interest in marine life, they might spend their time reading books about marine biology, watching documentaries, visiting aquariums, and even volunteering with local conservation organizations.

- **Project-Based Learning:** Unschooling allows children to engage in long-term projects driven by their interests. For instance, a child passionate about photography might spend weeks or months mastering different techniques, studying the work of famous photographers, and creating their own portfolio.

- **Real-World Experiences:** Unschooling recognizes that learning happens naturally in everyday life. Children might accompany their parents on trips to the grocery store and learn about budgeting, measurement, and nutrition. They might participate in household chores and gain practical skills like cooking, cleaning, and managing finances.

- **Community Involvement:** Unschooling often involves actively engaging with the local community. Children might join clubs, attend workshops, or take part in community events that align with their interests. For example, a child interested in music might join a community band or attend local concerts.

- **Travel and Cultural Immersion:** Unschooling families often take advantage of the flexibility of their educational approach to travel and immerse themselves in different cultures. Children can learn about history, geography, languages, and traditions by exploring new places, interacting with locals, and experiencing different customs firsthand.

UNSCHOOLING ADVANTAGES

Unschooling is like the cool, laid-back uncle of the education world—it's all about letting the kids lead the way and learn on their own terms. Picture this: instead of a daily schedule packed tighter than a subway at rush hour, each child gets to follow their own curiosities, whether that means digging into dinosaurs or writing their own comic book series. It's about as personalized as education gets, because who knows better what they want to learn than the kids themselves?

This chill approach isn't just about keeping the peace at the kitchen table. It's a full-on strategy for sparking genuine passion and deep dives into whatever catches their fancy. Young learners grow into self-driven seekers, armed with the skills to pursue knowledge without someone hovering over their shoulder with a red pen and a stopwatch. And for you, the parent-guide rather than the parent-instructor, it's less about lesson plans and more about observing, facilitating, and occasionally stepping in to help navigate the learning journey. It turns education into an adventure that the whole family shares—no permission slips required! Plus, it's a front-row ticket to seeing your kids blossom into unique individuals, each with their own set of dazzling skills and interests.

UNSCHOOLING DISADVANTAGES

While unschooling teases with its tantalizing advantages, it's wise to weigh the possible pitfalls too. It may not be the first choice for parents who'd rather not see their children entranced by all-day Minecraft marathons on YouTube. Be forewarned; this unconventional approach might earn you a few puzzled looks from your friends and family. Let's delve into a few potential downsides to consider:

- **Lack of Structure:** Unschooling relies heavily on child-led learning, which means there is often a lack of structured curriculum and predetermined learning goals. This can be challenging for parents who prefer a more organized and structured approach to education.

- **Gaps in Knowledge:** Without a set curriculum, there is a risk of unintentional gaps in knowledge. While children may excel in their areas of interest, they might have limited exposure to subjects they are less inclined to explore. It requires careful monitoring and supplementation to ensure a well-rounded education.

- **Limited External Recognition:** Traditional educational systems and institutions may not easily recognize unschooling or value it in the same way as more conventional forms of education. This can present challenges when it comes to college admissions, standardized testing, or transitioning to a more traditional learning environment.

- **Parental Commitment and Resources:** Unschooling often requires a significant commitment from parents in terms of time, effort, and resources. Parents play a vital role in facilitating their child's learning experiences, providing access to materials, resources, and opportunities for exploration.

- **Socialization:** Unschooling may present challenges when it comes to socialization with peers, as the learning environment is less structured and less likely to provide regular opportunities for interaction with other children. Parents need to actively seek out social activities, groups, or community programs to ensure their child has ample social interactions.

- **Parental Comfort Zones:** Unschooling can push parents outside their comfort zones, especially if they are accustomed to a more traditional educational approach. It requires trusting in the child's natural learning process and allowing them to take charge of their education, which can be a significant mindset shift for some parents.

---------- **Summary** ----------

So there you have it, the grand tour of unschooling—a method that throws the traditional school playbook out the window to let learning roam free, where curiosity leads the charge. It's a bit like turning the whole world into a classroom without walls, schedules, or a bell dictating when to switch gears. Unschooling is a testament to trusting your kids' innate drive to learn, letting them dive headfirst into passions that light up their eyes, from deciphering the mysteries of marine life to orchestrating their very own symphony with a community band.

As we wrap up this chapter, remember: unschooling isn't just an educational choice; it's a lifestyle. It's about embracing a bit of the unknown, the spontaneous, and sometimes, the messy. But, let's not gloss over the caveats—it's not all sunshine and free-range learning. Without structured curriculum, there's a risk that some subjects might fall by the wayside, leaving gaps in a traditional education sense. And let's face it, not every college or formal institution will tip their hat to an unschooled background without some convincing. Plus, this path demands a hefty dose of parental involvement—think of it as less 'set it and forget it' and more 'always on your toes.' If the idea of education as one grand, glorious adventure appeals to you—if you're ready to be less of a stern conductor and more of a co-explorer—then unschooling might just be your family's ticket to an extraordinary, personalized learning journey. Buckle up, toss out the old maps, and see where this learning road takes you!

For Further Research:

Unschooling.com: This website provides insights, resources, and support for families interested in the unschooling approach, where learning is driven by the child's interests rather than a structured curriculum. You can visit them here at: https://www.unschooling.com.

25

The Waldorf Approach

Cultivating Renaissance Kids with Rhythm and Rhyme

Where is the book in which the teacher can read about what teaching is? The children themselves are this book. We should not learn to teach out of any book other than the one lying open before us and consisting of the children themselves.

— Rudolf Steiner

I MAGINE STEPPING INTO A cozy, organic farm-to-table restaurant, where each dish is prepared with love, intention, and a deep respect for the natural world. The Waldorf method of education, developed by Rudolf Steiner in the early 20th century, emphasizes holistic development by nurturing the intellectual, artistic, and practical skills of children. This approach integrates academics with hands-on activities and creative arts, fostering a well-rounded education that respects the interconnectedness of body, mind, and spirit.

HOW DOES THE WALDORF APPROACH WORK?

Just as a farm-to-table experience offers locally sourced, wholesome ingredients, Waldorf education invites children to savor the joy of learning and cultivate a deep connection with the world around them. This approach presents a menu of storytelling, art, music, and hands-on crafts, complemented by a healthy portion of academic subjects. It's a holistic, organic, and artistic journey that nourishes children's intellectual, emotional, and physical growth.

In the Waldorf classroom, you'll find a rich tapestry of activities that engage the head, heart, and hands. Children immerse themselves in captivating stories, expressing their creativity through art and music and engaging in practical activities that develop practical skills. Academic subjects are seamlessly interwoven with artistic experiences, fostering a well-rounded education that goes beyond conventional textbook learning.

WALDORF KEY FEATURES

- **Morning Circle:** A typical Waldorf day often begins with a morning circle, where children gather together to sing songs, recite poems, engage in movement exercises, and participate in rhythmic activities. This helps foster a sense of community, develops fine motor skills, and sets a harmonious tone for the day.

- **Imaginative Play:** Waldorf education encourages imaginative play as a key component of learning. Children engage in open-ended, unstructured play with simple, natural toys such as wooden blocks, dolls, and play silks. Through play, they develop creativity, problem-solving abilities, social skills, and language proficiency.

- **Main Lesson Blocks:** Waldorf curriculum organizes subjects into "main lesson blocks," where children immerse themselves in a specific topic for a few weeks. For example, during a main lesson block on Ancient Egypt, your child might create elaborate drawings, write stories, build models of pyramids, learn about hieroglyphics, and even prepare Egyptian-inspired meals. This immersive approach allows for deep exploration and understanding of the subject matter.

- **Handwork and Crafts:** Waldorf education emphasizes the development of practical skills and the use of hands in learning. Children engage in various handwork activities such as knitting, sewing, woodworking, and felting. These activities promote fine motor skills, focus, patience, and creativity while producing beautiful and useful creations.

- **Nature-Based Learning:** Waldorf education values a strong connection with nature. Children spend time outdoors, engaging in activities like gardening, nature walks, and seasonal celebrations. They observe and learn about the natural world, fostering an appreciation for its beauty, cycles, and interdependence.

- **Arts Integration:** Artistic expression is woven throughout the Waldorf curriculum. Children engage in activities such as watercolor painting, drawing, modeling with beeswax, and playing musical instruments. Artistic experiences support cognitive development, self-expression, and emotional well-being.

- **Storytelling and Oral Tradition:** Storytelling plays a central role in Waldorf education. Teachers skillfully tell stories, often using rich language and vivid imagery, to ignite children's imaginations and cultivate a love for literature. Children also have opportunities to retell stories through dramatic play, puppetry, and creative writing.

WALDORF ADVANTAGES

- **Holistic Development:** Waldorf education focuses on nurturing the whole child—intellectually, emotionally, physically, and spiritually. By integrating academics with artistic and practical activities, it fosters well-rounded development and encourages children to engage deeply with their learning.

- **Creativity and Critical Thinking:** The Waldorf method emphasizes creative expression and independent thinking. Through activities like storytelling, music, and hands-on projects, children develop their creativity and problem-solving skills, preparing them to think critically and innovatively in various aspects of life.

- **Developmentally Appropriate Learning:** The curriculum is tailored to align with the natural developmental stages of children. This approach ensures that the learning experiences are age-appropriate and engaging, helping students build a strong foundation at each stage of their growth and fostering a lifelong love of learning.

WALDORF DISADVANTAGES

While the Waldorf method offers a unique and holistic educational experience, it's important to consider some aspects. The emphasis on artistic activities and the relatively limited use of technology may not align with the preferences of all families. Additionally, parents seeking a more structured, academically focused approach might find the Waldorf method less suitable for their needs. Here are some challenges that may arise:

- **Limited Emphasis on Academic Skills:** Critics argue that the Waldorf approach places less emphasis on formal academic instruction during the early years, which may result in children entering traditional academic settings later with potential gaps in specific skills or knowledge. Some parents may be concerned about how this approach aligns with standardized testing requirements or college preparation.

- **Limited Use of Technology:** Waldorf education traditionally limits the use of technology, especially in the early years. While this approach aims to protect children from excessive screen time and promote imaginative play, it may pose challenges for families who rely on digital resources for certain subjects or skills development. In today's digital age, finding a balance between technology use and hands-on learning can be a consideration for some families.

- **Lack of Individualized Instruction:** The Waldorf approach often follows a group-oriented model, where children progress together through the curriculum without strict differentiation based on individual abilities or interests. This may present challenges for children who require more personalized instruction or have advanced skills in specific areas. Additionally, children who struggle with certain subjects may not receive immediate targeted support.

- **Limited Exposure to Modern Technologies:** Waldorf education tends to delay or limit exposure to modern technologies, such as computers and tablets. While this is done to protect children's development and encourage hands-on engagement with the physical world, it may result in children having limited exposure to essential digital literacy skills that are increasingly relevant in today's society.

- **Parental Commitment and Understanding:** Implementing the Waldorf approach requires a high level of commitment and understanding from parents. Families need to be willing to embrace the principles and philosophy of Waldorf education, which may involve making significant lifestyle adjustments and actively supporting their child's learning at home. This level of involvement and dedication may not be feasible for all families.

---------- Summary ----------

For families yearning for a nurturing and well-rounded educational journey, Waldorf education serves up a recipe for success. It instills a deep sense of wonder, fosters a connection with nature, and nurtures children's intellectual, emotional, and creative potential. Like a delightful meal made with love and intention, Waldorf education invites children to embrace their unique gifts and become Renaissance individuals ready to make a meaningful impact on the world.

For Further Research:

The Association of Waldorf Schools of North America (AWSNA): Provides information about Waldorf education, resources for parents and educators, and a directory of Waldorf schools. https://www.waldorfeducation.org.

26

The Worldschooling Approach

A Globetrotter's Guide to Experiential Education

The world is a book and those who do not travel read only one page.
— Saint Augustine

I MAGINE STROLLING THROUGH VIBRANT street markets, trying new flavors, and engaging in meaningful conversations with people from different backgrounds. Well, gather your globes, travelogues, and the spirit of curiosity because worldschooling captures this essence by cultivating an insatiable appetite for adventure and a broad palate for knowledge. It breaks down the walls of traditional classrooms and encourages hands-on exploration of the world's wonders. Let the planet transform into your child's vast, open-air classroom, where the languages, landscapes, histories, and human connections construct a living, breathing, and indelible educational expedition.

HOW DOES WORLDSCHOOLING WORK?

The worldschooling approach works by using the world as a classroom, integrating travel and real-world experiences into the educational process. As you travel with your family, your children immerse themselves in the sights, sounds, and flavors of each destination. They learn about geography by traversing diverse landscapes, absorbing history through visiting ancient sites, and embracing languages by engaging with locals. They also practice math through exchange rates, calculating travel times and distances, budgeting for trips, and understanding architectural measurements and conversions. It's an adventurous feast for the senses that expands horizons and stimulates curiosity. Through worldschooling, your child not only gains academic knowledge but also develops essential life skills like adaptability, cultural understanding, and open-mindedness. They become global citizens, appreciating the diversity and interconnectedness of our world.

WORLDSCHOOLING KEY FEATURES

The worldschooling approach offers countless opportunities for learning through travel and cultural experiences. Here are a few examples to give you a taste of what it can entail:

- **Historical Expeditions:** Imagine exploring ancient and past civilizations firsthand. Your family could travel to Egypt to witness the majestic pyramids, explore the ancient Inca city of Machu Picchu in Peru, and admire the intricate architecture of the Taj Mahal in India. Through these immersive experiences, your children could learn about the history, architecture, and cultural significance of these ancient wonders.

- **Language and Cultural Immersion:** Worldschooling provides the perfect opportunity for language learning and cultural immersion. You might spend a month in Spain, where your children take Spanish classes, converse with locals, and experience the vibrant culture firsthand. By living and interacting with native speakers, they develop a deeper understanding of the language and its cultural context.

- **Environmental Exploration:** Traveling to diverse ecosystems allows children to learn about environmental conservation and sustainability. You might explore the Amazon rainforest or the Great Barrier Reef, learning about their biodiversity and the challenges they face. Your children could participate in fieldwork, assisting scientists and researchers and gaining a firsthand understanding of environmental issues.

- **Culinary Adventures:** Worldschooling also involves sampling local cuisines and exploring the culinary traditions of different regions. Your family might attend cooking classes in Thailand, learning to prepare authentic Thai dishes. Through this experience, your children not only develop their cooking skills but also gain insight into the country's culture, traditions, and ingredients.

- **Art and Cultural Heritage:** Imagine visiting renowned art museums and historical landmarks around the world. Your children could explore the Louvre in Paris, marveling at masterpieces like the Mona Lisa, or visit the Royal Palace of the Oba of Benin in Nigeria, learning about the rich heritage and advanced metalworking skills of the Benin Kingdom. They could also explore Cahokia Mounds in Illinois, the largest pre-Columbian settlement north of Mexico, which showcases the complex society and advanced engineering skills of the Mississippian culture. These experiences foster a deep appreciation for art, history, and cultural heritage, making learning tangible and memorable for children.

- **Community Engagement:** Worldschooling often involves engaging with local communities and volunteering. Your family might spend time in a rural village, helping with community projects or teaching English to local children. Through these interactions, your children develop empathy, cross-cultural understanding, and a sense of global citizenship.

WORLDSCHOOLING ADVANTAGES

- **Hands-On Learning:** Provides children with hands-on learning experiences that go beyond traditional classroom education. By exploring different countries and cultures, children engage directly with the material they are studying. This method makes learning tangible and memorable, helping children retain information more effectively.Immersive Learning Experiences

- **Development of Life Skills:** Develops crucial life skills that are often overlooked in conventional education systems. These skills include adaptability, problem-solving, and resilience, as they navigate new environments and face unexpected challenges. Fosters cultural awareness and sensitivity, teaching children to appreciate and respect the diversity of the world.

- **Strong Family Bonds and Personalized Education:** Often involves close family involvement, strengthening family bonds through shared experiences and adventures. Parents can tailor the educational journey to fit their child's unique interests, learning pace, and educational needs. This personalized approach ensures that children are engaged and motivated, as their education is directly relevant to their experiences and passions.

WORLDSCHOOLING DISADVANTAGES

Of course, world schooling isn't without its challenges. It requires careful planning, logistical considerations, and an adaptable mindset. It may disrupt regular routines and necessitate flexibility in education. However, the rewards of exposing your child to a world of experiences, forging lifelong memories, and fostering a love for learning are immeasurable. Nonetheless, it's important to consider the potential drawbacks as well. Here are a few to keep in mind:

- **Financial Considerations:** Traveling extensively can be expensive, and worldschooling often requires a significant financial investment. Costs associated with transportation, accommodation, visas, and experiences can add up quickly. Families need to carefully budget and plan for these expenses to sustain long-term worldschooling.

- **Disruptions to Stability:** Constant travel can disrupt routines, social connections, and a sense of stability for both children and parents. It can be challenging for children to establish long-term friendships and maintain consistent educational routines. Additionally, frequent transitions and adjusting to new environments may cause some level of stress and uncertainty.

- **Educational Challenges:** While worldschooling offers incredible opportunities for experiential learning, it may present challenges in terms of academic structure and continuity. Children may miss out on traditional classroom settings, standardized curricula, and formal assessments, which could impact their transition to more conventional educational settings in the future.

- **Limited Local Support:** Access to educational resources, support networks, and specialized services may be limited while traveling. Finding suitable educational materials or connecting with local homeschooling or worldschooling communities can be more challenging in unfamiliar locations.

- **Cultural and Language Barriers:** Traveling to different countries and immersing in diverse cultures can present communication and cultural challenges. Language barriers may hinder full engagement and understanding, especially in non-English-speaking countries. Adapting to cultural norms, customs, and expectations can also be a learning curve for both children and parents.

- **Logistical Considerations:** Constant travel requires careful planning, organization, and flexibility. Managing logistics such as visas, transportation, accommodation, and healthcare needs can be complex and time-consuming. Parents need to be resourceful, adaptable, and prepared for unexpected challenges that may arise during their world schooling journey.

---------- **Summary** ----------

Worldschooling is a personalized adventure—what ignites inspiration for one family may look entirely different for another. While there might be a few unexpected turns along the way, embracing these challenges alongside the abundant rewards ensures this exciting lifestyle harmonizes with your family's values, budget, and lifelong learning goals. With worldschooling, the globe transforms into a vibrant classroom bursting with endless opportunities for discovery and growth. So, pack your curiosity and enthusiasm, and prepare for the journey of a lifetime. Safe and joyful travels!

For Further Research:

Worldschooling Central is a comprehensive platform that provides insights, tips, and resources tailored for families embarking on global learning adventures. Embrace the world as your classroom and make the most of every travel opportunity to educate and inspire. Visit here: http://www.worldschoolingcentral.com.

27

The Afterschooling Approach

Outsmarting the Bell—The "Unofficial" Lessons

The bell might ring at three, but the real learning starts when school ends.

— Ebony Jackson

A FTERSCHOOLING DOES NOT FIT the traditional homeschool approach, but it's a fantastic option for those who have the homeschooling spirit but can't commit full-time. This is actually the route I took before I pulled my oldest child out of public school when he was in second grade. If you love the idea of personalized, flexible learning but are tied to a conventional school schedule, afterschooling is your secret weapon. Think of it as the cherry on top of your child's educational sundae. It's a chance to go deeper into their passions, whether they're budding scientists, aspiring artists, or hands-on project enthusiasts. With afterschooling, you can sprinkle in that extra bit of magic and creativity that a regular school day just can't cover, making sure your child's learning is as unique and exciting as they are.

THE WHY BEHIND AFTERSCHOOLING

So, why jump on the afterschooling bandwagon? For starters, think about how much of the world there is to explore and how little of it fits into the school curriculum. There's only so much time between math and lunch break to learn about the wonders of the universe or the intricacies of ancient civilizations.

Enter afterschooling. It's your ticket to filling in the gaps. Your child loves music but only gets a brief music class at school? Time for afterschool guitar lessons or a family jam session. Obsessed with dinosaurs? Plan a weekend dig at a nearby fossil site. The goal is to fill in those gaps, turning curiosity into expertise and passion into projects.

Also, use school breaks, teacher development days, and holidays to really dig deeper into subjects. These are perfect opportunities to embark on special projects, visit museums, or take educational trips that align with your child's interests. Afterschooling isn't just about filling time; it's about enriching your child's educational journey in a fun and engaging way.

HOW DOES AFTERSCHOOLING WORK?

Here's the scoop: instead of zoning out with mindless screen time when your child comes home from school, your child dives into projects that make their hearts race. They might whip up culinary masterpieces in the kitchen-turned-chef's lab, design their own video game using coding platforms like Scratch, build a volcano that rivals Vesuvius in your living room or pen the next great novel in a cozy writing nook, creating worlds and characters that leap off the page. It's all about harnessing their natural interests and sprinkling a little educational glitter over the top.

Overcome Resistance and Spark Motivation

It's no secret that kids (and, let's be honest, adults too) can be resistant to new things, especially if it smells even remotely like extra work. The key to overcoming this resistance is to find their currency—what excites them, intrigues them, makes them tick. Once you've got that, use it to fuel their motivation. And remember, praise goes a long way. Celebrate the effort, not just the outcome.

Find the Right Balance

The trick to effective afterschooling isn't more work; it's finding the right balance. After a full day of school, your children need time to play, relax, and just be kids. Afterschooling isn't about replacing downtime; it's about making learning so exciting that it becomes a part of their playtime. I cannot stress this enough: the key is not to overload your kids.

So, what's the magic formula? As mentioned earlier, start with your child's passions—whether it's painting, karate, coding, or reenacting historical battles—and blend in some hands-on activities, tech tools, or a dash of real-world exploration. The goal? To turn "homework" into "home-fun" and make every moment a learning adventure. Here's a sample day of what afterschooling could look like.

Sample Afterschool Day

Elementary:
Your child gets home, grabs an apple, and talks about their day. Homework is done first, followed by an outdoor bug hunt. They're armed with a magnifying glass and a journal to observe critters up close. Once inside, it's time for a math game on an app that reinforces multiplication tables. After dinner, the family gathers for a read-aloud of Charlotte's Web, sparking a discussion about kindness and friendship. Before bed, your little explorer listens to a story-based science podcast, dreaming of the mysteries under the sea.

Middle School:
After school, your preteen needs a few minutes to scroll through funny memes before buckling down for homework. With assignments completed, they head outside to build a DIY weather station, tracking daily temperatures and conditions in a journal. Next up, they log into their coding platform, crafting a simple video game using Scratch or Python. Dinner comes with a conversation starter: "Would you rather live in ancient Rome or Egypt?" and a family jam session. The day ends with a riveting historical fiction audiobook that brings the Middle Ages to life.

High School:
Your teen comes home, eats a snack, and decompresses with a 20-minute walk around the block. After wrapping up homework, they head to the backyard greenhouse to check on their ongoing hydroponics project. Next, they focus on their personal passion project, like designing a 3D model for a CAD class or scripting a short film. Dinner becomes a debate about current events—everyone takes a stance. To close the day, the family sits together for an hour-long deep dive into a philosophy podcast or a TED Talk, sparking conversations about life's big questions.

These are just examples to give you an idea of what is possible. By integrating small but impactful activities into the evenings, you can create an enriching learning environment that complements traditional schooling. Afterschooling isn't about piling on more tasks; it's about sparking curiosity, pursuing passions, and connecting as a family—one bug hunt, coding session, and conversation at a time.

AFTERSCHOOLING KEY FEATURES

Afterschooling thrives in the flexibility of where and how it can happen. Transform your kitchen into a culinary school, your backyard into a biology lab, or your living room into an art studio. The whole world is your classroom.

For the Budding Artist

Remember the days of finger painting and fridge-worthy art projects? Well, the digital age has taken this to a whole new level. If your little Picasso loves drawing, why not introduce them to digital art? Tablets and apps like Procreate or Adobe Fresco can transform their creativity, offering endless brushes, colors, and effects that physical art just can't compete with. Plus, it's mess-free, which is a nice bonus for the clean-up crew (aka you).

Future Scientists

Science isn't just memorizing cell structures or elements on the periodic table—it's about curiosity and problem-solving. That's where coding comes in: the universal language of solutions. Platforms like Scratch, Tynker, or code.org give kids a hands-on introduction to coding through game creation, animations, and storytelling. It's like learning a new language, but instead of talking to people, they're having conversations with computers.

Young Historians

Who said history has to be boring? There's more to it than old dates and dusty textbooks. Podcasts and YouTube documentaries can be incredible ways to immerse yourself into history, telling stories that make the past as compelling as any Netflix drama. Imagine learning about the Roman Empire through the lens of a detective story or understanding the significance of the Silk Road through an adventure tale.

Integrate Tech Like a Pro

There are countless educational apps and websites out there that disguise learning as gaming, storytelling, educational, and more. Platforms like Commonsense Media offer reviews and ratings of movies, TV shows, books, apps, and games, helping parents ensure their kids can enjoy worry-free, safe, and age-appropriate content. This way, you can make learning something your kids love to do, without any concerns about inappropriate material.

AFTERSCHOOLING ADVANTAGES

- **Personalized Learning:** Tailor the educational experience to your child's unique interests and learning style.

- **Flexible Schedule:** Afterschooling fits around your family's life, offering a customizable learning pace.

- **Enrichment Opportunities:** Go beyond the school curriculum to explore subjects and skills not covered in traditional classrooms.

- **Strengthened Parent-Child Bond:** Engage in shared learning experiences, fostering closer relationships.

- **Creative Freedom:** Encourage your child's creativity through hands-on projects and innovative approaches to learning.

AFTERSCHOOLING DISADVANTAGES

- **Time Management:** Balancing afterschool activities with downtime and other commitments can be challenging.

- **Resource Intensive:** Afterschooling may require additional materials, technology, and sometimes financial investment.

- **Potential Overload:** Without careful planning, there's a risk of overwhelming your child with too many activities.

- **Consistency and Discipline:** Maintaining a regular afterschool routine can be difficult amidst the demands of daily life.

- **Parental Involvement:** Can require a significant commitment from parents to plan, facilitate, and participate in afterschool activities.

---------- **Summary** ----------

Afterschooling allows you to plug the gaps that school curricula can't cover, tailoring the learning experience to your child's passions. It's not about piling on more work; it's about transforming learning into such fun that it feels like play. It's maintaining a balance between learning and downtime to keep your child engaged without feeling overwhelmed. You can transform your home into anything from a culinary school to a biology lab, as the flexibility of afterschooling turns every space into a potential classroom. Overcoming resistance by finding what excites your child and celebrating their efforts turns any reluctance into eager participation. It's your secret weapon to make learning an exhilarating part of your child's everyday life. So go ahead, outsmart the bell, and sprinkle some extra magic onto their educational sundae!

For Further Research:

Afterschool Alliance: Offers resources and strategies for effectively engaging children in educational activities after school hours. You can visit the website at: http://www.afterschoolalliance.org.

28

The Religious Approach

Blending Beliefs and Values With Learning

Train up a child in the way he should go; even when he is old he will not depart from it.

— Proverbs 22:6

RATHER THAN BEING MERELY an "approach" or "methodology," incorporating a religious perspective into homeschooling provides a unique way to blend beliefs and values with learning. Some families prefer to view their educational journey through the lens of their faith, which adds a distinct perspective to subjects like science, reading, and history, to name a few.

These faith-based glasses are not limited to a single educational style. Whether you're following the traditional path, exploring the experiential route of unschooling, or adhering to the rigorous methods of classical education, incorporating religious values can enhance the experience. It's all about the particular emphasis you want to bring to your educational journey. This approach can be enriched with perspectives from various faiths, adding diverse insights to the learning process.

Disclaimer: In writing this chapter, my goal is to present the best available information with the utmost respect. Please note that while discussing faith, it is not my intention to offend or trigger any readers. I recognize that there are many ways to practice faith, and some perspectives may be sensitive to others. This book is meant to educate, and I feel it is my duty to provide basic information or exposure so you can make informed decisions. Thank you for your understanding.

HOW DOES A BIBLICAL/RELIGIOUS APPROACH WORK?

Integrating a religious or biblical approach into homeschooling offers a robust moral and ethical framework, enriches literary knowledge, and enhances cultural understanding. Each religious perspective presents unique teachings and texts that guide character development and offer profound literary and historical insights. This approach emphasizes the importance of spiritual growth alongside academic development, using scriptures and religious texts as foundational tools for learning. Lessons often incorporate moral and ethical discussions, fostering a holistic understanding of the world through a faith perspective. By seeking to cultivate not only intellectual proficiency but also character and values, this method aligns educational goals with the family's religious beliefs, providing a cohesive and spiritually enriched learning environment. Such an approach ensures that education is not just about knowledge, but also about nurturing well-rounded individuals.

BIBLICAL/RELIGIOUS KEY FEATURES

Incorporating a biblical or religious approach to homeschooling offers a profound way to intertwine faith with education, enriching the learning experience beyond academic achievements. Key features of this approach include:

- **Robust Moral and Ethical Framework:** Utilizing religious texts and teachings as foundational tools, homeschooling can emphasize moral values and ethical principles. This framework guides character development through lessons that might integrate biblical commandments, Quranic virtues, or Buddhist precepts, cultivating qualities like integrity, compassion, and respect.

- **Enhanced Literary Knowledge:** The rich literary and historical content in religious texts such as the Bible, Quran, and Tripitaka provides students with unique insights into language, storytelling, and historical contexts. This not only enhances their understanding of both religious and secular literature but also fosters a greater appreciation of cultural heritage.

- **Deepened Cultural Understanding:** This approach connects religious history with global civilizations, broadening students' perspectives and helping them see the interconnectedness of faith, culture, and history. It prepares them to engage with the world knowledgeably and respectfully, appreciating the diverse tapestry of human belief and experience.

BIBLICAL/RELIGIOUS ADVANTAGES

Christian Approach

- **Moral and Ethical Framework:** A Christian lens provides a strong moral and ethical framework. The Ten Commandments and other biblical teachings offer valuable guidance for character development.

Example: Lessons can be designed to illustrate biblical principles, such as showing kindness to others (Luke 6:31) or the importance of honesty (Proverbs 12:22).

- **Literary Knowledge:** The Bible is a major literary work containing various forms of literature, such as poetry, narrative, law, and prophecy. This knowledge can enhance understanding of other literature and historical events.

Example: Understanding biblical allusions in literature like "Moby Dick" or "The Chronicles of Narnia".

- **Cultural Understanding:** Christianity has had a major influence on Western civilization. Teaching from a biblical lens can enhance understanding of this cultural heritage.

Example: Studying art history with a focus on Christian themes and symbolism.

Islamic Approach

- **Moral and Ethical Framework:** An Islamic lens provides a strong moral and ethical framework. Teachings from the Quran and Hadith offer valuable guidance for character development.

Example: Lessons can emphasize the importance of honesty (Surah Al-Baqarah 2:42) or the significance of charity (Surah Al-Baqarah 2:177).

- **Literary Knowledge:** The Quran is a major literary work, rich in poetry, narrative, and law. This knowledge can enhance understanding of other literature and historical events.

Example: Understanding Quranic allusions in works like "The Arabian Nights" or the poetry of Rumi.

- **Cultural Understanding:** Islam has had a profound influence on global civilization. Teaching from an Islamic lens can enhance understanding of this cultural heritage.

Example: Studying the contributions of Islamic scholars to science and mathematics, such as Al-Khwarizmi and Avicenna.

Jewish Approach

- **Moral and Ethical Framework:** A Jewish lens provides a strong moral and ethical framework. The Torah and Talmud offer valuable guidance for character development.

Example: Lessons can highlight the importance of justice (Deuteronomy 16:20) or kindness to strangers (Leviticus 19:34).

- **Literary Knowledge:** The Hebrew Bible is a major literary work containing poetry, narrative, law, and prophecy. This knowledge can enhance understanding of other literature and historical events.

Example: Understanding biblical allusions in works like "Paradise Lost" or "The Merchant of Venice".

- **Cultural Understanding:** Judaism has had a significant influence on Western civilization. Teaching from a Jewish lens can enhance understanding of this cultural heritage.

Example: Studying Jewish contributions to philosophy, such as the works of Maimonides.

Buddhist Approach

- **Moral and Ethical Framework:** A Buddhist lens provides a strong moral and ethical framework. The teachings of the Buddha, such as the Four Noble Truths and the Noble Eightfold Path, offer valuable guidance for character development.

Example: Lessons can focus on the importance of compassion (karuna) and non-violence (ahimsa).

- **Literary Knowledge:** Buddhist texts, such as the Tripitaka, contain rich narratives, poetry, and philosophical discourses. This knowledge can enhance understanding of other literature and historical events.

Example: Understanding Buddhist themes in literature like Herman Hesse's "Siddhartha" or modern works like "Life of Pi" by Yann Martel.

- **Cultural Understanding**: Buddhism has had a major influence on Eastern civilization. Teaching from a Buddhist lens can enhance understanding of this cultural heritage.

Example: Studying art history with a focus on Buddhist themes and symbolism, such as the depiction of the Buddha in various cultures.

Spiritual Approach

- **Moral and Ethical Framework:** A spiritual lens provides a broad moral and ethical framework, emphasizing universal principles like compassion, mindfulness, and interconnectedness.

Example: Lessons can focus on the importance of empathy and mindfulness practices to foster inner peace and well-being.

- **Literary Knowledge:** Spiritual texts from various traditions, such as the Bhagavad Gita, Tao Te Ching, and writings of mystics, offer profound narratives and philosophical insights.

Example: Understanding spiritual themes in works like "Siddhartha" by Herman Hesse or "The Alchemist" by Paulo Coelho.

- **Cultural Understanding:** A spiritual approach encompasses a wide range of beliefs and practices, enhancing understanding of global spiritual traditions and their impact on culture.

Example: Exploring the influence of spirituality on art, music, and architecture, such as meditation practices influencing modern wellness movements.

BIBLICAL/RELIGIOUS DISADVANTAGES

Christian Approach

- **Limited Perspective:** A strictly biblical lens can lead to a narrow worldview. It may limit exposure to other religious beliefs, cultures, and scientific theories which may contradict biblical teachings.

Example: Potential conflict with the theory of evolution if interpreted literally from the Genesis creation story.

- **Interpretation Difficulties:** The Bible has been interpreted in many different ways over centuries. It can be challenging for parents or children to discern the intended meanings of biblical texts.

Example: The book of Revelation's symbolic language can lead to a variety of interpretations.

- **Potential Bias:** There is a risk of indoctrination if differing viewpoints aren't also presented and discussed. This could potentially limit critical thinking skills.

Example: If a curriculum only teaches biblical creation and does not discuss or even mention the theory of evolution, it can lead to a biased understanding of biology.

Jewish Approach

- **Cultural Isolation:** Focusing exclusively on Jewish teachings might limit students' exposure to other cultural and religious perspectives.

Example: Students may miss learning about important historical events from non-Jewish perspectives, such as the Renaissance or the Reformation.

- **Resource Limitations:** There may be fewer homeschooling resources tailored specifically for Jewish education, making it challenging to find comprehensive materials.

Example: Limited availability of Jewish-themed science and math textbooks that align with religious teachings.

- **Balancing Secular and Religious Education:** Integrating Jewish laws and traditions with secular subjects can be complex, requiring careful planning to ensure both aspects are adequately covered.

Example: Ensuring that students meet standard educational benchmarks while also studying the Torah and Talmud can be demanding.

Islamic Approach

- **Curriculum Constraints:** An Islamic-focused curriculum may restrict exposure to diverse viewpoints and educational content outside the Islamic framework.

Example: Excluding significant world literature or scientific theories that are not aligned with Islamic teachings.

- **Complex Interpretations:** Islamic texts, like the Quran and Hadith, have multiple interpretations, which can lead to confusion or differing views within the educational setting.

Example: The varying interpretations of Sharia law can make it challenging to present a unified understanding.

- **Community Support:** Depending on the region, there may be limited community support or resources for Islamic homeschooling, making it harder to access quality educational materials.

Example: Difficulty finding extracurricular activities or social groups that align with Islamic values.

Spiritual Approach

- **Lack of Structure:** A broad spiritual approach may lack the structured framework that traditional religious curricula provide, leading to inconsistencies in teaching.

Example: Difficulty in establishing a consistent moral and ethical guideline without a specific religious text.

- **Vagueness:** Spiritual teachings can be abstract and open-ended, which might be challenging for younger children to grasp and apply practically.

Example: Concepts like "universal love" or "interconnectedness" may be hard for children to understand without concrete examples.

- **Potential for Misinformation**: Without a standardized curriculum, there's a risk of incorporating inaccurate or superficial interpretations of various spiritual traditions.

Example: Oversimplifying or misrepresenting complex spiritual practices from different cultures.

---------- **Summary** ----------

So, a family might weave their religious worldview into a classical education approach, enriching their educational tapestry with threads of faith. Maybe they'll opt for one of the many religious-based curricula in the homeschool market. Another might introduce religious studies as a side dish while following a secular curriculum as the main course. They're not redrawing the map; they're just adding a splash of their own color to the journey. But remember, those lenses can always be taken off, swapped, or adjusted to suit the learner's needs. In the end, the magic of homeschooling lies in its adaptability. Whether through a religious lens or a secular one, the panorama of knowledge stretches out invitingly, and the choice of viewpoint is in the hands of the explorer.

For Further Research:

For those interested in exploring religious-based curricula or incorporating faith into their homeschooling approach or philosophy, consider visiting the website: http://www.cathyduffyreviews.com. This site offers thorough reviews of both secular and religious homeschool curricula, helping you find the best fit for your family's educational philosophy and religious beliefs. The resources and insights provided can assist you in weaving your religious worldview seamlessly with various educational methods, ensuring your homeschooling experience is both enriching and aligned with your values.

PART V - ADAPTING TO SPECIFIC NEEDS

Welcome to Part V, where we focus on the heart of tailored homeschooling! Think of this section as your trusty guidebook for navigating the unique quirks and challenges each child brings to the table. Whether you're crafting a personalized plan for your special-needs superstar, wrangling the boundless energy of little ones, guiding elementary kids through their next big leap, cracking the code of middle school complexities, or gearing up high schoolers for the real world, this part has you covered. I've loaded these chapters with practical tips and insights to keep your homeschooling journey as smooth and successful as possible. Buckle up; it's going to be a fun ride!

29

The Special-Needs Child

Expect the Unexpected With Grace and Grit

While we try to teach our children all about life, our children teach us what life is all about.

— Angela Schwindt

HOMESCHOOLING A SPECIAL-NEEDS CHILD can feel akin to helming a blockbuster movie—exhilarating, demanding, and immensely gratifying, with a dash of off-camera mayhem. Your unique superstar needs a director who appreciates their uniqueness, scripts a tailored narrative, casts a supportive ensemble, promotes social camaraderie, and throws the grandest wrap parties for every scene/milestone well done. The purpose of this chapter is to be your trusty guide and cheerleader as we cover everything from understanding your child's unique needs, building community and emotional resilience, adapting curricula, incorporating necessary therapies, and gracefully navigating the inevitable challenges.

Whew! That's a tall order which is why this is the longest chapter in this book. By the end of this chapter, you'll have a toolkit full of practical tips, a heart full of encouragement, and a clearer path forward in your homeschooling journey, ensuring your child's specific needs are met with compassion and expertise.

Disclaimer: *Please note that I am not a medical professional or specialist. The strategies, resources, and recommendations in this section are drawn from nearly 15 years of personal experience with my own special needs child, insights gained from collaborating with parents, therapists, and behaviorists in the special-needs community, and my science-based research as a graduate student in education. These insights are meant to offer general guidance and support; however, they should not be considered a substitute for professional medical advice. For information specific to your situation, I strongly recommend consulting with licensed professionals, such as occupational therapists, behavioral therapists, speech language pathologists, or pediatric physicians/neurologists/psychologists. You will find a list of resources throughout this chapter and in the Selected Notes section at the back of the book.*

CAST YOUR STAR—GET TO KNOW YOUR CHILD

The Superpower of Knowing

Before you can start crafting those perfect lesson plans or setting up the ultimate learning space, you need to understand your child's unique needs. Think of this as your homeschooling superpower. Knowing what makes your child tick is like having a secret weapon in your parenting arsenal. Consider these suggestions:

- **Observe and Listen:** Spend time watching how your child interacts with the world. What excites them? What frustrates them? Pay attention to these cues. For example, if your child is excited by music but frustrated by reading, you might integrate songs and musical activities into reading lessons.

- **Learning Styles:** Identify whether your child is a visual, auditory, or kinesthetic learner. This will help you choose the best teaching methods and materials. For instance, a visual learner might benefit from colorful charts and diagrams, while a kinesthetic learner might excel with hands-on activities and experiments.

- **Strengths and Challenges:** Make a list of your child's strengths and areas where they struggle. This will be your guide in creating a balanced and effective learning plan. For example, if your child is strong in math but struggles with writing, you can use their math skills to build confidence while incorporating writing exercises that align with their interests.

UNCOVER THE PLOT TWISTS—UNDERSTAND YOUR CHILD'S CHALLENGES

Raising and educating a child with special needs can be a rewarding yet challenging experience. It's crucial to understand the unique hurdles these children face to provide the necessary support and create an environment conducive to their growth and development. Below is an exploration of some key challenges and how they impact special needs children, along with strategies and resources to address them.

Communication Difficulties

Many special needs children have trouble expressing themselves verbally, leading to frustration and misunderstandings. *Using communication aids such as picture exchange systems (e.g., PECS) or speech-generating devices (e.g., Dynavox) can help bridge this gap and improve their ability to communicate effectively.*

Social Interaction

Special needs children often struggle with understanding social cues, making friends, and maintaining relationships. *Social skills training programs, like those offered by the Social Thinking® curriculum, and group activities designed for special needs children can enhance their social interaction abilities and help them build meaningful relationships.*

Sensory Sensitivities

Many children with special needs experience heightened sensitivities to sensory stimuli, such as loud noises, bright lights, or certain textures. Creating a sensory-friendly environment and using tools like noise-canceling headphones or sensory toys (e.g., fidget spinners, weighted blankets) can help manage these sensitivities. *Resources like the STAR Institute for Sensory Processing can provide additional support and information.*

Behavioral Issues

Challenges with self-regulation can lead to behaviors that are difficult to manage, such as impulsivity, aggression, or meltdowns. Behavioral interventions, such as Applied Behavior Analysis (ABA), can be effective in managing and improving these behaviors. *Organizations like the Autism Society can provide resources and support for behavioral issues.*

Learning Disabilities

Special needs children often face difficulties with specific academic skills like reading, writing, or math. Specialized instructional strategies, such as those found in the Orton-Gillingham approach for reading, can support their learning and help them achieve academic success. *Websites like Understood.org offer resources for parents and educators on learning disabilities.*

Emotional Regulation

Managing emotions can be particularly tough for special needs children, leading to frequent feelings of anxiety, frustration, or depression. Techniques such as mindfulness, therapy, and emotional regulation training can assist in managing these emotions. *Programs like Zones of Regulation provide structured approaches to help children understand and manage their emotions.*

Physical Disabilities

Motor skills and physical coordination can be affected, making it harder for these children to participate in physical activities or perform daily tasks independently. Physical therapy and adaptive equipment (e.g., wheelchairs, specialized utensils) can support their physical development and independence. *The American Physical Therapy Association (APTA) offers resources for finding appropriate physical therapy services.*

Executive Functioning

Skills such as planning, organizing, and completing tasks can be particularly challenging, affecting both academic and everyday activities. Executive functioning training and tools like planners and checklists can support these skills. *Resources like the Smart but Scattered book series by Dr. Peg Dawson and Dr. Richard Guare provide practical strategies for improving executive functioning skills.*

BOOST THEIR SUPERPOWER—BUILD THEIR EMOTIONAL RESILIENCE

Developing emotional resilience in children is like building a fort—it provides a safe space for managing stress and overcoming challenges. For special needs children, this ability to adapt to adversity is vital for their well-being and success. In this section, we'll explore educational and life strategies with useful resources for you to nurture emotional resilience in your child. By implementing these strategies, you'll help your children construct their own fortresses of emotional strength, equipping them to face any obstacle with confidence.

Bounce Back Basics—Building Resilience in School Subjects

Math

Teach emotional resilience through mathematical setbacks. If your child struggles with a problem, encourage them to take deep breaths, break it down into smaller steps, and try again. Emphasize that it's okay not to get it right the first time.

- **Book Recommendations (for parent & child):** *Mathematical Mindsets* by Jo Boaler, *Math Curse* by Jon Scieszka and Lane Smith

- **Example Activity:** When faced with a difficult math problem, use a "step-by-step" chart to visually break down the problem into manageable parts. Reward effort rather than just correct answers.

Science

Use scientific failures as life lessons. If an experiment doesn't turn out as expected, explain that many scientific discoveries came from unexpected outcomes. Emphasize that it's all part of the learning process.

- **Book Recommendations (for child):** *Epic Fails: The Wright Brothers: Nose-Diving into History* by Erik Slader and Ben Thompson; *Ada Twist, Scientist* by Andrea Beaty and David Robe

- **Example Activity:** Conduct simple experiments and discuss famous scientific failures and their unexpected successes, such as Thomas Edison's many attempts before inventing the light bulb.

Reading

Books provide a treasure trove of characters facing challenges and overcoming them. Use these narratives to teach emotional resilience and empathy.

- **Book Recommendations (for child):** *Charlotte's Web* by E.B. White, *Thank You, Mr. Falker* by Patricia Polacco

- **Example Activity:** After reading a story, discuss how the characters faced their challenges and what they learned from them. Relate these lessons to your child's own experiences.

Writing

Encourage your child to write about their feelings or maintain a journal. This can be a great emotional outlet and a tool for self-reflection.

- **Book Recommendations (for child):** *How to Write Your Best Story Ever!* by Christopher Edge, *The Creativity Project: An Awesometastic Story Collection* edited by Colby Sharp

- **Example Activity:** Provide daily journal prompts that encourage your child to reflect on their day, express their feelings, and explore solutions to any challenges they faced.

Art

Art can be a powerful way for children to express emotions and build resilience. Encourage creative activities like drawing, painting, or crafting.

- **Book Recommendations (child):** *The Dot* by Peter H. Reynolds, *Art Before Breakfast: A Zillion Ways to be More Creative No Matter How Busy You Are* by Danny Gregory

- **Example Activity:** Use art projects to help your child depict their feelings or create visual stories about overcoming obstacles.

History

Teach resilience by discussing historical figures who overcame significant challenges. Highlight their perseverance and the lessons learned from their experiences.

- **Book Recommendations (for child):** *Mistakes That Worked* by Charlotte Foltz Jones, *The Brilliant Disaster: JFK, Castro, and America's Doomed Invasion of Cuba's Bay of Pigs* by Jim Rasenberger.

- **Example Activity:** Create a timeline of a historical figure's life, focusing on the obstacles they faced and how they overcame them. Discuss how these lessons apply to everyday life.

SET THE SCENE—CREATE A SUPPORTIVE LEARNING SPACE

Creating the perfect learning environment is like setting up a stage for a play – everything needs to be just right for the performance to shine. When homeschooling a child with special needs, your 'stage' needs a bit of extra attention to ensure it's both comforting and stimulating. For more information on crafting an ideal environment, see Chapter 5, "Getting Organized." For now, consider these tips:

- **Lighting:** Proper lighting can have a significant impact on mood and concentration. Utilize natural light when possible and choose soft, warm lighting to minimize glare and harshness, creating a soothing atmosphere that enhances focus and calmness.

- **Seating:** Flexible seating options such as bean bags, yoga balls, or standing desks can accommodate your child's sensory and comfort needs, promoting better engagement and focus during lessons.

- **Sensory Tools:** Incorporate sensory tools like fidget spinners, weighted blankets, or tactile toys to provide essential sensory input so your child can self-regulate, stay calm, and maintain concentration throughout their learning activities.

- **Organization:** Keep the learning space organized with clear containers and labeled shelves to ensure materials are easily accessible and reduce potential distractions. This aids in smoother transitions between tasks and better overall focus.

Real-World Examples:

1. Rachel has ADHD and struggles with maintaining focus during her homeschooling sessions. Her parents have set up a flexible learning environment that allows her to move around and take frequent breaks. They've provided a standing desk, an exercise ball chair, and various fidget tools to help Mia channel her energy in a productive manner. They've also implemented a visual schedule and timers to help her manage her time effectively and stay on task.

2. Greg has autism and is sensitive to loud noises and bright lights. His parents have created a space tailored to his sensory needs. They've installed dimmable lights, added soft and calming colors to the room, and provided noise-canceling headphones to minimize auditory distractions. Additionally, they've incorporated a sensory corner with various tactile objects and fidget toys to help Greg self-regulate and focus during his lessons.

ENHANCE SOCIAL SKILLS

Socialization can be a challenge for special needs children, but homeschooling provides an opportunity for you to foster social inclusion and emotional intelligence. By providing opportunities for community involvement and extracurricular activities, you can help your children build relationships and develop social skills through social stories and role-playing exercises that teach social norms and etiquette. See Chapter 14, "The Socialization Myth" for more details. Here are some ways to foster these social skills:

- **Social Stories:** Use social stories to teach appropriate social behaviors and responses in various situations.

- **Role-Playing:** Practice social interactions through role-playing different scenarios.

- **Social Skills Programs/Workshops:** Enroll in programs like "PEERS" or "Social Thinking" which provide structured social skills training. Online social skills workshops like on the platform Outschool.com, can help your child interact with peers and practice social behaviors in a structured environment.

TEACH PROBLEM-SOLVING SKILLS

Effective problem-solving skills help children handle frustration and setbacks. Equip your child with strategies to navigate challenges.

- **Breaking Down Problems:** Teach your child to break down problems into smaller, manageable steps.

- **Brainstorming Solutions:** Encourage brainstorming multiple solutions to a problem.

- **Role-Playing Scenarios:** Use role-playing to practice problem-solving in a controlled environment.

- **Problem-Solving Chart:** Create a visual problem-solving chart that your child can use when they encounter a challenge. Include steps like "Identify the problem," "Think of solutions," and "Choose the best solution."

BUILD SELF-ESTEEM AND CONFIDENCE

A strong self-esteem is foundational to emotional resilience. It also reinforces your child's strengths and achievements. Here are three ways to start the building process.

- **Strength-Based Learning:** Focus on your child's strengths and interests in their learning activities.

- **Encouragement:** Provide consistent encouragement and support, emphasizing effort and improvement over perfection.

- **Self-Esteem Activities:** Engage in activities that build self-esteem, such as keeping a "pride journal" where your child records their accomplishments and positive experiences.

STORYTIME SCRIPTS—STRENGTHEN RESILIENCE WITH CHILDREN'S BOOKS

Books are crucial for building emotional resilience in children because they provide exposure to diverse experiences and challenges, allowing young readers to learn through the characters' journeys. These stories offer role models who demonstrate perseverance and problem-solving skills, inspiring children to adopt similar attitudes. Moreover, books help children understand and process complex emotions in a safe environment, fostering self-awareness and emotional growth. By engaging with literature, children develop empathy and the ability to cope with adversity, enhancing their overall emotional resilience. Below is a brief curated list of fiction, nonfiction, and picture books that offer valuable lessons in perseverance, empathy, and overcoming adversity. For a comprehensive list of recommended books, please visit my website at www.homeschoolknockouts.com.

Fiction:

- *Fish in a Tree* by Lynda Mullaly Hunt — The story of Ally, a young girl with dyslexia, who struggles in school but learns to overcome her difficulties with the help of a supportive teacher and friends.

- *Wonder* by R.J. Palacio — The story of Auggie Pullman, a boy with a facial difference who faces challenges and bullying at school but ultimately finds acceptance and friendship.

- *Freak the Mighty* by Rodman Philbrick — The story of Max and Kevin, two boys who form an extraordinary friendship that helps them overcome their individual challenges and adversities.

Nonfiction:

- *The Boy Who Harnessed the Wind*: Young Readers Edition by William Kamkwamba and Bryan Mealer — This inspiring true story follows William Kamkwamba, a young boy in Malawi who builds a windmill to bring electricity to his village despite numerous setbacks and failures.

- *El Deafo* by Cece Bell — A graphic memoir that chronicles Cece Bell's experiences growing up deaf and how she turns her challenges into strengths, using humor and determination to navigate school and friendships.

- *Grit for Kids: The Book - A Growth Mindset and Grit Guide for Kids, Parents, and Educators* by Lee David Daniels — This book provides practical advice and stories to help children develop grit and resilience, emphasizing the importance of persistence and a growth mindset.

Picture Books/Poem:

- *The Most Magnificent Thing* by Ashley Spires — This delightful picture book tells the story of a little girl who attempts to create the most magnificent thing but faces many failures along the way. She learns the value of perseverance and creativity through her journey.

- *After the Fall (How Humpty Dumpty Got Back Up Again)* by Dan Santat — This book reimagines the classic tale of Humpty Dumpty, focusing on his journey to overcome his fear of heights and get back up after his great fall, teaching children about resilience and courage.

- *The Undefeated* by Kwame Alexander — A powerful and inspiring poem that celebrates the achievements and resilience of African Americans throughout history, with stunning illustrations by Kadir Nelson.

Using these books, you can engage in discussions with your child about how the characters faced their challenges, what they learned from their failures, and how these lessons can apply to their own lives. This helps to build emotional resilience and empathy in a relatable and enjoyable way.

WRITE ADAPTABLE SCRIPTS—PLAN FLEXIBLE LESSONS

Lesson planning for special needs homeschooling is like planning a road trip with multiple scenic routes. Flexibility is key, and sometimes the detours offer the best experiences. For more detailed information, see Chapter 8, "Lesson Planning for Couch Potatoes."

Suggestions:
- **Short, Engaging Activities:** Break lessons into small, manageable chunks to maintain your child's attention.

- **Movement Breaks:** Incorporate regular breaks for physical activity to help your child reset and refocus.

- **Visual Aids:** Use charts, pictures, and other visual tools to help explain concepts.

Example: For children with ADHD, long, uninterrupted lessons can be a recipe for disaster. Instead, break down each lesson into 10-15-minute segments with plenty of movement breaks in between.

CUSTOMIZE THE ROLES—TAILOR CORE SUBJECTS TO THEIR NEEDS

Next, we head into the realm of adaptation. Traditional schooling can often feel like trying to fit a square peg into a round hole, but with homeschooling, you've got the tools to reshape that hole! We'll discuss common challenges in core subjects and adaptations you can make with the curriculum to help your child succeed.

MATHEMATICS

Children with special needs face unique challenges in math that require tailored strategies for their specific difficulties. Here are some common challenges with adaptations:

Working Memory Limitations

Many children with special needs struggle with working memory, which is the ability to hold and manipulate information in the short term. Math often requires holding several pieces of information in mind simultaneously, such as remembering the steps of a problem while calculating numbers. Difficulties with working memory can make it hard to follow multi-step procedures, leading to challenges with complex problem-solving.

Adaptations

- **Chunking and Simplifying:** Break math problems into smaller, more manageable parts. Presenting information in chunks can help children process and retain details more effectively.

- **Visual Aids**: Use visual supports like number lines, charts, and graphs to provide external memory aids, helping your children keep track of information without having to hold it all in their heads.

- **Repetition and Practice:** Regular, consistent practice with math concepts can help strengthen working memory related to math. Incorporating varied practice methods (worksheets, oral repetition, digital games) can keep engagement high

Spatial Awareness and Visual-Spatial Skills Issues

Some children have trouble understanding and organizing spatial information. This can affect their ability to grasp concepts such as geometry, measurement, and spatial relationships, which are integral to understanding math. Problems visualizing shapes, understanding diagrams, or remembering the layout of numbers on a page can all stem from challenges with spatial awareness.

Adaptations

- **Hands-On Activities:** Utilize physical objects and manipulatives (e. g., blocks, shapes, measuring tapes) to teach spatial concepts. Physical interaction with materials can help develop a stronger grasp of spatial relationships and measurements.

- **Visual Representations:** Incorporate clear, detailed diagrams and visual cues in lessons. Highlighting and color-coding can draw attention to important spatial information and relationships.

- **Spatial Reasoning Games:** Engage in games and activities that specifically build spatial reasoning skills, such as puzzles, construction toys (e.g., LEGO), and drawing tasks that require understanding of space and dimension.

Dyscalculia

Dyscalculia is a specific learning disability in math. Children with dyscalculia may have difficulty understanding number concepts, counting sequences, performing basic arithmetic operations, and grasping the value of numbers. This challenge goes beyond typical math anxiety or struggle; it's a fundamental difficulty in making sense of numbers and math concepts.

Adaptations

- **Multisensory Instruction:** Engage multiple senses through tactile activities (using fingers or objects for counting), visual aids (charts and pictures for concepts), and auditory methods (songs or rhymes for mathematical operations).

- **Use of Technology:** Implement apps and software designed to support math learning in children with dyscalculia. These tools often offer interactive, visual ways to understand and practice math concepts.

- **Individualized Learning Plans:** Develop personalized learning strategies that focus on the child's strengths. For example, if a child excels in verbal comprehension, incorporating story-based problems can help them better understand mathematical concepts.

Grasping Abstract Concepts

Understanding abstract concepts can be difficult for those who don't have physical examples to relate to, especially for children whose thinking skills are still developing. Language and prior knowledge also play a role; without strong language skills or foundational knowledge, abstract ideas can be hard to understand. Visualization and memory challenges, different learning styles, and emotional factors like anxiety can add to the difficulty.

Adaptations

- **Use Concrete Examples:** Visual aids, graphic organizers, stories, mind maps, hands-on activities, step-by-step learning, and real-life applications can make abstract ideas easier to understand.

- **Physical Interaction:** The use of physical objects or manipulatives helps in making math operations concrete. Have children manipulate objects themselves as much as possible to form a deeper connection with the material and enhance memory.

- **Break Down Problems:** Break down problems into smaller, more visual steps to aid in comprehension and retention.

- **Analogies and Metaphors:** Use analogies and metaphors that relate to the learner's experiences to make abstract concepts more relatable and easier to understand.

SCIENCE

Special needs children often face challenges in science due to difficulties with abstract thinking, language comprehension, and fine motor skills. Let's examine some challenges with adaptations.

Sensory Processing Issues

Sensory Processing Disorder (SPD) is a condition where the brain has trouble receiving and responding to information that comes in through the senses. In the context of science education, children may be overly sensitive to sensory input such as loud noises, bright lights, strong smells, or certain textures. For example, the noise of a bubbling experiment, the smell of chemicals, or the texture of lab materials can be overwhelming. Conversely, children with under-sensitivity (hyposensitivity) might seek out more sensory input and may not respond to stimuli that others find typical. They might not notice subtle chemical smells or need extra stimulation to focus on an experiment.

Adaptations
- **Controlled Environment:** Adjust the learning environment to minimize sensory overload. Use noise-canceling headphones for children sensitive to sound, ensure good ventilation to handle strong smells, and use gloves for those sensitive to textures.

- **Hands-On Experiments:** Incorporate tactile experiments where children can touch, smell, and see the materials they are learning about. This can help ground abstract scientific concepts in concrete experiences.

- **Sensory Breaks:** Allow children to take breaks to manage sensory overload, providing a quiet and calming space.

Difficulty with Abstract Concepts

May struggle to understand ideas that are not concrete or tangible, such as the structure of an atom or the concept of an ecosystem. Often needs more concrete examples and visual aids to make abstract ideas more relatable.

Adaptations
- **Use Models and Visuals:** Employ 3D models, detailed illustrations, and virtual reality apps to make abstract concepts (like atoms or ecosystems) tangible.

- **Concrete Examples:** Tie lessons to real-world examples that are relevant to the child's experiences, making abstract concepts more relatable.

- **Step-by-Step Instruction:** Break down complex ideas into smaller, more manageable steps with clear, concrete examples at each stage.

Limited Attention Span

Difficulty staying focused during lengthy science lessons or experiments, often becoming easily distracted or restless. Might struggle to follow through with multi-step procedures.

Adaptations
- **Short, Varied Activities:** Break lessons into short segments with varied activities (discussion, video, experiment) to keep children engaged.

- **Interactive Learning:** Utilize interactive platforms and technology that require active participation, catering to varied attention spans.

- **Frequent Breaks:** Incorporate short breaks between activities to help children stay focused and prevent fatigue.

Language Comprehension

Struggles with understanding scientific terminology and complex instructions.

Adaptations
- **Pre-Teaching Vocabulary:** Introduce and review key vocabulary before starting a new lesson to build familiarity with the terms.

- **Visual Supports:** Provide visual aids like diagrams, pictures, and videos to accompany verbal explanations.

- **Simplified Language:** Use straightforward and simple language to explain scientific terms and instructions, avoiding jargon.

Memory Retention

May struggle to remember the steps in scientific processes or retain detailed information about scientific concepts. Children might forget critical stages of an experiment or have trouble recalling key terms and definitions, leading to incomplete tasks and frustration.

Adaptations

- **Repetition and Review:** Frequently review and repeat key concepts and steps to reinforce memory.

- **Visual Reminders:** Use posters, charts, and visual aids in the classroom to remind children of important information and steps.

- **Mnemonics and Memory Aids:** Teach mnemonic devices and memory aids to help children remember scientific concepts and procedures.

Organizational Skills

Struggles to keep track of materials, follow multi-step procedures, and maintain an orderly workspace. This can lead to missed steps in experiments, misplaced materials, and overall disorganization, which hinders ability to complete tasks effectively.

Adaptations

- **Structured Routines:** Establish clear and consistent routines for science activities and lab work.

- **Checklists and Guides:** Provide checklists and step-by-step guides to help your child follow multi-step procedures.

- **Organizational Tools:** Use folders, binders, and labeled containers to help your child keep materials organized and easily accessible.

READING

Special needs children often face a variety of challenges in reading that can hinder their ability to effectively process and comprehend written material. These challenges can stem from cognitive, sensory, or physical difficulties, impacting their reading fluency, comprehension, and overall learning experience.

Dyslexia

Dyslexia is a specific learning disability characterized by difficulties with accurate and/or fluent word recognition and by poor spelling and decoding abilities. These difficulties typically result from a deficit in the phonological component of language, making reading a laborious and challenging task.

Adaptations

- **Structured Literacy Programs:** Implement programs, such as Orton-Gillingham Approach, Wilson Reading System, Barton Reading or Spelling System, specifically designed for dyslexia, emphasizing phonics and structured language. ***Resources:*** *International Dyslexia Association (IDA), Understood.org*

- **Reading Technology:** Use text-to-speech software and audiobooks like Kurzweil 3000, Learning Ally, or Bookshare to support reading comprehension and fluency. ***Resources:*** *Dyslexia Help at the University of Michigan, Reading Rockets*

Limited Working Memory

Limited working memory affects a child's ability to hold and manipulate information in their mind for short periods. This limitation can make it difficult to follow multi-step instructions, retain details from a text, and understand complex sentences, all of which are crucial for effective reading comprehension.

Adaptations

- **Graphic Organizers:** Use visual aids like story maps, sequence charts,

Venn diagrams, flowcharts, or mind maps to help organize and retain information. ***Resources:*** *Education.com, TeachersPayTeachers.com, Re adWriteThink.org*

- **Chunking Text:** Present texts in small, manageable chunks, to allow for focus on understanding without overwhelming memory. Break paragraphs into sentences, summarize sections after reading. ***Resources:*** *ADDitude Magazine, Learning Disabilities Association of America (LDA)*

Visual Impairments

Visual impairments can include a range of conditions that affect a child's ability to see clearly, making reading standard print materials difficult. These impairments can slow reading speed, reduce comprehension, and cause eye strain or fatigue.

Adaptations

- **Large Print and Braille Books:** Provide access to books with larger text or in Braille to accommodate visual needs. ***Resources:*** *American Printing House for the Blind (APH), National Library Service for the Blind and Print Disabled (NLS)*

- **Assistive Technology:** Use screen readers and magnification tools like JAWS (Job Access With Speech) or ZoomText to enhance readability and comprehension. Adjust the font size on electronic devices (usually under the 'accessibility' tab) for better viewing. ***Resources:*** *Perkins School for the Blind, AFB (American Foundation for the Blind)*

WRITING

Special needs children often encounter significant challenges with writing that can impact their ability to express ideas and complete assignments. These challenges can stem from various cognitive, motor, and emotional difficulties, making writing a frustrating and anxiety-inducing task. Addressing these challenges with appropriate adaptations and resources can help improve their writing skills and overall learning experience.

Dysgraphia

Dysgraphia is a learning disability that affects writing abilities, causing difficulties with spelling, handwriting, and putting thoughts on paper. This condition can make writing tasks laborious and can hinder a child's ability to produce legible and coherent written work. ***Resources:*** *International Dyslexia Association, Learning Disabilities Association of America (LDA)*

Adaptations
- **Graphic Organizers:** Use pre-writing tools to organize thoughts visually, reducing the burden on fine motor skills. ***Resources:*** *Understood. org, ADDitude Magazine*

- **Speech-to-Text Technology:** Implement speech-to-text tools to allow children with dysgraphia to articulate their thoughts verbally, which the software then converts into written text. This method reduces the physical strain of writing and helps them focus on content creation. ***Resources:*** *DyslexiaHelp at the University of Michigan, Tech Finder by Learning Disabilities Association of America (LDA)*

- **Writing Software:** Utilize programs like Google Docs templates that offers structured writing environments, like templates or planning tools. ***Resources:*** *Common Sense Media, Edutopia*

Fine Motor Skill Weakness

Weakness in the fine motor skills required for writing can make the physical act of writing laborious and tiring. Children may struggle with poor handwriting and slower writing speed because of a lack of hand strength, dexterity, and coordination, which may cause fatigue quickly when writing. ***Resources:*** *Occupational Therapy Tools, Therapy Street for Kids*

Adaptations
- **Adaptive Tools:** Use tools such as pencil grips or ergonomic pens that are designed to reduce the strain of writing. ***Resources:*** *Special Supplies, National Center for Learning Disabilities (NCLD)*

- **Hand Strengthening Exercises:**
  Engage children in activities that build hand strength and dexterity, such as using therapy putty, squeezing stress balls, or playing with clay. These exercises can improve fine motor skills, making writing tasks less strenuous. ***Resources:*** *Understood.org, Your Therapy Source*

Anxiety and Frustration

Anxiety and frustration can significantly impact a child's willingness and ability to engage in writing tasks. These emotions often arise from previous negative experiences or the pressure to meet high expectations, leading to avoidance and decreased confidence. ***Resources:*** *Scholastic's Book Wizard, TeachThought*

Adaptations

- **Positive Feedback:** Focus on strengths and improvements in writing, building confidence gradually. ***Resources:*** *Psychology Today, Positive Psychology*

- **Mindfulness Techniques:** Incorporate mindfulness exercises, such as deep breathing, guided imagery, or progressive muscle relaxation, to help manage anxiety and frustration related to writing tasks. These techniques promote relaxation and improve focus, making writing a more positive experience. ***Resources:*** *Mindful Schools, KidsHealth*

SOCIAL STUDIES

Special needs children often face challenges in social studies due to difficulties with abstract thinking, comprehension of complex concepts, and retaining vast amounts of information. These challenges can make it hard to grasp historical events, understand geographical data, and engage with social theories.

Understanding Cause-and-Effect Relationships

Children may find it difficult to connect historical events and understand their impact over time because these concepts require abstract thinking and the ability to see connections between events that are not immediately obvious. *Resources: Interactive History Websites - History for Kids, BBC Bitesize*

Adaptation

- **Role-Playing and Simulations:** Engage children in role-playing activities or simulations to bring historical events or civic concepts to life. *Resources: iCivics, BrainPOP, National Geographic Kids, TimeMaps*

Remembering Dates and Key Facts

Retaining large amounts of information, such as dates, names, and key facts, can be overwhelming and difficult to manage because it requires strong memory skills and the ability to organize and retrieve information efficiently.

Adaptations

- **Simplified and Chunked Text:** Break down complex texts into smaller, manageable sections to help children focus on understanding each part without being overwhelmed by too much information at once. *Resources: Newsela, Simple English Wikipedia*

- **Graphic Organizers:** Visual tools like timelines, charts, and mind maps help children organize and visualize information, making it easier to remember and retrieve key facts. *Resources: Education.com, ReadWriteThink.org*

Challenges with Reading Comprehension

Special needs children often struggle with reading comprehension due to difficulties in decoding text, understanding vocabulary, and making inferences. These challenges can hinder their ability to grasp the full meaning of the material, affecting their overall learning experience.

Adaptations

- **Audiovisual Resources:** Supplement reading materials with watching a documentary about a historical event being studied, listening to an audiobook of a history text, or exploring an interactive geography website. These resources can help children better understand and retain information by engaging multiple senses. ***Resources:*** *National Geographic Kids, Audible, BBC Bitesize*

- **Guided Reading Sessions:** Use guided reading strategies to focus on comprehension skills, asking predictive and analytical questions during reading. For example, read a passage together and pause to ask questions like "What do you think will happen next?" or "Why do you think this event was important?" to enhance comprehension. This approach helps children engage with the text, think critically, and improve their understanding. ***Resources:*** *Reading Rockets, Scholastic Guided Reading.*

CELEBRATE EVERY AWARD—APPLAUD MILESTONES AND PROGRESS

It's party time for every win, big or small. Cheering on your kiddo's victories is just as crucial as being their guide on the journey. Heap on the high-fives, dish out the rewards, and hand over those awesome 'You Did It!' certificates to turn each big step into its own little fest. In your homeschooling journey, especially with special-needs children, progress is measured in many ways – and every bit of progress deserves recognition. Celebrations can be both academic and non-academic, and acknowledging these milestones can boost your child's confidence and motivation, making learning a joyful experience. Here are some ways to recognize small and big wins:

1. Think about a child with autism who finds it challenging to make eye contact. After consistent practice and gentle encouragement, they manage to hold eye contact for a few seconds during a conversation. This small yet significant progress can be celebrated in a fun and tangible way by adding colorful marbles to a jar each time eye contact is made. Watching the jar fill up can be a visual and rewarding way for the child to see their progress, and once the jar is full, the family could enjoy a special outing to the child's favorite place, reinforcing their efforts and making them feel valued.

2. Consider a child who struggles with reading. After weeks of practice, they manage to read a short story independently. This achievement, no

matter how small it may seem, is monumental for the child and deserves celebration. The family could mark the occasion with a special reading night where the child gets to pick the story and read it aloud to everyone. Also, the family could create a 'Reader of the Month' certificate to present to the child, making them feel proud of their hard work.

3. Developing communication skills is a significant milestone for children with special needs. If a child starts to use a communication device or begins to express their needs verbally, it's a notable achievement. Parents could celebrate this progress by creating a 'communication treasure hunt,' where the child uses their new skills to follow clues and find a hidden treasure. This fun and interactive celebration not only reinforces the new skill but also makes the child feel accomplished and supported.

ASSEMBLE YOUR CREW—FIND COMMUNITY SUPPORT AND RESOURCES

It Takes a Village – Really!

Homeschooling can sometimes feel isolating, especially when you're raising special-needs children. But guess what? There's a whole village out there ready to support you because building a support network is crucial! From online resources to local support groups and social media spaces, we'll explore the lighthouse locations that can guide you through the stormy seas of homeschooling our differently-abled children. These communal spaces are great for finding guidance, inspiration, and motivation. Plus, by joining online communities, attending local meetups, and seeking out specialized resources, you'll not only get the support you need but also connect with like-minded families to share ideas and experiences. Remember, URLs change over time so if you encounter a broken link just go to the main page on the website and do a search for "special needs."

Online Forums and Communities

Forums:

1. **Wrong Planet** - www.wrongplanet.net/forums — A popular forum for individuals with autism and their families to discuss various topics, including education and therapy integration.

2. **The Well-Trained Mind Special Needs SubForum** —– www.welltrainedmind.com —– A dedicated space within The Well-Trained Mind Forum for discussing homeschooling strategies and support for children with special needs.

3. **ADDitude** – www.additudemag.com— An active community where parents of children with ADHD can share strategies and resources, including those for homeschooling.

4. **Parent to Parent USA** – p2pusa.org: — For parents of special needs children to share experiences and resources.

5. **Homeschooling Special Needs Children Meetup Groups on Meetup.com** - Various local groups available through Meetup.com where parents can find and join communities of others homeschooling children with special needs.

Facebook Groups:
- **Special Needs/IEP Homeschool Support - ADHD, Dyslexia, Autism spectrum, etc.** - A supportive community for parents homeschooling children with special needs, offering resources, advice, and encouragement. Group Name: <u>Homeschooling Special Needs</u>

- **Special Needs Homeschooling** - A group where parents can discuss and share resources specifically for homeschooling children with special needs. Group Name: <u>Special Needs Homeschooling</u>

- **Autism & Homeschooling** - A dedicated space for parents who homeschool children with autism to exchange tips, support, and resources. Group Name: <u>Homeschooling Autism</u>

Books:
- *The Zones of Regulation* by Leah Kuypers,

- *Marva Collins' Way* by Marva Collins and Alex Haley

- *The Out-of-Sync Child* by Carol Kranowitz

These resources can provide you with a wealth of information and support as you work to create a homeschooling routine that integrates both academic and therapeutic needs.

Disclaimer: This list is not exhaustive. There are numerous additional resources and communities available that offer valuable support and guidance for homeschooling children with various special needs. For a comprehensive list of all the resources mentioned here, please refer to the Selected Notes section at the back of the book.

---------- **Summary** ----------

So, building emotional resilience in homeschooled special needs kids is like crafting a blockbuster movie—there's action, adventure, and a whole lot of heart. You've been the director all along: creating a safe and supportive set, sprinkling in mindfulness and relaxation scenes, enhancing their social skills, and developing problem-solving plots that make them feel like superheroes. You've boosted their self-esteem with uplifting storylines and established a strong support system, like a loyal cast and crew. By leveraging a treasure trove of resources and practical examples, you've helped your special needs child become the star of their own story, ready to face life's challenges with confidence and grace.

So, grab your director's chair, be creative, and get ready for "Action!"

30

Toddlers & Preschoolers

Meltdowns & Snack Negotiations

Play is the highest form of research.

— Albert Einstein

S O, WHY HOMESCHOOL TODDLERS and preschoolers? Home education can foster a close parent-child bond that lays a strong foundation for lifelong learning. Plus, if you're already homeschooling older children, it just makes sense to include the younger ones. It streamlines your day and provides enriching opportunities for everyone to learn together. Picture your little one tagging along on a nature walk, marveling at the bugs and flowers, or sitting next to their older sibling during a read-aloud session, eyes wide with wonder. Or imagine your preschooler happily coloring or counting blocks at the kitchen table while you teach a math lesson to your older child. These shared experiences are not only educational but also help strengthen family bonds and create a supportive learning environment for all your kids.

In this chapter, we'll start by focusing on strategies and activities specifically designed for homeschooling toddlers. Then, we'll explore approaches tailored for preschoolers, ensuring that you have the tools and ideas you need to engage and educate both age groups effectively.

THE TODDLER & PRESCHOOLER FACE-OFF—WHO'S WHO IN EARLY CHILDHOOD

Ah, the exhausting world of early childhood – where toddlers and preschoolers roam free, each with their own unique set of quirks and milestones. Let's break it down.

Toddlers, those adorable little hurricanes aged 1-3 years, are busy mastering the basics. Picture them toddling around, conquering the art of walking, running, and, of course, self-feeding – though half of their meal often ends up on the floor. Their language? Think caveman chic: simple words and phrases. Playtime for these tiny tots is more about parallel play – hanging out side-by-side with their buddies without actually interacting much.

Now, enter the preschoolers, aged 3-5. These slightly older kiddos have refined their motor skills and boast a vocabulary that's expanding faster than a balloon at a birthday party. Their playtime is a theatrical masterpiece, full of interaction and imagination. Social skills? Check. Following simple instructions? Double check. And let's not forget, they're already dipping their toes into the academic pool, starting to recognize letters and numbers. Meanwhile, our toddler friends are still happily exploring the world through sensory and motor adventures.

In a nutshell, toddlers are in the training camp of early childhood, while preschoolers are stepping up their game, gearing up for the big leagues.

TODDLERS—KEEP IT SHORT, SWEET, AND HANDS-ON

Note: Some of the following examples and activities are suitable for both toddlers and preschoolers.

Let's face it. Toddlers have the attention span of a goldfish—blink, and they're onto the next thing. So, the key is to keep things quick and peppy. Cap activities at 15 minutes or you'll be performing to an audience of one—yourself. This is also a good stage to start teaching your toddler how to interact with others. Here are some ideas to get you going.

Design a Structured, Yet Flexible, Schedule

First things first—let's talk about routines. Kids thrive on routine, but that doesn't mean you need a military-style schedule. Think of it more as a flexible framework. Here's an example:

Sample Daily Routine:

- **Morning Routine:** Wake-up, breakfast, and a bit of free play.

- **Learning Time:** Short, engaging activities (more on those later).

- **Snack Break:** Healthy snacks to keep those little engines running.

- **Creative Play:** Arts, crafts, or sensory bins.

- **Lunch and Nap:** Refuel and recharge.

- **Afternoon Adventures:** Outdoor play, park visits, or community classes.

- **Wind Down:** Quiet time with books, puzzles, or calm activities.

- **Evening Routine:** Dinner, bath, and bedtime stories.

Sample Weekly Routine

- **Monday Mingle:** Start the week with a morning at the playground. Encourage your toddler to invite a new friend to join them on the jungle gym.

- **Wednesday Walkabouts:** Midweek, explore a new part of the neighborhood or a local museum, fostering curiosity and conversation with others.

- **Friday Fun Day:** End the week with a themed playdate. Pirates, princesses, or paleontologists—each week can be a new adventure in play-pretend and collaboration.

LEARN THROUGH PLAY

The best way for toddlers to learn is through play. Let's look at some fun and educational activities.

Basic Academic Skills

- **Counting and Numbers:** Use toys, building blocks, or snacks and start a counting game. "Can you give me three blocks? How about five?" Turn it into a game by making funny noises every time they get it right.

- **Cup and Spoon Size Party:** Got measuring cups and spoons? It's a size and volume party! Ask them which cup is the giant and which is the baby—it's a big deal in the toddler world.

- **Alphabet and Letters:** Flashcards are your friends. Get some decked out with bright colors and letters. Turn them into a treasure hunt around the house—"A is for apple, but can you find one?" or around the yard, "Find something that is green!"—and watch them run around in excitement.

Creative Arts

- **Art Projects:** Set up an art station with crayons, markers, paper, and stickers. Let them create masterpieces. Remember, the messier, the better!

- **Music and Movement:** Have a daily sing-along or dance session. Use simple instruments like tambourines or shakers to add to the fun.

- **Cereal Box Puppet Theater:** Transform an empty cereal box into a stage for their little puppet friends. It's showtime in the living room with storytelling!

Science and Nature Exploration

- **Simple Experiments:** Show them the magic of mixing colors with water and food coloring. Plant seeds in small pots and watch them grow together.

- **Nature Walks:** Take them on nature walks to collect leaves, rocks, and flowers. Talk about the different things you find.

Music and Movement

- **Daily Sing-Along:** Have a set time each day for a sing-along session. Choose a variety of songs, including nursery rhymes, classic children's songs, and even some of their favorite tunes. Incorporate hand movements and actions to make it more interactive.

- **Dance Session:** Create a playlist of upbeat songs and have a daily dance session. Encourage children to express themselves through movement. You can also introduce simple dance routines or just let them freestyle dance to the music.

- **Simple Instruments Play:** Use simple instruments like tambourines, shakers, or homemade instruments (e.g., a container filled with beans). Let children play along to music, exploring different rhythms and sounds. This can be a structured activity or free play.

Fine Motor Skills

- **Clothespin Pincer Showdown:** Strengthen those tiny fingers with clothespins. Can they pick up small objects? Provide clothespins and a variety of small objects and challenge children to pick up the objects using the clothespins. This helps strengthen their pincer grasp, which is important for writing and other fine motor tasks. Make it a game and watch those fine motor skills level up.

- **Bead Stringing:** Use large beads and string to create necklaces or bracelets. Encourage children to thread the beads onto the string. This activity improves hand-eye coordination and fine motor precision. You can also use different shapes and sizes of beads for added complexity.

- **Play Dough Fun:** Provide children with play dough and tools such as plastic cookie cutters, rolling pins, and plastic knives. Encourage them to shape, mold, and cut the play dough. This activity strengthens their hand muscles and improves dexterity. They can create different shapes, animals, or even simple objects like balls and snakes.

Gross Motor Skills

- **Climbing:** Toddlers are natural climbers, whether it's scaling the couch, climbing up playground equipment or your leg, or tackling a set of stairs. This activity helps them build strength, coordination, and problem-solving skills as they figure out how to navigate different heights and obstacles safely. Plus, it's a great way for them to burn off some of that endless energy!

- **Running:** Toddlers love to run. It's more about figuring out how to balance and move quickly on two feet without taking a tumble. Preschoolers, on the other hand, can run with better coordination and control, often adding a bit of flair with changes in direction and speed.

- **Jumping:** This skill starts to emerge in the toddler years, with little ones experimenting with getting both feet off the ground at the same time. By preschool age, kids are not just jumping – they're leaping, hopping, and even mastering the art of jumping from small heights or over objects.

Sensory Play

- **Sensory Bin Wonderland:** Fill up a bin with stuff like rice, sand, or those squishy water beads. Toss in some cups and spoons, maybe a couple of their favorite tiny toys, and let them explore the textures and engage in imaginative play. You can change the contents of the bin regularly to keep it interesting.

- **Texture Exploration:** Create a tactile board or tray with different materials such as sandpaper, sponges, textured balls, fabric swatches, cotton balls, and bubble wrap. Let children touch and feel the different textures. Discuss how each one feels and use descriptive words to expand their vocabulary.

- **Water Play:** Set up a water table or a large container filled with water. Add items like cups, spoons, sponges, and small floating toys. Let children explore pouring, scooping, and squeezing. You can also add a few drops of food coloring or a bit of soap to create bubbles, adding an extra sensory element to the play.

SOCIALIZATION OPPORTUNITIES

Even though you're homeschooling, it's important for your child to interact with other kids and adults. This isn't just play—it's essential for their development to interact with other children and adults. So, weave playdates, park visits, and other interactive activities into your homeschooling routine.

Unlike the hands-on crafts that might occupy 10-15 focused minutes before interest wanes, these social escapades should stretch beyond 15 minutes to allow for meaningful engagement. If your child is shy, start with short interactions and gradually increase the time as they become more comfortable. If scheduling is tough, look for local parent groups online that meet in person—they often have events that can fit into your busy life. The key is consistency and patience.

Playdates and Group Activities

- **Playdates:** Arrange regular playdates with other homeschooling families. Not only does it give the kids a chance to play together, but you also get some adult conversation!

- **Community Classes:** Look for local music, dance, or art classes. They're great for learning new skills and making friends.

Community Engagement

- **Library Story Times:** Many libraries offer story times for young children. It's a great way to introduce them to books and the joy of reading.

- **Park Visits:** Take your children to the park regularly and let them play with other children. Playgrounds are perfect for socializing, plus all that running around will tire them out (hello, early bedtime). Encourage them to share toys and take turns on the swings.

- **Playdates:** Arrange playdates with other homeschooling families in your area. It's an excellent way for your toddler to meet new friends and practice social skills.

- **Community Classes:** Enroll your toddler in community classes such as music, dance, or art. These classes are a fantastic opportunity for your child to learn new skills in a structured group setting, allowing them to interact with peers who share similar interests. It also gives them a chance to follow group instructions and collaborate on projects, which can boost their confidence and social development.

INCORPORATE MOVEMENT AND PHYSICAL ACTIVITY

Little ones have boundless energy. Channel that energy into fun physical activities.

Structured Physical Activities

- **Yoga for Kids:** Simple yoga poses can help them with balance and flexibility. Plus, it's a calming activity.

- **Interactive Games:** Play games like "Simon Says" or "Follow the Leader" to keep them moving and learning.

Unstructured Play

- **Free Play:** Give them time to play freely, whether it's in the backyard, at a local park, or in an indoor play area.

- **Rainy Day Fun:** On rainy days, set up an indoor play area with tunnels, balls, and soft mats.

MAKE LEARNING FUN AND ENGAGING

Let's face it, toddlers can be tough critics. Keeping their attention requires a bit of creativity.

Use Themes and Interests

- **Follow Their Interests:** If your child is obsessed with trucks, incorporate trucks into your lessons. Teach shapes by looking at different truck parts, or count how many trucks they see during a walk.

- **Themed Learning Weeks:** Dedicate each week to a different theme. One week could be all about space—read space books, do space crafts, and watch educational videos about planets.

Incorporate Games

- **Educational Games:** Use puzzles, matching games, and educational apps to teach new concepts.

- **Interactive Learning:** Turn learning into a game. Play "I Spy" with letters or numbers, or create a scavenger hunt for shapes around the house.

Develop Social and Emotional Skills

Social and emotional skills are just as important as academic ones.

Teach Social Skills

- **Sharing and Taking Turns:** Use games to teach sharing and taking turns. Board games and cooperative play activities work wonders.

- **Role-Playing:** Role-play different social scenarios with dolls or stuffed animals to teach empathy and problem-solving.

Emotional Development

- **Books About Feelings:** Read books that talk about different emotions. Discuss the feelings of the characters and relate them to your child's experiences.

- **Discussing Emotions:** Talk about emotions regularly. Ask how they feel and help them express their feelings in words.

RESOURCES FOR PARENTS

You're not in this alone—there are plenty of resources to help you on your homeschooling journey.

Books

Invest in a few good educational or idea books for ideas and inspiration. Some of my favorites include:

- *The Toddler's Busy Book: 365 Creative Games and Activities to Keep Your 1 1/2- to 3-Year-Old Busy* by Trish Kuffner

- *The Ultimate Toddler Activity Guide: Fun & Educational Activities to Do with Your Toddler* by Mrs. Autumn McKay

Online Resources

Websites like ABCmouse, Starfall, and PBS Kids offer a wealth of learning games and printables.

PRESCHOOLERS— KEEP IT ENGAGING, INTERACTIVE, AND FUN

Note: Some of these examples and activities are suitable for both toddlers and preschoolers.

Let's face it. Preschoolers have a bit more focus than toddlers, but they still need activities that capture their imagination and energy. So, the key is to keep things dynamic and interactive. Aim for engaging sessions that last about 20-30 minutes, as their attention span is growing but still limited. At this stage, preschoolers are honing their social skills and starting to follow routines. Here are some ideas to keep your preschooler entertained and learning:

Create a Balanced and Fun Daily Schedule

Preschoolers thrive on routine, but flexibility is crucial. Think of it as a balanced blend of structure and spontaneity. Here's an example:

Sample Daily Routine
- **Morning Routine:** Wake-up, breakfast, and a bit of free play.

- **Learning Time:** Engaging activities focused on basic academic skills (more on those later).

- **Snack Break:** Healthy snacks to keep those little engines running.

- **Creative Play:** Arts, crafts, or sensory bins.

- **Lunch and Nap:** Refuel and recharge.

- **Afternoon Adventures:** Outdoor play, park visits, or community classes.

- **Wind Down:** Quiet time with books, puzzles, or calm activities.

- **Evening Routine:** Dinner, bath, and bedtime stories.

Sample Weekly Routine
- **Monday Music and Movement:** Start the week with a music and dance session. Explore different musical instruments and dance styles.

- **Wednesday Wonders:** Midweek, explore a new place or try a new activity, like a nature walk or a trip to a children's museum.

- **Friday Fun Day:** End the week with a themed playdate. Superheroes, chefs, or explorers—each week can be a new adventure in imaginative play.

CREATE MONTHLY THEMES

Creating monthly themes for preschoolers is a fantastic way to structure learning and exploration, integrating fun with educational content like books, crafts, and games. Here are sample themes that align with seasonal changes and developmental interests, covering September through May.

Additionally, a weekly component to each monthly theme can help break down the concepts into manageable chunks and keep the learning fresh and engaging. Here's how you could structure each month into exciting weekly sub-themes:

September: "All About Me"

- **Week 1: My Body**

  - Activities: Create body part collages, play Simon Says focusing on body parts.

- **Week 2: My Family**

  - Activities: Draw family portraits, discuss family traditions and share stories.

- **Week 3: My Favorites**

  - Activities: Crafts and discussions about favorite foods, colors, and animals.

- **Week 4: My Home**

  - Activities: Build model houses from cardboard, create a neighborhood map.

October: "Harvest and Helpers"

- **Week 1: Autumn Leaves**

  - Activities: Leaf collecting and sorting, leaf rubbing art projects.

- **Week 2: Pumpkin Patch**

  - Activities: Visit a pumpkin patch, pumpkin painting, and carving.

- **Week 3: Apple Adventures**

  - Activities: Apple tasting, making apple stamps, and reading stories about apple orchards.

- **Week 4: Community Helpers**

  - Activities: Dress-up days for various helper roles, guest speakers from the community.

November: "Thanksgiving and Traditions"

- **Week 1: Family Traditions**

  - Activities: Share family stories, make a family tree, and discuss different family traditions around the world.

- **Week 2: Gratitude Week**

   ○ Activities: Create gratitude jars or a thankful wall, write thank-you cards.

- **Week 3: Feast and Fun**

   ○ Activities: Cooking simple recipes together, learn about the history of Thanksgiving.

- **Week 4: Native American Heritage**

   ○ Activities: Learn about Native American cultures, crafts like bead necklaces or dream catchers.

December: "Winter Holidays Around the World"

- **Week 1: Christmas Celebrations**

   ○ Activities: Christmas ornament crafts, storytime with Christmas-themed books.

- **Week 2: Hanukkah Happenings**

   ○ Activities: Make menorahs, play dreidel, and explore the story of Hanukkah.

- **Week 3: Kwanzaa Culture**

   ○ Activities: Learn about the seven principles of Kwanzaa, make Kwanzaa crafts like unity cups.

- **Week 4: New Year's Festivities**

   ○ Activities: Create a time capsule, make New Year's Eve party hats, discuss New Year traditions from around the world.

January: "Winter Wonders"

- **Week 1: Snow and Ice**

- Activities: Snow painting with colored water, experiments with freezing and melting.

- **Week 2: Winter Animals**

  - Activities: Animal track matching games, create animal masks, and learn about hibernation.

- **Week 3: Winter Sports**

  - Activities: Indoor "ice skating" on wax paper, mini hockey games.

- **Week 4: Staying Warm**

  - Activities: Explore how animals and humans stay warm, make winter clothes for dolls or teddy bears.

February: "All About Animals"

- **Week 1: Pets and Domestic Animals**

  - Activities: Learn about pet care, create pet portraits, visit a local animal shelter.

- **Week 2: Wild Animals**

  - Activities: Explore different habitats, create animal fact cards, watch documentaries about wild animals.

- **Week 3: Under the Sea**

  - Activities: Ocean-themed crafts, learn about marine life, create a mini aquarium.

- **Week 4: Birds and Bugs**

  - Activities: Bird watching, make bird feeders, insect scavenger hunt.

March: "Budding Botanists"

- **Week 1: Seed Starters**

  - ○ Activities: Plant various seeds in clear containers to watch roots develop, discuss what plants need to grow.

- **Week 2: Flowers and Trees**

  - ○ Activities: Go on a nature walk to identify local flowers and trees, flower pressing.

- **Week 3: Insects and Pollinators**

  - ○ Activities: Bug hunts, crafting bees and butterflies, learning about how insects help plants.

- **Week 4: Fruits and Vegetables**

  - ○ Activities: Plant a small vegetable garden, taste test different fruits and vegetables, learn about where food comes from.

April: "Earth and Environment"

- **Week 1: Planet Earth**

  - ○ Activities: Earth Day crafts, learn about the Earth's layers, and discuss how to take care of our planet.

- **Week 2: Weather Wonders**

  - ○ Activities: Weather charting, make a simple weather station, discuss different types of weather.

- **Week 3: Plants and Gardens**

  - ○ Activities: Start a spring garden, learn about plant life cycles, visit a botanical garden.

- **Week 4: Recycling and Conservation**

  - Activities: Learn about recycling, upcycle old materials into art, discuss the importance of water conservation.

May: "Growth and Renewal"

- **Week 1: Insects and Butterflies**

  - Activities: Observing caterpillars turn into butterflies, learning about insect life cycles, and going on a nature walk to spot insects.

- **Week 2: Seeds and Sprouts**

  - Activities: Planting seeds, tracking their growth, and discussing what plants need to grow.

- **Week 3: Birds and Nests**

  - Activities: Birdwatching, making bird feeders, and learning about different types of nests.

- **Week 4:** Springtime Celebrations

  - Activities: Exploring spring holidays around the world, creating spring-themed crafts, and hosting a spring festival.

These weekly focuses allow for deeper exploration of each theme and provide ample opportunities for thematic crafts, songs, and field trips that reinforce the learning objectives.

LEARN THROUGH PLAY

As with toddlers, the best way for preschoolers to learn is through play. Here are some fun and educational activities (some of these activities overlap with the toddler activities).

Basic Academic Skills

Alphabet Treasure Hunt

- **Flashcard Hide and Seek:** Create a set of brightly colored flashcards with both the uppercase and lowercase letters. Hide them around the house. Say, "A is for apple. Can you find the apple card in the living room?" or "Can you find the letter 'S' hidden in the kitchen?" This turns letter recognition into an adventurous game of hide and seek.

- **Outdoor Alphabet Adventure:** Take the learning outside. Say, "Let's find something that starts with the letter 'B' in the yard." Look for items like a ball, a butterfly, or a bench. This makes learning letters a part of their outdoor play and exploration.

Letter Craft Time

- **Alphabet Art:** Use large cut-out letters and let the preschoolers decorate each letter with items that start with that letter. For example, glue apple stickers on the letter 'A', buttons on the letter 'B', and cotton balls on the letter 'C'. This helps reinforce letter sounds and associations in a creative, hands-on way.

- **Letter Matching Game:** Create pairs of letter cards with both uppercase and lowercase letters (feel free to decorate). Lay them out and have them match the pairs. Turn it into a memory game by flipping the cards over and finding matching pairs.

Interactive Games

- **Alphabet Soup:** Fill a large bowl with plastic letters and use a ladle to scoop out letters. Have them identify the letter and say a word that starts with it, making it a fun and interactive way to learn letters and their sounds.

- **Counting and Numbers:** Use colorful building blocks or animal-shaped toys for counting games. Ask, "Can you give me ten blue blocks?" or "How many toy dinosaurs do we have?" Turn it into a playful challenge with funny sounds or cheers when they get it right to keep it fun and engaging.

- **Measurements:** Set up a water play station with various containers like cups, bowls, and pitchers of different sizes. Ask them to pour water from one container to another and observe which holds more or less. Say, "Which bowl can hold all the water from the big pitcher?"

Creative Arts

- **Nature Collage:** Take a walk to collect leaves, flowers, and twigs. Use these natural items to create a collage on construction paper. This combines art with a nature exploration.

- **DIY Instruments:** Make simple musical instruments using household items, like a shaker with rice in a sealed container or a drum with a pot and a wooden spoon. Decorate them with stickers or paint.

- **Cooking Helper:** Involve them in cooking or baking. Ask them to help measure ingredients using different-sized measuring cups and spoons. Discuss the quantities: "We need one cup of flour. Can you find the biggest cup?"

Science and Nature Exploration

- **Simple Experiments:**

  - Ice Melting: Freeze small toys in ice cubes and let them melt in the sun or with warm water. Talk about how the ice changes from solid to liquid.

  - Magnet Fun: Explore with magnets and various objects to see what sticks. Discuss why some objects are magnetic and others are not.

- **Nature Walks:**

  - Bug Hunt: Go on a bug hunt with a magnifying glass. Look for different insects and talk about their features and habitats.

  - Rock Painting: Collect smooth rocks and bring them home to paint. Use the opportunity to discuss the textures and shapes of the rocks.

Music and Movement

- **Action Songs:** Sing songs that involve actions, like "Head, Shoulders, Knees, and Toes" or "If You're Happy and You Know It." Encourage them to follow along with the movements.

- **Parachute Play:** Use a large sheet or parachute and have fun lifting and lowering it to the rhythm of music. Place lightweight balls on top and watch them bounce with the movements.

GROSS MOTOR SKILLS

- **Running:** Preschoolers can run with better coordination and control, often adding a bit of flair with changes in direction and speed.

- **Jumping:** Preschoolers are not just jumping – they're leaping, hopping, and even mastering the art of jumping from small heights or over objects.

- **Climbing:** Preschoolers love to climb, whether it's playground equipment or a jungle gym. This helps them build strength and coordination while burning off some of that endless energy!

SENSORY PLAY

- **Themed Bins**: Create themed sensory bins like a beach bin with sand, seashells, and small beach toys, or a farm bin with dried corn, toy animals, and small farm equipment. Rotate themes to keep it engaging.

- **Mystery Objects:** Fill a bin with rice or beans and hide small toys inside. Have them dig in and find the hidden items, guessing what each object is by touch.

Texture Exploration
- **Texture Walk:** Create a path with different textures to walk on barefoot, such as soft fabric, bubble wrap, grass, and sandpaper. Talk about how each texture feels under their feet.

- **Texture Books:** Make a touch-and-feel book using different materials glued to cardboard pages. Each page can have a different texture like felt, cotton, or foil for them to explore.

SOCIALIZATION OPPORTUNITIES

Earlier, we discussed how socialization looks for toddlers, but let's shift our focus to preschoolers. Preschoolers are more advanced in their social development compared to toddlers. They engage in cooperative play, where they interact and play games together. Preschoolers begin to form friendships, understand the concept of empathy, and develop better communication skills. They can participate in group activities with more structure and follow simple rules, making their social interactions more complex and meaningful. By incorporating socialization opportunities suited to their developmental stage, preschoolers can greatly benefit from interacting with their peers and adults.

Playdates and Group Activities

- **Playdates:** Arrange regular playdates with other homeschooling families. Not only does it give the kids a chance to play together, but you also get some adult conversation!

- **Community Classes:** Look for local music, dance, or art classes. They're great for learning new skills and making friends.

Community Engagement

- **Library Story Times:** Many libraries offer story times for young children. It's a great way to introduce them to books and the joy of reading.

- **Park Visits:** Take your children to the park regularly and let them play with other children. Playgrounds are perfect for socializing, plus all that running around will tire them out (hello, early bedtime). Encourage them to share toys and take turns on the swings.

Incorporate Movement and Physical Activity

Little ones have boundless energy. Channel that energy into fun physical activities.

Structured Physical Activities

- **Yoga for Kids:** Simple yoga poses can help them with balance and flexibility. Plus, it's a calming activity.

- **Interactive Games:** Play games like "Simon Says" or "Follow the Leader" to keep them moving and learning.

Unstructured Play

- **Free Play**: Give them time to play freely, whether it's in the backyard, at a local park, or in an indoor play area.

- **Rainy Day Fun:** On rainy days, set up an indoor play area with tunnels, balls, and soft mats.

MAKE LEARNING FUN AND ENGAGING

Preschoolers are famously discerning judges. Capturing their attention demands a healthy dose of creativity.

Use Themes and Interests

- **Follow Their Interests:** If your child is obsessed with trucks, incorporate trucks into your lessons. Teach shapes by looking at different truck parts, or count how many trucks they see during a walk.

- **Themed Learning Weeks:** Dedicate each week to a different theme. One week could be all about dinosaurs—read dinosaur books, create fossil imprints, and watch documentaries about prehistoric life.

Incorporate Games

- **Educational Games:** Use puzzles, matching games, and educational apps to teach new concepts.

- **Interactive Learning:** Turn learning into a game. Play "I Spy" with letters or numbers, or create a scavenger hunt for shapes around the house.

DEVELOP SOCIAL AND EMOTIONAL SKILLS

Social and emotional skills are just as important as academic ones.

Teach Social Skills

- **Sharing and Taking Turns:** Use games to teach sharing and taking turns. Board games and cooperative play activities work wonders.

- **Role-Playing:** Role-play different social scenarios with dolls or stuffed animals to teach empathy and problem-solving.

Emotional Development

- **Books About Feelings:** Read books that talk about different emotions. Discuss the feelings of the characters and relate them to your child's experiences.

- **Discussing Emotions:** Talk about emotions regularly. Ask how they feel and help them express their feelings in words.

RESOURCES FOR PARENTS

Don't worry, you're not flying solo here—there's a wealth of resources available to support your homeschooling adventure. Here are a few to get you started:

Books and Workbooks

Invest in a few good educational or idea books for ideas and inspiration:
- *The Preschooler's Busy Book: 365 Creative Games & Activities to Occupy 3-6 Year Olds* by Trish Kuffner

- *Preschool Big Fun Workbook (Highlights™ Big Fun Activity Workbooks)* by Highlights Learning

Online Resources

Websites like Khan Academy Kids, Scholastic Early Learners, Education.com, ABCmouse, Starfall, PBS Kids are great resources to use in your homeschool.

---------- **Summary** ----------

As Albert Einstein said, "Play is the highest form of research." Homeschooling toddlers and preschoolers isn't just about academic readiness; it's about embracing the natural curiosity and boundless energy of young children. Through play, we cultivate a love of learning, build strong family bonds, and create an environment where every moment is an opportunity for exploration. Whether they're counting blocks, crafting masterpieces, or embarking on neighborhood adventures, your little ones are engaged in the most important work of childhood—learning through play. So, as you guide them on this journey, remember that the foundation you're building now is setting the stage for a lifelong love of learning. Keep it playful, keep it flexible, and most importantly, keep it fun.

31

Elementary Years

Crayons, Chaos, and the Quest for Quiet

Children are not a distraction from more important work. They are the most important work.

— C.S. Lewis

A<small>H, THE ELEMENTARY YEARS</small>—<small>WHEN</small> your homeschool morphs from a cozy learning den into a bustling beehive of activity. Kids at this age are on a developmental roller coaster, evolving and growing at breakneck speeds. Getting a grip on these transformative years and understanding these key stages can seriously up your homeschooling game. We'll slice it up by age groups because, as any seasoned homeschooler will tell you, keeping up with these kids is like trying to track a firefly at a rave—blink and the game changes!

AGES 5-7—THE ABCs & 123s

For the sprightly 5- to 7-year olds, we're talking the big basics: reading, writing, and 'rithmetic, all served up with a healthy side of play. These kids are honing those brain cells with hands-on activities that make learning as fun as a barrel of monkeys. They're also mastering the art of sharing and playing nice, so throw in plenty of playdates and group gigs to spice up their social skills. And let's not forget those busy little fingers—cutting, drawing, and scribbling are key to getting their fine motor skills in shipshape.

Ages 5-7 (Early Elementary)
- **Cognitive Development**: Children at this age are developing basic reading, writing, and math skills. They learn best through hands-on activities and play.

  ○ **Example:** Use phonics games to teach reading, incorporate counting and simple math into daily activities, and engage in storytelling to develop language skills.

- **Social Development**: They are learning to cooperate, share, and understand others' perspectives. Playdates and group activities can be very beneficial.

  ○ **Example:** Organize group activities like building a simple project together, cooperative games, or reading circles where they can discuss stories with peers.

- **Physical Development**: Fine motor skills are improving, so activities that involve cutting, drawing, and writing are important.

  ○ **Example:** Provide plenty of art supplies for drawing and crafting, and incorporate activities like building with blocks or simple science experiments.

AGES 8-10—DEEP DIVES AND HIGH FIVES

Moving on to the 8 to 10 crowd, things get a notch trickier. These kids are diving into deeper waters with more complex reading, a dash of advanced math, and a sprinkle of logic and problem-solving. Social life's a big deal now—think group projects and team efforts that are as crucial as the academics. Physically, they're ready to tackle more challenging feats that require slicker motor skills, so keep those activities coming.

Ages 8-10 (Middle Elementary)
- **Cognitive Development**: Children become more proficient readers and can handle more complex math problems. They begin to develop logical thinking and problem-solving skills.

- **Example:** Introduce chapter books, use educational software for math practice, and engage in science experiments that require hypothesis testing and observation.

- **Social Development**: Peer relationships become more important. Group work and collaborative projects can enhance learning.

  - **Example:** Encourage group projects like creating a class newspaper, collaborative science projects, or history reenactments.

- **Physical Development**: They have better control over fine motor skills and can engage in more complex physical activities.

  - **Example:** Include activities like sports, dance, or detailed crafts and model building that require precision and coordination.

AGES 11-12—THE BRAVE NEW WORLD OF TWEENS

By the time they hit 11 and 12, strap in because abstract thinking enters the arena. These pre-teens are ready to wrestle with the big-ticket items in science and history, and they're carving out a stronger sense of who they are in this wild world. Independence is the name of the game, along with a hefty dose of responsibility. And with puberty knocking on the door, it's high time to ramp up that physical and health education.

Ages 11-12 (Upper Elementary)
- **Cognitive Development**: Abstract thinking begins to develop. Children can understand more complex concepts in subjects like science and history.

  - **Example:** Explore topics like basic physics or world history, and engage in discussions that require critical thinking and analysis.

- **Social Development**: They are developing a stronger sense of self and are more aware of social dynamics. Encouraging independence and responsibility is key.

  - **Example:** Assign independent research projects, encourage leadership roles in group activities, and discuss ethical and moral issues in literature and history.

- **Physical Development**: They are approaching puberty, and their bodies are beginning to change. Physical education and health education become more relevant.

  ○ **Example:** Provide opportunities for physical activity through sports or structured exercise, and include lessons on health and wellness.

Understanding these whirlwind stages allows you to tailor a homeschooling experience that's not just educational, but downright delightful. It's about nurturing those young minds and bodies comprehensively, ensuring they grow up not just smart, but well-rounded. Ready, set, educate!

ELEMENTARY TEACHING TIPS WITH EXAMPLES

- **Offer More In-Depth Lessons**: Elementary schoolers are ready for more in-depth lessons, so consider incorporating longer lessons and more complex topics.

  ○ **Example:** Instead of a brief overview of the solar system, dive into each planet's characteristics, explore the history of space exploration, and conduct experiments like creating a model rocket or simulating craters with flour and marbles.

- **Get Creative with Activities**: Elementary-aged kids love to create and get their hands dirty. So, use this to your advantage and incorporate fun activities like art projects, science experiments, or building challenges into your lessons.

  ○ **Example:** Create a homemade weather station to teach about meteorology. Use materials like thermometers, barometers, and rain gauges, and have the kids record weather data and create their own weather forecasts.

- **Use Technology**: Kids these days are practically born with a tablet in their hands, so use technology to your advantage. There are tons of educational apps, websites, and online games that can help reinforce learning.

- **Example:** Use Duolingo for language learning, Math Playground for math practice, or educational games like Prodigy for a fun way to practice math skills. Utilize YouTube channels like CrashCourse Kids for science and history lessons.

- **Use Humor**: Kids love to laugh, so use humor to your advantage. Incorporate funny stories, silly songs, or even jokes into your lessons to keep them engaged and entertained.

  - **Example:** Tell funny anecdotes about famous inventors' mishaps, use silly songs to memorize multiplication tables, or read humorous books like "Captain Underpants" to encourage a love for reading.

- **Encourage Curiosity**: Elementary schoolers are naturally curious. Encourage this by allowing them to ask questions and explore topics that interest them.

  - **Example:** If your child is fascinated by dinosaurs, build a unit study around paleontology, including reading books, watching documentaries, and visiting a natural history museum. If they love space, delve into astronomy with stargazing nights and building a model of the solar system.

- **Incorporate Physical Activity**: Young children have lots of energy, so incorporating physical activity into your homeschooling routine can be beneficial.

  - **Example:** Start the day with a family yoga session, take breaks for a quick dance party with songs from "GoNoodle," or include a nature walk as part of the science curriculum to explore local flora and fauna.

- **Celebrate Achievements**: Recognize and celebrate your child's achievements, no matter how small. activity into your homeschooling routine can be beneficial.

  - **Example:** Create a "Wall of Fame" where you display completed assignments and projects, have a special "achievement day" with fun activities and treats, or use a reward system with stickers and small prizes to motivate progress.

Understanding and addressing the developmental stages of elementary-aged children can help you create a more effective and engaging homeschooling experience tailored to their needs and interests.

---------- Summary ----------

As your child enters the elementary years, the homeschooling journey takes on new dimensions. Understanding their developmental stages is crucial to creating an engaging and effective learning environment. For children aged 5-7, cognitive development focuses on basic reading, writing, and math skills through hands-on activities and play. Socially, they learn to cooperate and share, making playdates and group activities beneficial. Physically, fine motor skills are improving, so activities involving cutting, drawing, and writing are important.

For children aged 8-10, cognitive abilities advance to more complex reading and math, logical thinking, and problem-solving skills. Socially, peer relationships gain importance, and collaborative projects enhance learning. Physically, they engage in more complex activities requiring better motor control.

By ages 11-12, abstract thinking develops, allowing children to grasp complex concepts in science and history. They gain a stronger sense of self and social awareness, making independence and responsibility key focuses. Physically, they are approaching puberty, making physical education and health education more relevant.

Understanding where your elementary-aged kids are developmentally helps you whip up a homeschooling experience that's both effective and enjoyable. You'll hit all the right academic notes while also giving their social, emotional, and physical growth a solid boost. It's like creating a balanced education with a splash of fun!

32

Middle School Years

Field Trips to the Fridge & Other Elective Courses

The best way to predict the future is to create it.

— Peter Drucker

S O, YOU'VE MADE IT to the middle school years. Congratulations! Your child is growing up, and so is their attitude. This is the age where they begin to push boundaries, question everything (including your sanity), and develop a keen sense of independence. Navigating the choppy waters of middle school can be daunting, but it's also an incredibly rewarding time. You'll see your child evolve from a curious kid into a critical thinker with burgeoning interests and passions. It's a journey that will challenge your patience, creativity, and yes, it might just triple your coffee consumption. But don't worry; there are ways to keep your middle schooler engaged in their homeschooling education. Here are some tips:

HOW TO KEEP THE EYE ROLLS TO A MINIMUM

Get Them Involved

Middle schoolers are at an age where they want to have a say in what they learn. Let your child choose a topic they want to learn about, and then have them research and create a presentation to share with the family. This not only gives them a sense of ownership but also makes learning more enjoyable.

Example: If your child is passionate about marine biology, let them explore different marine ecosystems, culminating in a presentation about the Great Barrier Reef or the Mariana Trench. The excitement in their eyes when they teach you something new is worth the effort!

Use Real-World Examples

Middle schoolers are starting to think more abstractly and are keen to see how their lessons apply to the real world. Instead of focusing solely on abstract concepts, use practical scenarios.

Example: Have them figure out how many pizzas to order for a party or the cost of tickets for a family outing. Spice things up by incorporating financial literacy, like budgeting or calculating taxes. It's all about making learning relevant and engaging!

Give Them Choices

Middle schoolers want to feel like they have some control over their education. Give them choices in how they learn or what projects they work on. If your child is studying a historical figure, give them the choice to either write a research paper or create a short video summarizing their life and achievements.

Example: While studying the American Revolution, offer the option to either write an essay on George Washington or create a comic strip depicting key events. By providing choices, you cater to different learning styles and keep the subject matter interesting.

Use Multimedia

Middle schoolers are growing up in a multimedia world, so use videos, podcasts, virtual reality experiences, and other multimedia sources to reinforce learning and keep them engaged.

Example: If your child is interested in space, have them research a specific planet or the history of space exploration and create a presentation using PowerPoint or Google Slides. Or, if your child is studying a science topic like the human body, use virtual reality experiences like "The Body VR" or "Anatomyou VR" to provide a more immersive learning experience.

Allow for Independence

Middle schoolers are becoming more independent, so allow them to take ownership of their learning by giving them more responsibility for their projects and assignments.

Example: If your child is interested in photography, give them a photography project to complete on their own, such as taking pictures of different animals or plants and creating a photo album to present to the family. Or, assign a long-term science project, like building a simple weather station to track and report weather patterns. This encourages independent research and problem-solving skills, critical for their development.

Relatability

When it comes to subjects like history or literature, make the content more relatable by discussing how past events or characters can relate to modern-day issues or situations. This can make the content more relevant and engaging for your middle schooler.

Example: While reading a classic novel, draw parallels to current events or popular culture. Discuss how the themes in "To Kill a Mockingbird" relate to today's social justice movements, making the material more resonant.

Hormones and More Hormones

Middle schoolers are in the midst of a whirlwind of physical and emotional changes. Patience and empathy will go a long way in handling their shifting moods and attitudes. Be sure to offer regular breaks and downtime to help them reset, and don't skimp on their sleep. Especially for boys, those growth spurts come fast and frequent, and sleep is essential for keeping pace with their rapid growth.

Tip: Create a flexible schedule that includes physical activity and relaxation time. Incorporating yoga or mindfulness exercises can help them manage stress and stay centered.

Foster Engagement

Incorporate social activities into their homeschooling routine. Middle schoolers are at an age where they are developing their social skills and crave interaction with their peers. Joining a homeschooling group, participating in group projects or activities, or even just having a study group with friends can provide opportunities for socialization and collaboration.

Example: Look for local homeschooling co-ops or online communities like Outschool.com, where your child can take live, interactive classes with peers from around the world.

RESOURCES FOR MIDDLE SCHOOLERS

1. **Khan Academy:** A free resource offering lessons in math, science, history, and more. The interactive exercises and instructional videos are perfect for self-paced learning.

2. **Outschool:** A platform providing live online classes in a wide range of subjects, from academic topics to hobbies and life skills. It's a great way to keep your middle schooler engaged and connected with other learners.

3. **CrashCourse:** This YouTube channel offers quick, engaging overviews of various subjects, from world history to biology. The humorous and energetic delivery keeps middle schoolers interested.

4. **Duolingo:** If your child is interested in learning a new language, Duolingo offers gamified lessons in dozens of languages. The bite-sized lessons are perfect for daily practice.

5. **CK-12 Foundation:** Provides free and customizable K-12 textbooks and learning materials in subjects like math, science, and social studies. The interactive simulations and practice problems are great for middle schoolers.

6. **National Geographic Kids:** Offers a wealth of articles, videos, and games about geography, animals, and cultures. It's an excellent resource for making learning about the world fun and engaging.

7. **Scholastic Learn at Home:** Offers daily learning journeys divided by grade level. The interactive lessons and projects are designed to keep kids engaged and learning.

8. **Mystery Science:** Provides open-and-go science lessons for elementary and middle school students. Each lesson begins with a question and unfolds into a mini-adventure with hands-on activities.

9. MiddleWeb: Teacher focused for grades 4-8, MiddleWeb provides resources, strategies, and support for teaching and learning in the middle school years. https://www.middleweb.com

PRACTICAL TIPS FOR PARENTS

Maintain a Flexible Schedule

A rigid schedule can stifle creativity and lead to frustration. Instead, establish a flexible routine that allows for both structured learning and free time. This balance helps middle schoolers stay focused and motivated.

Encourage Curiosity

Allow your child to explore topics that pique their interest, even if they fall outside the traditional curriculum. Curiosity-driven learning fosters a love for education and can lead to unexpected and rewarding discoveries.

Be a Learning Role Model

Demonstrate your own love for learning. Whether it's reading a book, taking an online course, or exploring a new hobby, let your child see that learning is a lifelong journey. Your enthusiasm can be contagious.

Stay Organized

Keep track of assignments, projects, and deadlines with a planner or digital calendar. Middle schoolers are developing time management skills, and a bit of organization can go a long way in helping them stay on top of their work.

Take Breaks

Learning should be engaging, not exhausting. Incorporate regular breaks into your schedule to give your child time to relax and recharge. Short breaks can improve focus and productivity.

Embrace Technology

Use educational apps and online resources to supplement traditional learning materials. Technology can provide interactive and dynamic ways to explore new concepts.

Foster a Growth Mindset

Encourage your child to view challenges as opportunities for growth rather than obstacles. Praise their effort and resilience, and remind them that mistakes are a natural part of the learning process.

---------- **Summary** ----------

Homeschooling a middle schooler is like embarking on an epic adventure—one full of growth spurts and brainy breakthroughs. Spice things up with real-world examples, let them flex their independence, and keep them engaged with multimedia and social activities. Remember, patience and flexibility are your secret weapons during these whirlwind years of change. With the right mix of approach and resources, you'll navigate these middle school years with confidence and maybe even a chuckle or two. So, grab another cup of coffee, take a deep breath, and dive into the homeschooling journey with gusto!

33

High School Years
Graduating from Sanity High with Honors

When I was a boy of fourteen, my father was so ignorant I could hardly stand to have the old man around. But when I got to be twenty-one, I was astonished at how much he had learned in seven years.

— Mark Twain

YOU'VE MADE IT TO the high school years. Congratulations! Your child is growing up, and so are their eye-rolls. But don't worry; there are ways to keep your high schooler engaged in their homeschooling education while also preparing them for the future. As a homeschooling parent, it can be daunting to design a high school plan, navigate college admissions, and secure scholarships. However, with the right resources and approach, homeschoolers can not only survive but thrive during the high school years. In this chapter, we will discuss how to celebrate your decision to homeschool by exploring different aspects of high school planning, from designing a plan to securing scholarships.

HIGH SCHOOLER—PREPARE FOR THE FUTURE (AND MORE EYE ROLLS)

- **Encourage Exploration:** High school is a time for exploring interests and potential career paths. Encourage your child to take classes or engage in activities that align with their passions. If your child is interested in writing, encourage them to take writing classes or participate in a writing workshop. You can look for local writing workshops or check out online resources like Gotham Writers Workshop or the Young Writers Project. If they love animals, suggest they volunteer at a local animal shelter or take a course in animal behavior. Many animal shelters offer volunteer opportunities for high schoolers, or you can look for online courses through organizations like the Animal Behavior Institute.

- **Provide Opportunities for Independence:** High schoolers are preparing for adulthood, so give them more independence in their studies. Let your high schooler choose their own courses, set their own schedules, and take ownership of their learning. Have them create a research project on a topic of their choice, like the history of fashion or the science behind cooking. You can also encourage them to design their own experiment to test a scientific hypothesis, like studying the effect of caffeine on memory retention or the effects of music on plant growth.

- **Incorporate Real-World Experiences:** High schoolers are preparing for life after graduation, so incorporate real-world experiences into their education. Encourage them to take on internships or volunteer work in areas of interest. If your child is interested in medicine, encourage them to volunteer at a hospital or shadow a doctor. If they're interested in business, they can start a small online business selling handmade crafts or offer their services to help a local business with social media marketing. Or, they can simply apply for jobs in retail, grocery stores, restaurants, etc., to get direct work experience.

- **Offer More Advanced Classes:** High schoolers are ready for more advanced classes, so consider incorporating classes like calculus, chemistry, and foreign languages into your curriculum.

- **Trade Schools:** If your child has a strong interest in areas like carpentry, automotive repair, culinary arts, or other trades, encourage them to explore vocational training schools. Many high schools offer vocational programs, or they can enroll in a trade school post-graduation. Trade skills are in high demand and can lead to stable, high-paying jobs. Allow them to intern or apprentice to gain hands-on experience in their chosen field.

- **Military:** The armed forces offer a range of opportunities for young adults, from scholarships to job training to life-long careers. If your child is considering the military, schedule visits to local recruiting offices of different branches to gain a comprehensive view. Encourage them to participate in programs like the Junior Reserve Officer Training Corps (JROTC), if available. These programs instill leadership, discipline, and teamwork. Research military academies and their requirements if your child shows an interest.

- **College-Ready Concentration:** For many high school students, the journey leads to college. Enhance their homeschool experience with college-grade material, exam readiness, campus visits, and help with applications. Engage them in AP classes, SAT or ACT prep, and college exploration. They can pursue online AP classes via platforms like Khan Academy or attend courses (online/onsite) at nearby community colleges for dual credit. For test prep, resources such as The Princeton Review or College Board are invaluable, and they can explore colleges physically or via virtual tours.

DESIGN A HIGH SCHOOL PLAN—NO PRESSURE, RIGHT?

Navigating the high school years as a homeschooler offers a unique opportunity to tailor education to your child's needs, interests, and post-high school aspirations. Whether the goal is college, a trade, the military, or the workforce, a well-thought-out plan can set the foundation for success without the pressure of striving for perfection. The truth is, there is no one-size-fits-all approach to high school planning. Instead, we can focus on creating a plan that aligns with our child's goals.

While post high-school prep can seem like an epic saga, if broken down year by year, it's more like a four-part sitcom. Totally manageable. And yes, there might be a cliffhanger or two. So, let's break it down from the Freshman Frenzy to the Senior Sprint!

Freshman Year – Laying the Foundations

- **Students**: Kick off with essential core classes like math, science, history, and English. Explore electives that catch your interest and start a portfolio to document your academic and extracurricular activities.

- **Parents**: Understand your state's graduation requirements, begin a transcript (it's easier to add as you go than to remember two years later), and attend homeschool conferences or webinars focused on post-secondary pathways, including college prep, military, trade schools, and the workforce. Knowledge is power.

Sophomore Year – Deepening the Dive

- **Students**: Continue with advanced core subjects and start exploring post-high school options. Research colleges, trade schools, and consider potential career fields or military service. Keep a dedicated binder to track options and prerequisites. Consider PSAT or other prep exams. It's good practice for later.

- **Parents**: Ensure the curriculum supports your child's interests and potential career paths. Attend educational fairs or open houses with your child. Start early with scholarship and financial aid research, including opportunities specific to trade schools and military benefits. It's never too early to find free money.

Junior Year – Crunch Time

- **Students**: If college-bound, consider taking the SAT or ACT. Research colleges more in-depth. For those considering trades or the workforce, look into apprenticeships or vocational courses. For military aspirations, research the ASVAB requirements and speak with recruiters to understand the commitments involved. Engage in extracurriculars, volunteering, or work.

- **Parents**: Continue updating that transcript. Like a plant, it needs regular love. Explore financial aid, including scholarships and grants for vocational training and ROTC scholarships for future military personnel. Organize visits to colleges, trade schools, and job fairs to help your child make informed decisions.

Senior Year – The Final Countdown

- **Students**: Finalize decisions on post-high school paths and take necessary actions like college applications, trade school enrollment, or military enlistment. Ensure all applications are meticulously completed, and gather recommendations if needed. Celebrate your high school accomplishments and prepare for the next steps.

- **Parents**: Finalize the transcript and assist with applications for financial aid, scholarships, and enrollment procedures. Provide emotional support as your child transitions from high school to their chosen path, recognizing the significance of this milestone.

By integrating considerations for various post-secondary paths into your homeschool curriculum, you create a comprehensive plan that accommodates your child's aspirations. This approach not only prepares them academically but also gives them the confidence and clarity to step into the future, be it in academia, a skilled trade, the workforce, or the military.

For Further Research: Visit Let's Homeschool High School at: lets homeschoolhighschool.com. This redirects to homeschool.com (mentioned later in this chapter) and provides comprehensive guidance, curriculum resources, and support specifically tailored to homeschooling through the high school years.

DUAL ENROLLMENT—A JUMPSTART TO COLLEGE

Dual enrollment allows high school students to take college courses and earn college credit while still in high school or middle school. This can save money and time when it comes to pursuing a college degree. As homeschoolers, we can take advantage of dual enrollment programs, whether at a local college or online. Here's how to get started.

First, you'll want to research local community colleges, four-year colleges, and universities to see if they offer dual enrollment programs for high school students (or middle schoolers). Community colleges, in particular, offer accessible and affordable dual enrollment options that can be a great fit for many families (in some states, like California, tuition is waived). Here are a few examples of colleges known for their strong and homeschool-friendly dual enrollment programs, including options for middle school students. If a link is broken, simply type "dual enrollment" in the search bar on the college's homepage.

1. **Arizona State University (ASU):** ASU offers a comprehensive dual enrollment program that allows high school students to take university-level courses. This program not only gives students a taste of college-level work but also enables them to earn credits that can be transferred to many other institutions. ASU does not have residency requirements for its dual enrollment program, making it accessible to out-of-state students as well. ASU is also known for its flexibility with homeschoolers. https://asuonline.asu.edu/what-it-costs/discounts/dual-enrollment/

2. **Miami Dade College (MDC):** MDC's dual enrollment program is designed to provide high school students with the opportunity to take college courses and earn college credits tuition-free. This program is particularly beneficial for students aiming to reduce the overall cost of their college education. Generally, students must be residents of Miami-Dade County to enroll in this program. MDC is supportive of homeschool students and offers resources to help them succeed in the dual enrollment program. https://www.mdc.edu/dual-enrollment/

3. **University of North Carolina at Charlotte (UNC Charlotte):** UNC Charlotte offers a robust dual enrollment program through its Early College program. High school students can take a variety of courses, gaining valuable experience and earning credits that count towards both their high school and college diplomas. Typically, North Carolina residency is required to participate in UNC Charlotte's dual enrollment programs. However, UNC Charlotte also offers online courses through its dual enrollment program, which are available to all students regardless of residency status. This flexibility makes it a great option for homeschoolers, including advanced middle school students. https://a

dmissions.charlotte.edu/early-college-dual-enrollment

4. **California Community Colleges (CCC):** California has an extensive system of community colleges offering dual enrollment programs that allow high school students to take college courses and earn credits. For example, **Los Angeles Community College District (LACCD) and San Diego Community College District (SDCCD)** both have well-established dual enrollment programs. These programs often provide a cost-effective way for students to get a head start on their college education. Residency requirements usually apply, so students generally need to be California residents to participate. Both districts are known for being accommodating to homeschool students, including middle schoolers. Here are the links.

   ◦ (CCC) https://www.cccco.edu/Students/High-School-Students/Dual-Enrollment

   ◦ (LACCD) https://www.laccd.edu/Students/opencccapply/Pages/dual-enrollment.aspx

   ◦ (SDCCD) https://www.sdccd.edu/students/new-students/high-school-students.aspx

5. **Local Community Colleges:** Many community colleges across the country offer excellent dual enrollment programs that provide a flexible and cost-effective way for high school students to start their college education. These programs often have lower tuition costs compared to four-year institutions and can serve as a bridge to a bachelor's degree. For example, **Austin Community College (ACC)** in Texas has a well-regarded dual enrollment program that allows high school students to take courses at any of ACC's campuses or online, earning college credits while fulfilling high school requirements. Residency requirements generally apply, meaning students typically need to be residents of the state or local district. ACC is also supportive of homeschool students and allows middle school students to participate on a case-by-case basis. https://www.austincc.edu/admissions/college-in-high-school/dual-credit

By exploring these opportunities, you can help your child maximize their educational potential and get a head start on their college career. Dual enrollment at community colleges can be particularly advantageous, offering a supportive learning environment and reducing the overall cost of higher education. Homeschool-friendly programs ensure that even younger students can benefit from these opportunities.

CAREER EXPLORATION—WHAT WILL THEY BE WHEN THEY GROW UP?

First off, why should we focus on career exploration? Well, when kids know what they like and what they're good at, it makes it easier for them to choose a direction in life. Career exploration helps students identify their interests and goals beyond high school. It gives them a sense of purpose and makes the transition from school to the "real world" a lot smoother. Plus, it helps avoid those "I have no idea what I want to do" moments. Let's discuss how to incorporate career exploration into your high school curriculum. It's easier than you might think and can fit any homeschooling style.

Activities and Resources for Career Exploration

- **Career Assessments:** There are online tools that help students identify their interests and skills and match them with potential careers. The O*NET Interest Profiler, which is a useful online tool for students to explore careers that align with their interests and skills, can be found on the "My Next Move" website. Websites like and O*NET Interest Profiler are great places to start. They're interactive and can give your kids a clearer picture of careers they might enjoy.

- **Job Shadowing:** This involves letting your child observe professionals in various fields to gain a better understanding of different career paths. It's like a behind-the-scenes look at a job. Reach out to friends, family, or local businesses to set up shadowing opportunities.

- **Internships and Apprenticeships:** These provide hands-on experience in a particular career field. Internships and apprenticeships offer a taste of the work environment and responsibilities.

- **Create a Career-Exploration Course:** Dedicate part of your high school curriculum specifically to career exploration. This could include researching different careers, taking career assessments, and learning about the education and skills required for various jobs. Dedicate a set amount of time each week on career exploration by taking some career assessments and then research the top three careers that interest your child the most.

- **Integrate Career-Related Projects:** Incorporate projects that relate to potential careers your child is interested in. This makes learning more relevant and helps them see the practical application of their studies.

- **Set Up a Mentorship Program:** Pair your child with a mentor in a field they're interested in. This could be someone from your community or an online mentor. Regular meetings with a mentor can provide guidance, answer questions, and offer insights into a particular career.

- **Encourage Volunteering:** Volunteering is a fantastic way to explore careers while giving back to the community. It can provide valuable experience and help students build important skills.

COLLEGE ADMISSIONS—THE FINAL FRONTIER

College admissions can be intimidating for any high school student, but homeschoolers may face additional challenges, such as proving their academic credentials without traditional transcripts. Here are some tips and resources for homeschoolers applying to college.

- **Create a homeschool transcript** that showcases both your academic achievements and extracurricular activities. This transcript should provide a comprehensive view of your educational journey and personal interests, highlighting the full scope of your accomplishments.

- **Consider obtaining recommendation letters** from non-academic sources like employers, community leaders, and supervisors from internships. These letters can provide valuable insights into your work ethic, character, and skills outside of homeschooling. For example, a letter from a summer job supervisor can highlight your reliability and teamwork, while a community leader can speak to your leadership and volunteer efforts. These diverse perspectives can offer a well-rounded view of your abilities and experiences.

- **Look into colleges that are familiar with working with home-schoolers,** especially those that have homeschool admissions counselors. These schools understand the unique backgrounds of homeschool students and can provide the support and guidance needed for a smooth transition to college life.

SCHOLARSHIPS—SHOW ME THE MONEY!

Scholarships can be a game-changer when it comes to paying for college. So start early! Begin your scholarship search early in your high school career. Many scholarships have deadlines well before the college application season. By starting early, you'll have plenty of time to gather necessary documents, write essays, and complete applications without feeling rushed. Here's how you can take advantage of scholarship opportunities:

1. **Keep Track of Deadlines!** Organization is key when applying for scholarships. Use a planner or digital calendar to keep track of application deadlines, essay requirements, and submission dates. Missing a deadline can mean missing out on free money for college. Use Google Calendar to set reminders and keep track of important scholarship deadlines.

2. **Write a Strong Personal Statement.** Many scholarships require a personal statement or essay. Take the time to write a compelling story about yourself, highlighting your achievements, goals, and why you deserve the scholarship. Have a teacher, parent, or mentor review your essays to provide feedback and help you improve. .

    ◦ **Purdue Online Writing Lab (OWL):** https://owl.purdue.edu— Offers tips and guidelines for writing effective scholarship essays.

3. **Many local organizations, community groups, and businesses o-ffer scholarships specifically for students in their area.** If you're

with a homeschool charter, start by checking with your local high school guidance counselor, who often has information about local scholarships. Additionally, public libraries and community centers can be valuable resources for scholarship listings. Another excellent resource are the community foundations, or non-profits, in your area, which frequently administers scholarships on behalf of local donors. For a comprehensive search, you can use websites like Scholarship America which allow you to filter scholarships by location.

- **Scholarship America:** https://www.scholarshipamerica.org

- **Unigo.com:** www.unigo.com – Lists both large and small scholarships, including unique and niche opportunities.

4. **Check with Colleges and Universities for Merit-Based Scholarships.** Many colleges and universities offer merit-based scholarships to students who excel academically or demonstrate exceptional talent in areas like music, art, or athletics. Reach out to the admissions offices of the colleges you're interested in to learn about the scholarships they offer. Don't forget to ask if they have specific scholarships for homeschoolers or if there are any additional steps you need to take as a homeschool applicant. Use the College Board Scholarship tool to help you find scholarships offered by colleges and universities.

- **College Board Scholarship:** https://bigfuture.collegeboard.org/scholarship-search

5. **Apply for Large/General and Small/Niche Scholarships Open to All High School Students.** There are countless scholarships available to all high school students, regardless of whether they attend a public, private, or homeschool. These can be based on a variety of criteria, including academic achievement, community service, leadership, and specific interests or talents. **Don't Ignore Small Scholarships!** While large scholarships are enticing, don't overlook smaller awards. Many smaller scholarships can add up to significant amounts and may have less competition. Every bit helps when it comes to funding your education.

- **Fastweb:** www.fastweb.comComprehensive online resource that helps students find scholarships, financial aid, and college information to support their educational journey.

- ○ **Scholarships.com:** www.scholarships.com— Offers a vast database of scholarships, grants, and financial aid opportunities, along with tools to navigate the college application process.

- ○ **Appily:** www.appily.com— Provides scholarship information, college search tools, and resources for navigating the admissions process.

- ○ **Scholarship Owl:** ScholarshipOwl.com — Streamlines the scholarship application process and helps manage multiple applications at once.

By exploring these resources and following these tips, you can increase your chances of securing scholarships to help fund your college education. Remember, the key is to be proactive, stay organized, and apply to as many scholarships as possible.

TRANSCRIPTS—CHANNELING YOUR INNER SCRIBE

All those late-night study sessions and impromptu science experiments have finally paid off: your homeschooler is ready to apply to college or enter the workforce. But first, they'll need a transcript—a detailed record of their academic accomplishments that demonstrates their readiness for the next chapter of life.

Creating a homeschool transcript can be a bit daunting, especially if you've never done it before. But don't worry. There are plenty of resources and templates available online to help you craft a professional-looking transcript that accurately reflects your child's achievements. Just remember to be thorough and honest, and don't be afraid to showcase your child's unique talents and interests.

Resources for Creating Homeschool Transcripts

Note: Only the homepages of these websites are listed, as individual links may become outdated over time.

1. **Home School Legal Defense Association Transcripts (hslda.org)** — Offers sample transcripts, templates, and a transcript service.

2. **Donna Young's Homeschool Printables (donnayoung.org)** — Free printable transcript forms and examples.

3. **Homeschool Tracker (homeschooltracker.com)** — Software for tracking coursework and generating transcripts.

4. **Transcript Maker (transcriptmaker.com)** — Easy-to-use online tool for creating professional transcripts.

5. **The Home Scholar (thehomescholar.com)** — Articles, webinars, and tools for transcript creation.

6. **The HomeSchool Mom (thehomeschoolmom.com)** — Free downloadable Excel spreadsheet that includes course plans, report cards, attendance, and transcripts. Great comprehensive tool for keeping all your homeschool records organized.

7. **HomeschoolGiveaways (homeschoolgiveaways.com)** — Free editable and printable homeschool transcript templates. They also offer guidance on how to fill out transcripts properly.

8. **Homeschool (homeschool.com)** — Provides a step-by-step guide to creating a homeschool transcript, along with a free high school transcript template. This template organizes information by subject, which is helpful for students who may not follow a traditional course sequence.

9. **Organized Home School (organizedhomeschool.com)** — Lists various formats for homeschool transcripts, including simple transcripts, detailed transcripts, and transcripts by subject. They also provide links to several free resources for creating these documents.

These resources should provide you with the templates and guidance needed to create a professional and comprehensive homeschool transcript for your senior.

GRADUATION—CAP, GOWN, AND TASSEL: THE TIMELESS TRIFECTA

Congratulations! You've successfully navigated the homeschooling journey, and now it's time to celebrate your child's accomplishments with a well-deserved graduation ceremony. But how do you go about getting that coveted diploma? Depending on the path you've chosen (charter, private, or DIY), the process of obtaining a diploma may vary. For example, if your child was enrolled in a homeschool charter or partnered with a private school, they may provide you with an official diploma. If you've opted for the DIY route, you can create a custom diploma yourself or purchase one from various online vendors that cater to homeschoolers.

When planning a graduation ceremony, think about what elements are most important to you and your child. You might want to hold a small gathering with close family and friends, complete with caps and gowns, speeches, and a diploma presentation. Or perhaps you'd prefer a more informal celebration, such as a backyard barbecue or a family vacation. The choice is yours—after all, homeschooling is all about customization and celebrating your child's unique journey. Onward and forward!

---------- **Summary** ----------

So, you've survived the high school years, and more impressively, so has your teenager! From navigating eye-rolls to conquering calculus, you've done it all. You've crafted a high school plan, explored career options, and even managed to fit in those all-important fridge field trips. Pat yourself on the back—you deserve it!

Remember, the high school years are about more than just academics. They're about preparing your child for adulthood, encouraging independence, and exploring passions. Whether your student is heading to college, the military, a trade school, or straight into the workforce, you've equipped them with the skills they need to succeed.

From the wide-eyed stare of freshman year to the final stretch of senior year, prepping for post high-school life is a marathon, not a sprint (though there might be some sprinting in the end). But with a game plan and maybe a big calendar with lots of colorful markers, you'll both cross that finish line ready for the next big adventure.

And as always, keep detailed records and transcripts. These will be essential for whatever path your student chooses next.

Homeschooling high school can seem daunting, but with the right resources and a bit of creativity, it's a rewarding journey. So, here's to celebrating your unique homeschooling adventure and looking forward to the bright future ahead. Cheers to you and your high schooler—you've got this!

> **Disclaimer:** *At the time of this book publication, my middle child is a freshman in public high school and my oldest child is a junior in public high school. Since I do not have direct experience homeschooling throughout high school (although my oldest took high school courses in middle school), I have interviewed and have had numerous paid consultations with homeschool college experts and free-advice-giving veteran homeschool parents about homeschooling throughout high school (when I planned on doing so). Additionally, many YouTubers and bloggers have successfully homeschooled through high school, and I will list so of them in the Selected Notes section in the back of the book. Just putting that out there. As always, do your due diligence.*

PART VI - CHALLENGES & TRIUMPHS

Every journey has its ups and downs, and Part VI honors this reality by sharing the potential challenges and unexpected perks of homeschooling. You'll find practical tips, a bit of tough love, and a whole lot of encouragement to help you stay on track. So, stay open to the surprises, tackle the challenges head-on, and celebrate the wins along the way—because this journey is as rewarding as it is unpredictable. Spoiler alert: It's totally worth it in the end!

34

Doubt Detox

Giving the Critics a Mute Button

What people think of you is none of your business.

—Tabitha Brown

S TARTING YOUR HOMESCHOOLING ADVENTURE means diving into a world
brimming with lesson plans, educational philosophies, and, of course,
boundless love for your kids. But just when you're feeling invincible in your cape,
here come the Doubters. They're the ones who pop up at family gatherings,
neighborhood events, and even among your friends. With their sharp questions,
perpetually raised eyebrows, and coffee cups clutched like faulty lifelines, their
skepticism can be hard to ignore.

To counter these Doubters, personal anecdotes, success stories, and solid statistics become your secret weapons. By sharing real examples of how homeschooling has positively impacted your family or others you know, you can transform
their theoretical concerns into tangible proof.

This chapter is your diplomatic toolkit, your shield, your armor, and yes,
your mute button for handling and maybe even winning over these relentless
skeptics. This is especially true if you're looking to sway the opinion of a spouse,
grandparent, or someone else who matters to you. So, let's talk about mastering
the art of managing, disarming, and converting those critics.

MEET THE DOUBTERS

First, let's identify the different species of Doubters lurking in the homeschooling jungle. Understanding what drives them can help you handle their criticism with confidence. For the record, I've kept the responses to the critics...polite. You, on the other hand, can feel free to let your inner lion roar.

The Well-Meaning Worrywart

This Doubter is often a close family member, like a concerned parent or grandparent. Their questions come from a place of love and genuine worry that homeschooling might disadvantage your child.

Typical Comments:
- "But what about socialization?"

- "How will they get into college?"

- "Are you really qualified to teach?"

Example Response to Socialization Worries: "I totally get why you're worried! The good news is, homeschoolers aren't isolated at all—they join co-ops, play on sports teams, and volunteer in the community. In fact, studies show they're often just as socialized, if not more, than kids in traditional schools. Who knew, right?"

Resource: *The Well-Adjusted Child: The Social Benefits of Homeschooling* by Rachel Gathercole. This book offers a wealth of information on the socialization of homeschooled children, complete with studies and anecdotes.

The Education Elitist

This doubter is often an educator or someone who places a high value on formal qualifications and traditional learning environments. They genuinely believe that teaching should be left to certified professionals, viewing institutional schooling as the gold standard for quality education.

Typical Comments:
- "Do you have a teaching credential?"

- "How can you ensure they're getting a well-rounded education?"

- "What about standardized testing?"

Example Response to Qualification Concerns: "I understand your point. However, despite having numerous certified teachers, the U.S. still ranks globally around 25th in the prestigious PISA (Programme for International Student Assessment) and 18th in TIMSS (Trends in International Mathematics and Science Study). After consulting experts like John Holt and thoroughly researching, I am confident that I can provide my children with a top-notch, well-rounded education." (a bit wordy, just say US schools perform abysmally in international tests and you think you can do better.)

Resource: *Teaching Your Own: The John Holt Book of Homeschooling* by John Holt. This classic guide provides reassurance and practical advice from one of the pioneers of the homeschooling movement.

The Competitive Parent

This Doubter isn't necessarily worried about your child's education—they're more focused on comparison. They may see your decision to homeschool as an indirect critique of their own choices, leading to a tendency to defend or highlight their approach.

Typical Comments:
- "My kids are thriving in public school. Why would you take yours out?"

- "Aren't you worried they'll miss out on sports and extracurriculars?"

- "Do you think you can do better than trained teachers?"

Example Response to Competitive Parents: "Every family is different, and what works best varies for each of us. For instance, there's a family in our homeschool group whose oldest child just got into an Ivy League school. They found that homeschooling let them dive deep into their interests and prepare for college in unique ways. And they still managed to play league volleyball and stay active socially."

Resource: *Homeschooling in America: Capturing and Assessing the Movement* by Joseph Murphy. This book provides a detailed look at the homeschooling movement in America, complete with data and analysis.

The Casual Critic

This group includes friends, acquaintances, or even strangers who've heard about your homeschooling and can't resist tossing in their two cents. Their comments are often off-the-cuff and not deeply thought out, but they can still catch you off guard if you're not prepared.

Typical Comments:
- "I could never do that. It seems so hard!"

- "Isn't homeschooling illegal in some places?"

- "Aren't you worried about sheltering them too much?"

Example Response to Casual Critics: "I get that it might seem overwhelming, but with the right resources and support, it's totally doable—and honestly, it's amazing to watch your kids learn and grow firsthand. And yep, homeschooling is legal in all 50 states!"

Resource: "Homeschooling and the Law: Your Rights and Responsibilities" by HSLDA (Home School Legal Defense Association). This resource provides comprehensive information on the legal aspects of homeschooling in the United States.

BUILD YOUR SUPPORT NETWORK

A strong support network can provide emotional bolstering, practical advice, and a sense of community. Here's how to build and maintain one:

- **Identify Key People:** Look for family, friends, and fellow homeschoolers who can offer support and encouragement.

- **Join Local Groups:** Participate in local homeschooling groups and co-ops to connect with others who share your experiences.

- **Utilize Online Communities:** Engage with online forums and social media groups focused on homeschooling.

- **Attend Workshops and Conferences:** Learn and network by attending events related to homeschooling and education.

- **Seek Professional Advice:** Don't hesitate to consult educators, counselors, or experienced homeschoolers for guidance.

- **Exchange Resources:** Share teaching materials, ideas, and tips with others in your network.

- **Regular Communication:** Keep in touch with your support network through regular meetings, calls, or messages to maintain strong connections.

OVERCOME SELF-DOUBT

Let's be honest—sometimes the most persistent Doubter is the one in the mirror. Here are some strategies to silence your inner critic:

Celebrate Small Wins

Keep a journal of daily or weekly achievements, no matter how small. These entries can be a powerful reminder of your progress and successes.

Continuous Learning

Invest in your own education. Attend workshops, read books, and take courses on homeschooling and child development. The more knowledgeable you become, the more confident you'll feel.

Self-Care

Don't forget to take care of yourself. Homeschooling is demanding, and you need to recharge. Schedule regular time for activities that bring you joy and relaxation.

Positive Affirmations

Create a list of positive affirmations to read each morning. Remind yourself that you are capable, resourceful, and dedicated to providing the best education for your children.

---------- **Summary** ----------

Homeschooling is a bold and gutsy choice, like deciding to bungee jump off a cliff with nothing but your wits and a really secure rope. Sure, there will always be Doubters lurking around, but remember—you're the one steering the ship of your children's future. You're crafting an educational adventure that's rich, fulfilling, and tailor-made just for them.

When the Doubters come knocking, greet them with a smile, a confident comeback, and maybe a cheeky joke. You've totally got this. Your homeschooling journey is yours to define, and every day you're proving that the best way to predict the future is to create it yourself.

And that mute button? Sometimes, it's about turning down the volume on the outside noise and cranking up your inner rock star voice—the one that knows you're on the right track. As Steve Jobs, the co-founder of Apple, once said, "Don't let the noise of others' opinions drown out your own inner voice." Remain calm and homeschool on!

35

Mid-Year Homeschool Start

Diving Into the Deep End With One Floatie

Leap, and the net will appear.

— John Burroughs

S TARTING HOMESCHOOLING MID-YEAR OR anytime during the school year is like being handed the lead role in a play at the last minute (and you weren't the understudy). You're not sure of the script, but the show must go on with your kids as your co-stars. But don't fret. Just as arriving late to a party can still lead to a great time, jumping on the homeschool train midway can be an unexpectedly delightful experience. Having started homeschooling midyear with my oldest child myself, I can assure you it's doable, and I'm here to guide you through it—floatie and all.

THE DECISION TO JUMP

Choosing to homeschool is like deciding to cook a gourmet meal without a recipe. You have the ingredients—your child, a stack of books, and plenty of enthusiasm—but what's the process? What's the final dish you're aiming for? That's what we're here to figure out together.

You might be starting mid-year for a variety of reasons – maybe the traditional school setting wasn't working out, perhaps you're seeking a more flexible schedule, or maybe the call of pajama school days was just too strong to resist. Whatever the reason, you've decided to leap, and that's half the battle won.

Now, let's talk logistics so we can get you started quickly.

Step 1: Deschooling

Before you start printing worksheets and assembling a mini classroom, you need to consider deschooling. Deschooling is the process of adjusting from a traditional school mindset to a homeschooling one. It's about letting go of the formal school structure and allowing your child to rediscover their natural love of learning.

The *general* rule of thumb is to spend one month deschooling for every year your child was in traditional school. This period helps them unwind, de-stress, and recalibrate their curiosity and enthusiasm for learning without the pressure of a structured curriculum.

Example: If your child has been in traditional school for five years, spend around five months deschooling. This doesn't mean doing nothing – it means engaging in informal learning activities like reading, exploring nature, playing educational games, and pursuing hobbies.

Step 2: Assess the Situation

Take a moment to breathe and assess. What does your child need? What subjects are they excelling in, and where do they need a bit more support? This isn't about recreating school at home – it's about tailoring an education to fit your child like a bespoke suit. You will assess the situation while you are deschooling.

Example: If your child struggles with math but loves history, you might focus on making math more engaging and fun while using history as a reward or break between challenging subjects.

Resource: Consider using the Khan Academy website, which offers free resources for a variety of subjects, allowing your child to learn at their own pace.

Step 3: Choose Your Transition Approach

The Transitional Week Approach
- Let's consider the scenario. It's the middle of the academic year, the leaves have fallen, and you've decided to start homeschooling. Instead of diving headfirst into the deep end, you can choose to wade in gradually. Begin with a "transitional week." This doesn't mean jumping into the

thick of algebra or Renaissance history right away. Instead, dedicate this week to understanding the homeschooling dynamics.

Example: Schedule visits to local libraries, engage in light reading or even take educational trips to local museums or historical sites. This helps your child (and you!) get used to the homeschooling rhythm. As for the curriculum, use this week to understand where your child stands academically. Perhaps get some diagnostic tests or just spend time discussing and reviewing what they've learned so far. This way, when you do start, you're not just picking up where the school left off; you're starting from a point that's comfortable for your child.

The Subject-by-Subject Transition

- If the thought of overhauling the entire educational process mid-year seems daunting, don't fret! You can always take a more piecemeal approach. Instead of transitioning all subjects into a homeschooling format at once, start with one or two that your child either enjoys or needs extra help with.

Example: If math is a favorite, kick off your homeschooling journey with some enjoyable math projects or exercises. Alternatively, if literature has been a tricky subject in traditional school, take the opportunity to explore it at home, maybe by reading a chosen novel together and discussing it. Gradually, as you both get the hang of it, introduce other subjects into your homeschooling routine. This method not only makes the transition smoother but also allows you to identify and cater to the specific needs and interests of your child.

Step 4: Legalities and Paperwork

I know, I know – the dreaded paperwork. But it's a necessary evil. Each state (if you're in the U.S.) has different regulations regarding homeschooling. Some require a letter of intent, others need you to submit an educational plan, and a few might want to check in periodically. **Check the laws in your state!**

Resource: The Home School Legal Defense Association is a great place to start. They offer detailed information on state-specific requirements and can even help with legal advice if needed.

Step 5: Choose a Curriculum

Ah, the curriculum. Think of it as your homeschooling roadmap. There are as many homeschooling curricula as there are opinions on whether pineapple belongs on pizza (it does, but that's a debate for another day). You've got your traditional, textbook-based curricula, online courses, unit studies, and even unschooling – which is less a curriculum and more a lifestyle. The key here is to find what resonates with you and your child. See Chapter 7, "The Curriculum Jungle" for more details.

Resource: Check out Cathy Duffy's reviews. She's the Oprah of reviewing homeschooling curricula – if she recommends it, you know it's worth a look.

Step 6: Set Up Your Learning Space

You don't need a dedicated classroom, but you do need a space where learning can happen. This could be the kitchen table, a cozy corner of the living room, or even a spot outside when the weather's nice. The goal is to create an environment that's conducive to learning but also flexible enough to change as needed.

Example: A small bookshelf, crate, or box with your child's current materials, a comfortable chair, a work surface, and a small whiteboard or corkboard for keeping track of daily tasks can transform a corner of your home into a mini-school.

Resource: Pinterest is a goldmine for creative homeschooling space ideas. Search for "homeschool room ideas" and prepare to be inspired (and slightly envious).

Step 7: Schedule Your Days

One of the biggest perks of homeschooling is the flexibility. Your schedule doesn't have to mimic a traditional school day. In fact, it shouldn't. Find a rhythm that works for you and your child. Some kids are early birds, ready to tackle math problems at dawn. Others might need a slower start with a morning walk or some quiet reading time.

Example: You might do academic work in the morning when your child is fresh, take a longer lunch break with some physical activity, and reserve afternoons for more relaxed subjects like art or science experiments.

Resource: The book "*Plan Your Year*" by Pam Barnhill offers excellent advice on creating a balanced and effective homeschool schedule.

Step 8: Find Your Tribe

Homeschooling can feel like an island, but you're far from alone. Finding a community – whether in person or online – can be a game-changer. Local homeschool groups often organize co-ops, field trips, and social events, providing both support and socialization opportunities for your child.

Example: Many areas have Facebook groups for local homeschooling families. Joining these can help you connect with others, share resources, and even set up playdates or group learning sessions.

Resource: Meetup.com and Facebook groups are great ways to find local homeschooling groups and events.

Step 9: Embrace the Chaos

Here's the thing – no matter how well you plan, there will be days when nothing goes right. The math lesson will devolve into tears, the science experiment will fail spectacularly, and you'll wonder why you ever thought this was a good idea. That's okay. It's all part of the journey. Homeschooling isn't about perfection. It's about growth, learning, and spending quality time with your child. It's about showing them that education isn't confined to a classroom – it's all around us.

Example: If a lesson isn't working, don't be afraid to switch gears. Watch an engaging documentary, bake cookies, listen to an audiobook, or take a nature walk. Learning happens in many forms.

Resource: The blog "Simple Homeschool" is full of stories and advice from real homeschooling parents, reminding you that you're not alone in the chaos.

Step 10: Measure Progress

Unlike traditional school, where progress is often measured by tests and grades, homeschooling allows for a more holistic approach. Keep track of your child's achievements through portfolios, projects, and regular assessments.

Example: Create a portfolio for each subject, including completed assignments, photos of projects, and notes on what your child has learned. This not only helps track progress but also creates a wonderful keepsake of your homeschooling journey.

Resource: The app Seesaw (web.seesaw.me) is a fantastic tool for creating digital portfolios, allowing you to easily share your child's work with family and friends.

Step 11: Stay Sane (Self-Care for Parents)

Homeschooling is rewarding, but it's also demanding. Don't forget to take care of yourself. Make time for your hobbies, connect with friends, and ensure you're getting enough rest. A happy, rested parent is a more effective teacher.

Example: Schedule regular "me time" into your week, whether it's a quiet coffee in the morning, a yoga class, or a night out with friends.

Resource: The book "The Brave Learner" by Julie Bogart offers not only educational insights but also encouragement and support for homeschooling parents.

---------- **Summary** ----------

Starting homeschooling mid-year is not just a leap into the unknown; it's an exciting opportunity to redefine education on your own terms. By embracing the initial phase of deschooling and assessing your child's needs, you're setting a solid foundation for a successful transition. Implementing a gradual approach—whether through a transitional week or focusing on subjects one at a time—ensures a smoother shift and helps build confidence. As you navigate the logistics and paperwork, remember that your journey is about more than just academics; it's about fostering resilience, curiosity, and a lifelong love of learning. So, while you may start with the support of a floatie, as you grow more confident, you'll find yourself equipped with something much sturdier—a life vest that will carry you both through the waves ahead.

36

Homeschool Burnout

Finding Your "Good Enough" Threshold

When my kids become wild and unruly, I use a nice, safe playpen. When they're finished, I climb out.

— Erma Bombeck

WELCOME TO THE BERMUDA Triangle of homeschooling—a place where scissors, math workbooks, and your sanity vanish mysteriously. Navigating through your day, you might feel like you're encountering magnetic anomalies with sibling disputes, pulling your plans off course. Sometimes, it even seems like time itself warps, with hours slipping away unnoticed.

And let's not talk about keeping up with household chores while striving for a Pinterest-perfect homeschool space. It can be exhausting. Those idealized setups make your home, with its lived-in mess and post-tornado decor, feel like a shipwreck in comparison, adding to the stress and potential burnout. But remember, those picture-perfect spaces are often more fantasy than reality. Embrace the realness of your home—it's a sign of a vibrant and active learning environment, not a failure.

Instead of feeling overwhelmed, let's tackle the issue head-on. In this chapter, we'll explore the causes, symptoms, and remedies for homeschool burnout, blending practical advice with a touch of humor to help you stay grounded and keep the educational flame alive. I've structured the chapter into key sections: recognizing burnout, managing time and responsibilities, and addressing unique homeschooling challenges. To illustrate these concepts, let's jump into the 'Morning Mayhem Chronicles' and meet Tracy—a story that might feel all too familiar.

MORNING MAYHEM—TRACY'S TALE

Meet Tracy, a once-enthusiastic homeschool mom now running on fumes and leftover mac 'n' cheese. Her day starts quietly at 7:00 a.m., with the soft hum of the refrigerator and gentle rain outside. She enjoys a brief moment of peace, sipping her coffee and mentally organizing the day's activities, feeling prepared.

At 7:15 a.m., Tracy enters her toddler's room, gently waking her and helping her pick out an outfit. Calmness quickly evaporates when her favorite tattered sequin cape is missing, leading to cries and frustration.

By 7:20 a.m., Tracy is in the kitchen, flipping pancakes while comforting her toddler with a cup of apple juice (the sippy cups are dirty or missing). The third grader bounces in, upbeat and hungry, and then quickly scowls at the morning basket of books on the table. He wants to do a science experiment instead.

Meanwhile, Tracy's pre-teen snoozes through alarms, responding with a muffled "five more minutes" when urged to get up. The clock is ticking, and Tracy can feel the pressure mounting.

At 7:25 a.m., she's barely had time to make two pancakes when her teen son trudges into the kitchen, eyes still half-closed. He plops down at the table and accidentally spills the toddler's juice, creating a sticky mess. You toss him a towel to start cleaning up all while trying to reassure your toddler (again), coaxing your third grader into reading, and yelling at your pre-teen to get out of bed.

By 7:28 a.m. (yes, that fast), peacefulness packs its bags, mutters "Peace out," and bolts out the front door. The once-serene morning has morphed into a whirlwind of chaos. Tracy stares at her empty coffee mug, sighing, and wonders where her homeschooling dream went off the rails.

Burnout, the stealthy villain, rubs its hands together with glee and slips out the window, chuckling to itself.

If this sounds familiar, you're not alone. Part of beating the burnout blues is to recognize when you might be under stress overload.

PART I—RECOGNIZE THE BURNOUT BEAST

First things first: How do you know you're burned out? Well, let's play a quick game of:

"You might be burned out if..."

- your eye twitches every time you hear the word *"lesson."* You're basically Pavlov's dog, flinching at the sound of a bell.

- at the farmer's market, someone asks what kind of apples you want. Without thinking, you blurt out, *"I don't care; just give me the ones that start with the letter A."*

- you spend more time browsing and organizing "pretty" lesson ideas than actually teaching them.

- you burst into tears when your child asks for help with simple addition because you've been doing math all day and can't take it anymore.

- you wake up on a Wednesday, panic because you think it's Friday, and scramble for lesson plans—only to remember it's still Wednesday.

- you're teaching dialogue for a narrative essay but keep eyeing the clock, counting down to your *"recess break"* so you can make a mimosa.

- you daydream about sending your kids to public school, imagining the blissful quiet while they ride the school bus every morning.

- you accidentally teach your kids a swear word during a Zoom meeting because you forgot they were in the room.

- you feel like you're constantly "on"—always teaching, always parenting. Rinse and repeat.

- your kids argue over the identical blue crayons, and suddenly the box of Thin Mints stashed behind the rice becomes your escape.

- Pinterest-perfect homeschooling moms are driving you to overspend, leaving you feeling inadequate, broke, and wondering if you should cut up your credit cards.

- your kids argue over who gets to use a blue crayon even though there are three *identical* blue crayons on the table. You suddenly remember the box of Thin Mints you've been hiding behind the 10-pound bag of rice. You sneak into your bathroom and start munching while trying to drown out the sound of your kids' bickering.

Recognizing these feelings is the first step to addressing them. If you see yourself in Tracy, it's time to take action. But before diving into solutions, let's first explore what's causing this burnout and how to tackle it head-on.

PART II—WHY WE BURNOUT: THE CULPRITS

The Over-Scheduler's Club—How Ambition Takes Over

It's easy to cram your day with every educational activity under the sun—math in the morning, followed by science experiments that inevitably spill into snack time. You're deep into history by noon, and suddenly it's time for lunch. But no break for you—it's on to art class and then a nature walk, followed by piano lessons squeezed in between racing to make it to the park for soccer practice and dinner. Finally, after dinner, there's just enough time for a family read-aloud before bed—if the kids aren't already passed out on the couch. It's no wonder you're running around like a headless chicken, wondering why everyone's melting down at 3 p.m. Your daily schedule looks more like a military operation than a school day

Perfectionism—Pinterest Boards vs. Reality

Do you spend more time creating the "perfect" lesson plan than teaching it? The quest for the perfect homeschool space or lesson plan is like chasing a unicorn—mythical and exhausting. You spend hours creating Pinterest-worthy lesson plans and activities that never go as intended. Perfectionism whispers in your ear that everything must be flawless, but the reality is, sometimes good enough really is good enough.

Lack of Support—Stranded on Solo Island

Isolation is the silent saboteur of homeschoolers everywhere. Without a network of fellow homeschool parents to share the triumphs and tribulations, it can feel like you're stranded on a deserted island—one where your only company is a cranky toddler and a stubborn tween. You need a tribe (virtual or local) to vent about the day's disasters and celebrate those small victories, like a tear-free math lesson (yours or the kids') with people who truly understand the struggle.

Sibling Rivalry—Household Smackdown

Sibling rivalry often feels less like minor disputes and more like officiating a non-stop wrestling match—minus the ring and fancy costumes. Whether it's over the last stick of glue or front seat privileges, these daily tussles can deplete your energy quicker than a sugar-loaded toddler. If every day feels like you're managing a wildlife sanctuary rather than educating future leaders, it may be time to introduce structured conflict resolution strategies that turn rivalry into teamwork.

Work-Life Balance—The High-Wire Act

Balancing homeschooling, work, and family life is like juggling flaming swords while riding a unicycle—possible, but highly risky. One minute you're helping your kid with fractions; the next, you're on a conference call trying to sound professional while your toddler is drawing on the wall behind you. It's a constant tightrope walk, and sometimes it feels like there's no safety net in sight. The result? You end up stretched thinner than a pizza crust, trying to be everything to everyone.

Low Motivation—When Zeal Fizzles

Ever feel like both you and your kids are just going through the motions, caught in a relentless cycle of "blah"? Loss of motivation is a common phase in the homeschool journey, where enthusiasm dips and even the most exciting projects seem dull. Reigniting this lost spark often requires stepping back to adjust your approach. Integrating more hands-on activities, field trips, or passion-led learning can transform drudgery into discovery, rekindling both your spirits.

Exhausted—Running on Fumes

Are you slogging through the day with the energy of a half-charged battery? Homeschooling can feel like you're constantly running a marathon—with no finish line in sight. From the early morning scramble to prep lessons to the late-night curriculum planning, exhaustion isn't just a possibility; it's a daily reality. It's crucial to acknowledge that you're not a machine and sometimes, a nap or a quiet moment with a cup of tea might be the most educational thing you can do—for you and your kids. Remember, an exhausted teacher can't ignite young minds, so take that well-deserved break.

Overwhelmed—Drowning in a Sea of Books and Expectations

Do you find yourself buried under a pile of educational materials, unsure of where to start? Overwhelm is the homeschool parent's constant companion. It sneaks up on you while you're trying to choose between five different math curricula or when you're attempting to track down the perfect historical novel that's age-appropriate, engaging, *and* historically accurate. The key to overcoming this deluge is not to find the perfect system but to simplify and prioritize. Strip back the extras, focus on what truly matters, and remember that sometimes, less really is more in the journey of lifelong learning.

As we close Part II of our exploration, we've peeled back the layers of homeschooling challenges—from overambitious schedules to overwhelming demands. These culprits, all too familiar in the homeschooling world, illustrate the multifaceted struggles that can lead to burnout. We've ventured through the chaotic daily battles, the silent pressure of perfectionism, and the echoing loneliness of a support-less journey. Now, as we transition into Part III, it's time to shift our focus from diagnosing these challenges to overcoming them. Let's dive into effective strategies designed to reignite your passion for homeschooling and transform this educational journey into one of joy and fulfillment.

PART III—STRATEGIES TO REIGNITE THE PASSION

Now that we've identified the burnout culprits, let's talk solutions. It's time to revive that homeschooling passion and banish burnout for good. Let's bring Tracy back into the story.

Simplify Your Schedule

Focus on core subjects and essential activities, creating a more manageable day. Remember, less is more.

Example: Instead of cramming five subjects into one morning, Tracy trims down her packed Monday to essentials, adding some fun science experiments mid-week.

Set Realistic Goals

Realistic goals are your best friends—they keep everyone motivated, reduce those hair-pulling moments, and give you and your child a reason to high-five each other. Start by breaking down those big, lofty goals into bite-sized, manageable steps.

Example: Tracy's goal for her child is to read more books. Instead of setting an overwhelming target like "My child will read 50 books this year," she sets a more realistic goal such as "My child will read one book every two weeks." This breaks down to about 26 books a year, a much more manageable number. To further simplify, she could start with shorter, age-appropriate books and gradually increase the difficulty as her child gains confidence and skill.

Practice Self-Care

Prioritize self-care. Making time for yourself is not selfish; it's necessary. Engage in activities or treats that bring you joy and help you relax (and make sure they're free if you're in debt). This could be gardening, crafting, massages, meditation, going for a walk, mani/pedis, enjoying a luxurious bubble bath, reading a good book or simply taking a quiet moment to enjoy a cup of tea.

Example: Tracy discovers that a 15-minute meditation session each morning helps her start the day with a clear mind. She schedules a yoga session or a coffee break with a good book. She finds what recharges her and makes it a *non-negotiable* part of her day by scheduling "me time" in her calendar to ensure she *consistently* makes time for herself.

Delegate and Outsource

Utilize online resources, tutors, and co-ops to help shoulder the teaching responsibilities. Expose your children to other educators who are passionate or experts in a particular subject, topic, or activity.

Example: Tracy enrolls her kids in an online math class, giving herself a much-needed break. She also joins a local co-op where parents take turns teaching different subjects, lightening everyone's load. You. don't. have. to. do. it. all.

Diffuse Sibling Rivalries

Sibling rivalries can turn your homeschool into a battleground, but with a few clever strategies, you can transform conflict into cooperation. Here's how Tracy does it:

- **Encourage Cooperation:** Assign tasks that require siblings to work together, like cleaning up after dinner or planning a family outing.

- **Individual Attention:** Spend one-on-one time with each child every day. Read a book together or go for a walk. This attention can help each child feel seen and valued, reducing the need for attention-seeking behavior.

- **Create Healthy Competition:** Encourage siblings to compete positively, like seeing who can finish their chores first or who can read the most books in a month (incentives are encouraged). This can help siblings learn healthy competition and cooperation.

- **Mediate Conflicts:** When conflicts arise, take the time to listen to each child's perspective and work together to find a solution that works for everyone. This can help siblings learn conflict-resolution skills and build stronger relationships with each other.

Shake Things Up

Stepping out of your comfort zone and trying something completely different can be just the ticket to shake things up and start fresh. Here are several suggestions that Tracy could try:

- **Outdoor Classroom:** Move your lessons to the backyard, a local park, or even a nearby beach. Fresh air and a natural setting can invigorate both you and your kids.

- **Field Trips:** Plan regular field trips to museums, zoos, botanical gardens, or historical sites. Real-world experiences can make learning more engaging.

- **Theme Days:** Dedicate specific days to fun themes, like Science Fridays or Art Mondays, where you focus on hands-on projects and experiments.

- **Interactive Learning:** Use educational games, apps, and virtual reality to make subjects like history and science come alive.

- **Guest Speakers:** Invite experts from various fields to speak to your kids (or co-op), either in person or via video call. This could be a local artist, a scientist, or even a grandparent with fascinating stories to tell.

- **Embrace the Chaos:** Sometimes, the best way to deal with homeschool burnout is to embrace the chaos and let your kids lead the lesson for the day or choose the topic/activity that *they're* excited about. This "Kid's Choice" day can be a great way to take some of the pressure off yourself and allow your kids to take ownership of their own learning.

Master Family Affairs

Tracy's days are so packed with responsibilities that weeks can go by without meaningful family interactions, leading to a sense of disconnection and burnout. It's crucial to anchor yourself to the reason behind all the juggling: your family.

Family Calendars
Example: Tracy uses a digital calendar accessible to the whole family. She inputs all work deadlines, virtual meetings, her high schooler's exams, dentist appointments, family movie nights, extracurricular activities, and "me time." This visual aid helps prevent scheduling conflicts and ensures everyone knows when quiet times are imperative and when the house can erupt into controlled chaos.

Family 'Status' Meetings
Example: Tracy starts the day with a quick family meeting over breakfast. She discusses the day's schedule, highlights times when she'll be unavailable, and sets expectations for noise levels and interruptions. It's a great way to involve kids in daily planning and make them feel part of the process.

Family Rituals
Example: Tracy establishes rituals like weekly movie nights, Saturday morning hikes, or cooking a family meal together once a week. These traditions become the glue holding her family together amidst the chaos.

Just Say No

Learn to set boundaries to protect your time and energy. It's perfectly okay to decline extra activities or commitments that add to your stress. When you're already juggling lesson plans, extracurricular activities, and household responsibilities, adding one more task to your plate can be overwhelming.

Example: Tracy is asked to join a planning committee for a local fundraiser. She politely, but firmly, declines with, "I appreciate the offer, but my current commitments don't leave me enough time to take on additional responsibilities." Don't waver!

Find Your Laugh Factory

Platforms like Facebook or Reddit have groups dedicated to homeschooling humor where you can share and enjoy relatable content. Laughter can be a great stress-reliever, and connecting with other homeschooling parents who understand your challenges can be both comforting and entertaining.

Example: Tracy browses popular homeschool humor groups on Instagram and Reddit for her morning laughs before she starts her day. The funny anecdotes, memes, and stories lift her spirits and remind her that she's not alone in the unique, sometimes chaotic, journey of homeschooling. Starting her day with a smile helps Tracy maintain a positive attitude and better handle the challenges that come her way.

These suggestions and resources can help you manage homeschool burnout more effectively, providing both immediate relief and long-term strategies to keep you and your family thriving.

---------- **Summary** ----------

Navigating the Bermuda Triangle of homeschooling, where the maelstrom of sibling squabbles and the ghostly haze of perpetual exhaustion loom large, can easily lead to feeling overwhelmed and burnt out. In this chapter, we've discussed finding your good enough threshold—a crucial step in recognizing and addressing burnout. By simplifying schedules, setting realistic goals, practicing self-care, and embracing the lived-in mess of your home, you can transform stress into success. Remember, those Pinterest-perfect setups don't always reflect reality. Embrace the imperfections, lean on your support network, and reignite your homeschooling passion with humor and resilience!

37

Persevering Through It All

Don't Throw in the Towel—You'll Need It to Wipe Your Victory Sweat

It does not matter how slowly you go, as long as you do not stop.
— Confucius

CONGRATULATIONS! YOU'VE BRAVED THE rollercoaster of lesson planning, weathered meltdowns (both yours and theirs), and discovered the blend of education and humor. Homeschooling is like running a marathon while juggling flaming torches – intense, impressive, and occasionally eyebrow-singeing. Yet here you are, at the finish line, likely with a bit of a tan from all that torchlight!

Homeschooling requires perseverance, creativity, and patience. Keep the big picture in mind, celebrate the small victories, and don't be too hard on yourself or your child. Both of you are learning and growing together.

The true triumph isn't just academic milestones, but fostering a lifelong love of learning, strengthening family bonds, and building resilience. The short-term rewards are daily discoveries and shared laughter, while the long-term benefits are curious minds and confident, independent individuals.

Reflect on the Madness

Remember when you thought a Pinterest-perfect homeschool space was a must? Or when you jumped on every new curriculum trend that popped up on your favorite YouTuber's channel or blog? Maybe you didn't fall for the decor frenzy, but you've definitely had your moments of homeschool mayhem. And guess what? Real learning doesn't need a shiny classroom or curated curriculum. It happens everywhere—on the couch, in the backyard, or even during a toddler's snack time.

Wisdom Nuggets

You've picked up some valuable nuggets of wisdom along the way. Like realizing that:

- **Perfection is a Myth:** Your child doesn't need a perfect teacher; they need you – imperfect, occasionally frazzled, but full of love and dedication.

- **Flexibility is Key:** Some days will be structured; others chaotic. Embrace the chaos; it's all part of learning.

- **Learning Happens Everywhere:** From grocery shopping math lessons to history discussions over movies, every moment is a teaching opportunity.

Passing the Baton

As you close this book, remember that homeschooling is both a marathon and a relay race. Like a marathon, it requires endurance and persistence. And like a relay race, it's about passing the baton of knowledge and values to your children. You've carried the baton with grace (and a few drops), and now it's time to pass it on with confidence.

So, here's to you, homeschooling warrior. And here's to the journey, the memories, and the countless cups of coffee that powered it all. May your future be bright, your patience be endless, and your sense of humor be intact. You've got this!

Now go forth and conquer the world – or at least the laundry pile.

Wow, you've made it to the end of *When Life Gives You Homeschool Lesson Plans*! I hope you found it as enjoyable and enlightening as I did writing it. If this book made you chuckle, inspired you, or simply helped make your homeschooling journey a little smoother, I'd love for you to spread the word and maybe even get involved. Here's how:

- **Share the Love**: Write a review online. Honest reviews help others find what they're looking for, whether it's a lifeline or a fun read.

- **Join the Community**: Sign up for my newsletter at www.hom eschoolknockouts.com/newsletter to stay updated on new book, homeschool tips, and more. Plus, when you join, you'll receive a **free copy of my digital Mega Homeschool Planner!**

Don't Miss My First Book in the *Homeschool S.O.S. Series*!

I'm thrilled to introduce the first book in my *Homeschool S.O.S.* series: *Homeschooling Boys*. In this guide, you'll explore the unique challenges and joys of educating boys, from their boundless energy to their hands-on learning style. It's filled with practical tips, fun strategies, and just the right dose of humor to keep your homeschool journey light-hearted and productive. Don't let this new release pass you by! Subscribe to my newsletter at **www.homeschoolknockouts.com/newsletter** to be in the know.

Looking for more ways to engage?

- www.youtube.com/homeschoolknockouts

- www.facebook.com/homeschoolknockouts

- www.instagram.com/homeschool_knockouts

BOOK EBONY JACKSON FOR YOUR NEXT EVENT!

Are you looking for an engaging, expert speaker to inspire and equip parents on their homeschool journey? With 15 years of hands-on experience, Ebony offers dynamic and informative presentations at a wide range of events, including:

- **Conventions & Conferences**

- **Homeschool Groups & Co-ops**

- **Workshops & Expos**

- **Book Events & Bookstores**

- **Podcasts & Webinars**

Ebony's talks are designed to empower both new and seasoned homeschoolers with stress-free strategies for creating successful, personalized learning experiences at home. Whether you're hosting a local group or a large event, her approachable style and practical tips resonate with parents looking for guidance on everything from curriculum planning to time management.

Interested in booking Ebony for your next event?

Visit **www.ebonyjacksonauthor.com** to learn more, or email **hi@homeschoolknockouts.com** to schedule a speaking engagement.

Scan the QR Code to Have Ebony Speak At Your Next Event:

Acknowledgements

First and foremost, I want to thank God for the guidance and strength that carried me through this homeschooling journey. Grace and wisdom have been at work beyond my understanding, and I'm deeply thankful for the blessings and support that appeared—often in the most unexpected moments.

To my husband, Don, who never blinked an eye as I commandeered room after room, turning each into its own homeschool kingdom. Whether it was the living room, dining room, or even a hallway art station, you took it all in stride. Most importantly, you gave me the priceless gift of staying home to teach our sons—something for which I'll be forever grateful. Your quiet support, infinite patience with the skyscraper of curriculum books, and ability to laugh through the chaos made this wild ride not only possible, but unexpectedly joyful.

To my three sons, who bravely endured the madness of being both students and test subjects for every wild idea I thought might work. Thanks for (mostly) not mutinying, for learning through my "creative" curriculum interpretations, and for turning documentary marathons and deep dives into current events into some of our best "classroom" discussions.

To my mom, whose encouragement has been the bedrock of my journey, thank you for always reminding me to believe in myself. Your strength and un-wavering support have been a constant inspiration.

To my sister, Aretha, thank you for being my voice of reason, my "Aha!" generator, and my biggest cheerleader. Your wisdom, humor, and love made all the difference.

A massive thank you to Niema Jefferson, my homeschooling lifeline and partner-in-crime. From survival schemes to shenanigans that cemented our bo-som buddy status, you reminded me that getting through the day—meltdowns or not—was a win. Our "quick" chats about life and homeschool that magically turned into three-hour therapy sessions kept me laughing and (semi) organized. Together, we probably bought half of all TeachersPayTeachers resources and most of Amazon's homeschooling supplies in our quest for the perfect resource (or at least the next distraction!). Your endless encouragement kept me sane and ready for the next adventure.

Major props to @LeadFarmer73 for those legendary, deep-dive YouTube marathon videos that tackle everything under the sun—and then some. You've schooled me on some of life's best lessons. Your videos were my saving grace during those endless late-night editing binges, keeping me sane and cracking up in the dead of night. The way you blend wisdom, wit, and raw authenticity didn't just make the grind tolerable; it actually made it fun. Thanks for the pep talks, the laughs, and the boost that got me through to the finish line. Keep being you, and keep the magic coming!

To my incredible YouTube family of homeschoolers—many of whom have become cherished friends—thank you for your constant support, shared laughter, and encouragement. You turned what could have been a lonely path into a vibrant, supportive community.

Finally, to all the homeschooling parents, online forums, and fellow adventurers on this wild journey—thank you for proving it's okay to skip the algebra lesson and call it a "home economics" day when the dishwasher breaks and everyone learns how to fix it.

About the Author

A Texas soul who's called California home for over 20 years, Ebony combines down-home practicality with laid-back humor in her one-of-a-kind homeschooling guide. With a Master of Science in Education and over 15 years of homeschooling experience, she's honed the art of transforming homeschool chaos into calm, productive days.

Now a retired homeschooler, Ebony is working on her new series, *Homeschool SOS*, where she continues to guide others toward stress-free educational days. Married with three sons, when Ebony's not reviewing curriculum, you'll find her planting exotic seeds in her garden or cheering on her favorite football team.

Discover more at her author website: www.ebonyjacksonauthor.com, or get in touch through the options below. She'd love to hear from you!

Website: www.homeschoolknockouts.com
YouTube: @homeschoolknockouts
Facebook: @homeschoolknockouts
Instagram: @homeschool_knockouts
Email: hi@homeschoolknockouts.com
Mail: That Homeschool Life
1601 N.Sepulveda Blvd., Suite #826
Manhattan Beach, CA 90266

Selected Notes

CHAPTER 3: HOMESCHOOLING LAWS

- The homeschooling statistics around the world information is based on insights from Christopher Klicka's articles in *Practical Homeschooling Magazine*, as printed in issue no. 35, 2001, and no. 55, 2003.

- Home School Legal Defense Association (HSLDA): Provides comprehensive legal support and resources to homeschooling families. https://www.hslda.org

- Christopher Klicka: Articles in *Practical Homeschooling Magazine*, issues No. 35 (2001) and No. 55 (2003). For insights into homeschooling statistics worldwide, check their online archive or library services.

CHAPTER 4: HISTORY OF HOMESCHOOLING

- "The Case for Homeschooling (Part 2): The History of Home Education", Posted by Christian PooleJune 10, 2020, ThinkingWest.com *Reviving the Great Conversation in the Digital Age.*

CHAPTER 6: HOMESCHOOL ROUTINES

- Pam Barnhill Homeschool Planning: Offers resources for effectively planning homeschool routines, including loop schedules. Visit: https://www.pambarnhill.com

CHAPTER 7: THE CURRICULUM JUNGLE

- S.M.A.R.T. Goals Template. A guide for setting effective and measurable goals. Find detailed templates and explanations at MindTools. https://www.mindtools.com/pages/article/smart-goals.htm

- Cathy Duffy's Reviews: For comprehensive curriculum reviews and recommendations. https://www.cathyduffyreviews.com

CHAPTER 8: LESSON PLANNING FOR COUCH POTATOES

- Resources like the Home School Legal Defense Association (HSLDA) can provide detailed information on state-specific regulations and help you ensure your calendar is compliant. https://www.hslda.org

CHAPTER 9: HOMESCHOOLING ON A BUDGET

- Homeschool Buyers Co-op: Learn how to obtain a free ID card for homeschooling discounts or explore DIY options. Website: https://www.homeschoolbuyersco-op.org

CHAPTER 10: TEACHING MULTIPLE CHILDREN

ABCmouse: Engaging educational content for preschool and kindergarten. https://www.abcmouse.com

Kids Discover Online: Provides interactive learning experiences in history. https://www.kidsdiscover.com

Mystery Science: Offers interactive science lessons. https://www.mysteryscience.com

Khan Academy: Features a wide range of educational content in many subjects including history and science. https://www.khanacademy.org

History Channel's History Here App: An app that allows exploration of historical sites across the United States. https://www.history.com/history-here

Labster: Provides virtual science lab simulations. https://www.labster.com

CHAPTER 15: THE SOCIALIZATION MYTH

- National Home Education Research Institute: Provides relevant statistics and studies debunking myths about homeschooling and socialization. Refer to educational studies and reports available at academic libraries and online educational journals. **(NHERI)** https://www.nheri.org

CHAPTER 16: ASSESSING PROGRESS

Calculating Weighted Average Grade

Definitions:

- **Grade**: The numerical score received for each assignment, test, or project.
- **Weight**: The importance of each grade, represented numerically. If all grades are equally important, the weight is 1 for each.

Formula: $\text{Weighted Average} = \frac{\sum (\text{Grade} \times \text{Weight})}{\sum (\text{Weight})}$

Steps:

1. Multiply each grade by its corresponding weight.
2. Sum all the results from step 1 to get the total weighted score.
3. Sum all the weights.
4. Divide the total weighted score by the total of the weights to get the weighted average grade.

Example:

- Grades: 85, 90, 80
- Weights: 2, 3, 1

$\text{Weighted Average} = \frac{(85 \times 2) + (90 \times 3) + (80 \times 1)}{2+3+1}$ $\quad \text{Weighted Average} = \frac{170 + 270 + 80}{6}$

$\text{Weighted Average} = \frac{520}{6} = 86.67$

Thus, the weighted average grade is 86.67.

CHAPTER 29: THE SPECIAL-NEEDS CHILD

- Using communication aids such as picture exchange systems (e.g. , PECS) or speech-generating devices (e.g., Dynavox).

- Social skills training programs, like those offered by the Social Thinking® curriculum, and group activities designed for special needs children can enhance their social interaction abilities and help them build meaningful relationships.

- Resources like the STAR Institute for Sensory Processing can provide additional support and information.

- Applied Behavior Analysis (ABA), can be effective in managing and improving these behaviors. Organizations like the Autism Society can provide resources and support for behavioral issues.

- Orton-Gillingham approach for reading, can support their learning and help them achieve academic success. Websites like Understood.org offer resources for parents and educators on learning disabilities.

- Programs like Zones of Regulation provide structured approaches to help children understand and manage their emotions.

- The American Physical Therapy Association (APTA) offers resources for finding appropriate physical therapy services.

- Smart but Scattered book series by Dr. Peg Dawson and Dr. Richard Guare provide practical strategies for improving executive functioning skills.

National Organizations

1. HSLDA (Home School Legal Defense Association) — Provides legal

support and resources for all homeschooling families, including those with special needs.

2. NATHHAN (National Challenged Homeschoolers Associated Network) — Christian-based platform that provides support and resources for homeschooling families with special needs children.

3. SPED Homeschool (Special Education Homeschool)— A nonprofit organization offering resources, support, and community for special needs homeschooling families.

4. The National Autism Association — Offers resources and support for families homeschooling children with autism.

5. CHADD (Children and Adults with Attention-Deficit/Hyperactivity Disorder) — Provides resources and support for homeschooling children with ADHD.

6. LDA (Learning Disabilities Association of America) — Offers resources and support for homeschooling children with learning disabilities.

7. Autism Speaks - Offers a wide range of resources, including toolkits for various aspects of autism management and education.

8. Understood.org — Provides resources for parents of children with learning and attention issues, including strategies for homeschooling and integrating therapies.

Index